HOUSE RULES

HOUSE RULES

A Freshman Congressman's
Initiation to the Backslapping,
Backpedaling, and Backstabbing
Ways of Washington

ROBERT CWIKLIK

VILLARD BOOKS
NEW YORK
1991

Grateful acknowledgment is made to *The Wall Street Journal* for
permission to reprint excerpts from "Congressional Crack."
Copyright © 1989 by Dow Jones & Company, Inc. All rights
reserved. Reprinted with permission of *The Wall Street Journal*.

Library of Congress Cataloging-in-Publication Data

Cwiklik, Robert.
House rules: a freshman congressman's initiation to the
backslapping, backpedaling, and backstabbing ways of
Washington/Robert Cwiklik.
p.   cm.
ISBN 0-394-58231-4
1. Hoagland, Peter.
2. Legislators—United States—Biography.
3. United States. Congress. House—Biography.
4. Nebraska—Politics and government.
I. Title.
E840.8.H63C85   1991
328.73′092—dc20
[B]   91-50059

Book design by Richard Oriolo

Manufactured in the United States of America

9 8 7 6 5 4 3 2

First Edition

ACKNOWLEDGMENTS

Many thanks to Peter Hoagland, his wife, Barbara, and his staff in Washington and Omaha; to Julie Sochalski for her heroic endurance; to Russell Shorto and Winston Wood for their priceless insights; to Alison Acker, who conceived this project, Anne Edelstein, who babysat it, and Emily Bestler, who edited it.

CONTENTS

HOUSE RULES

1
POLITICAL PLAINSONG

O n election night, Peter Hoagland and his wife, Barbara, planned to spend time alone in the low-budget motel room they'd taken across the street from the site of their victory party. But Hoagland didn't believe in his "victory"—in a journal entry he made for that night he surrounded the word with ironic quotation marks. His staff—most of them, anyway—didn't believe in it either.

Ever since Hoagland had seen the final *Omaha World-Herald* poll on Sunday night, putting him three points behind with less than two days to go, his mood had been dark. As his aides were plotting a last-ditch strategy over breakfast on election eve, the candidate was looking "very, very gray," said Tim Philips, his campaign manager. Hoagland was nursing a cold, along with some dark forebodings about his chances. He seemed to sense defeat. "I could see it in his eyes," Philips said.

The campaign had hoarded blocks of last-minute TV time in case of emergencies. They decided to record a new ad, to exhibit the soft-spoken sincerity that was Hoagland's strong suit. It would be a stripped-down affair, just the candidate, no gimmicks. In the language of Hoagland's image crafters, they would "do Peter right into the camera." The tight focus was a tool to convey candor and a certain vulnerability. In a sense the pose, not the medium, was the message.

For the taping session, Hoagland was wearing the same baggy blue suit he wore almost every day, with a blue shirt and red tie, his version of the unofficial politician's uniform. Blue shirts were thought to be better on TV. Hoagland owned practically no other type.

"I've told the hard truth throughout my years in public life," he assured the camera, "and I'll continue to do it. . . ."

Hoagland is tall and rangy, with wavy black hair and smooth, handsome features. But a pair of ears that extrude a bit too far give him a homey, disarming quality. Though he stands a good six foot three, his voice is surprisingly small. His soft-spokenness isn't so much timidity as a matter of style. Some politicians employ words as blunt instruments, but Hoagland's silky cadences are more like caresses.

". . . That is my pledge to you as your congressman," he concluded, almost hypnotically.

The tape was hurriedly edited. Then the finished cassette, labeled "credibility," was rushed to TV stations. For the next twenty-four hours, it flickered nearly continuously across the screens of Omaha.

The Hoaglands had prepared for election night by indulging in a last-minute taste of sour grapes. Believing they wouldn't win, they had "decided" that Peter really didn't want to go to Congress after all. They now seemed to agree that being a member of Congress was, as one friend said, "a crappy job." The hours were long, the work was crashingly dull, and new members had about as much clout as a corn dog. Besides, the $89,500 congressfolk made was a pittance next to the $250,000 Hoagland had earned the previous year practicing law. They would rather stay right here in Omaha, where Peter could earn sacks of litigation money, and they could go camping in Colorado whenever they wanted.

While Hoagland waited at the motel for his wife to show up, he began scribbling a pair of speeches, one for conceding defeat, one for claiming victory. Care would have to be taken with the first one. Concessions are trickier. It's tough to say only what should be said, to keep any bitterness you might be feeling from spilling out.

No matter what Hoagland said, underneath the rationalizations—and not far under—he wanted to win. He'd actually dreamed of going to Congress since he was in *fourth grade!* His "two-cylinder" law practice, as he described it, had never thrilled him. Hoagland was a personal-injury specialist, what impolite people call an ambulance chaser. In one case, he was laboring to snag a fat settlement for a poor soul disabled in a tractor-trailer accident —in which a swinging side of beef played a role—not exactly what a certain dreamy fourth-grader had had in mind.

If Hoagland didn't want to win, he wouldn't have tolerated the thousand indignities he had borne to get this far. He wouldn't have had the stomach to panhandle for campaign money from almost everyone he knew, and from old law school classmates, most of whom he really didn't know very well, and from those legions of anonymous voices on hundreds of cadging phone calls.

Then there was the gray zone of conduct, the dubious things one has to do, or one does, in order to win. Like telling a reporter on live television, as Hoagland had, "I served for two years in the United States Army back during the Vietnam days. . . . I'm proud to have been able to fight . . . er . . . do my part to preserve democracy then." Though he spent his entire hitch stateside, most of it based in Washington, D.C.—where he lived, off base in an apartment in Georgetown.

No, he wanted to win, and he'd taken his best shot. It was now or never. He was forty-seven years old, already a bit on the late side to be starting out in Congress, where you had to grovel some before you could walk. Besides, open seats don't come along every day. Omaha's hadn't been open for ten years, and it would be another ten at least before it was vacant again.

The only thing left was waiting for the vote to come in, "about the most miserable thing you can go through," Hoagland said. There was a sort of science to interpreting early results. The first returns were based on votes tallied at midafternoon. As common wisdom had it, if a Democrat was ahead, it was believed he or she would win, because Republicans vote early—since all they do during the day is clip coupons and horde money. Meanwhile, Democrats work all day, enslaved by the coupon-clippers, and can't vote till nightfall—or so the thinking goes. No matter how valid any of this logic is, or was, Hoagland braced for the first tally, due on the glowing screen just after 8:00 P.M.

Barbara got to the room at "about three minutes to eight," a nervously clock-watching Hoagland later recalled. She was two hours late for their quiet rendezvous. Despite her avowed longing to pitch a tent in Colorado, she worked the get-out-and-vote phones down to the last minute.

Hoagland had all his chips on one number. Besides his investment of eighteen months, plotting, preening, and pumping hands, he had now loaned over $293,000 to his campaign. If he won, solicitous lobbyists would no doubt attend his catered fundraisers, to help retire the annoying debt. But losing meant sweating it off among the side-of-beef victims.

In a few minutes, the first count popped onscreen—*Hoagland ahead by eighty votes!* If their "science" of the electorate was sound, *he had won!*

But Hoagland was hardly in a detached, scientific frame of mind. An eighty-vote margin didn't *feel* like victory yet. As the returns trickled in, however, his lead mounted. By 8:50 he was in front by fourteen hundred votes. That Colorado campsite was beginning to seem pretty dull.

But shortly after 9:00, Hoagland's slowly climbing little engine fell off the cliff. *Schenken surged ahead by six hundred votes!* Hoagland picked up the phone and called his staff across the street at the "victory" party—ironic jaws again snaring the word in his journal. What was going on? His lead was only supposed to mount!

Hoagland asked Dave Schinzel, a trusted aide, to come by the hotel. He needed someone to talk to. But bad news seemed to stalk him. On his way out to meet Schinzel, he noticed the TV in the lobby had Schenken up by thirteen hundred votes.

Hoagland and Schinzel decided to get away from televisions. They took a stroll in the bracing night air, to restore some perspective. But all Hoagland could do was say over and over, "I can't understand what's going on!"

The countryside around Omaha, Nebraska, is a place where one little adjective goes a long, long way: *flat.* Cast a hill-hungry eye in any direction, the prospect is wall to wall levelness, an epic regularity.

The flatness of the Great Plains echoes in the speech of Omahans; a cocked ear won't detect the faintest craggy twang. Locals define their accent as pure "American." They've made an asset of it. Omaha has become the 800-number capital of the continent, the busy tongue of telemarketing. Corporate America relies on the city's inoffensively neutral voice to answer a polyglot of toll-free calls, for everything from hotel and flight bookings to Civil War chess sets.

Just as Omahans are ordinary of speech, their politics tend to the plainsong variety. They don't go in for "attack videos" or other take-no-prisoners tactics of today's political combat. That's not to say they aren't "modern," that their campaigns don't rely on television and the simplifications and distortions of that medium. They would just prefer it if *their* distortions weren't so gaudy—and so mean-spirited.

But even by local standards, Peter Hoagland's stump style was fairly small beer. In late 1987, when he announced his candidacy for the district's open seat in Congress, not many people gave him much of a shot. Even non-fans agreed he was "a real nice guy." But his Mr. Rogers–like approachability didn't look like a match for the popularity of Cece Zorinsky, widow of the late, great Senator Ed Zorinsky, who led by forty-three points in early polls.

Cece had been "at the senator's side" on Capitol Hill for years, writing a folksy "Letter from Washington" column for the newspapers. She was well known. Hoagland's status, meanwhile, was best described as not exactly *un*known. He'd served eight years in Nebraska's unicameral legislature, retiring at the end of the 1986 session to devote himself full-time to his law practice. After all, the Unicameral—as Nebraskans fondly call their legislature, making a noun of the adjective—paid its senators only $400 a month throughout most of his stay. Polls said that people had positive feelings about Cece. They saw her as "caring." Their feelings about Hoagland—when they *had* feelings about him—ran no warmer than "neutral."

Nevertheless, Hoagland saw himself as well qualified for the job he sought. In one sense, it was hard not to agree. The halls of Congress were teeming with conformists like him. There were more former class presidents and class historians, more honors students and moot court team captains on Capitol Hill than anyplace outside the green room of *It's Academic*. Apparently, no office was too insignificant for the budding congress-type. One congress-woman had been elected "friendliest" person in her high school class and vice-president of her *homeroom.*

Conforming often means following the path of least resistance. But for those who aspire to Congress, conformity is a craft to be mastered. Peter Hoagland was a prodigy. As a boy, he was "very conscientious," says his mother, *"almost too good."* A former teacher remembered him talking about becoming a congressman since he was "a little boy," said his wife Barbara. Along the way, he did all the right things: high school ROTC, honors at Stanford, student government, enlistee in the Army, captain of the Yale Law moot court team, member of the national board of Common Cause. As a senior in college, Hoagland fretted over whether going out of state to law school would tarnish his later run for office.

One might think an open seat in Congress would draw quite a crowd of credible contestants. But for whatever reasons—the outrageous expense of campaigns, the stupendous odds against winning, Zorinski's perceived "lock" on the seat—not many Omaha Democrats seemed interested in the job. There were only four candidates. And apart from Zorinsky and Hoagland, there wasn't much competition.

During one Democratic debate, a candidate who had filed as a "pauper," rifled through a clipboard stuffed with soiled position papers whenever he was asked a question. He was a stoutish man in his late thirties who looked something like Bob Keeshan (of *Captain Kangaroo* fame), only sullen, with glasses. He got annoyed when asked to give an answer without using his clipboard. After ripping off a vague reply to a question about national health insurance, he snarled, "Off the top of my head . . . all right!"

Another candidate might have been credible. He was a former teacher and member of the Omaha school board. But he had an aloof, offhand attitude about sensitive issues that gave an unserious air to his campaign. While answering a benign query about his qualifications, he brought up the cancerous subject of taxes: "It hasn't been difficult to serve on the school board," he said, "even when it came time to raise property taxes . . . *every year.*" Later, he bluntly added, again without being asked, "I don't have any problem soakin' the rich."

As things worked out, Zorinsky wasn't a terribly strong candidate either. When you got past her celebrated espousal, there wasn't much of a résumé. She hadn't even graduated from college. And for all her Washington connections, her operation wasn't very sophisticated. Hoagland's primary-campaign manager, Gary Caruso, knew his candidate had a good shot at winning when he saw Zorinsky's people passing out *emery boards* embossed with the candidate's name—the kind used in low-rent elections for county sheriff.

Zorinsky was clearly uncomfortable discussing issues, which didn't help dispel some voters' doubts about handing a serious job to a "wife of." Her refusal to debate Hoagland didn't make the doubters feel any better. She attempted to reassure them. "I'm no star debater," she said, "but I understand things and have the ability to listen to people." Zorinsky suggested she would rely on her staff for help on issues, because "nobody can know everything about everything." Her presumed message, What's the point of debates when we're all creatures of our staffs, probably sounded a trifle self-serving even to adoring fans.

For sheer experience, Hoagland was head and shoulders above the field. He'd mastered the legislative process, having chaired committees and steered various bills through the backwaters of the Nebraska legislature. He'd even bucked the entrenched old-boy network some. He was also widely respected by colleagues for his intelligence and the ease with which he grasped the stuffy legalisms and archaic complexities of the legislative process.

What stirred doubts about Hoagland was not his competence but his motives. Vard Johnson, an old friend of Hoagland's, had served with him in the Nebraska legislature and was currently one of the congressman's issues advisors. Even Johnson believed his friend was often more concerned with political ambition than policy. Hoagland "yearns . . . to do the best thing for people," Johnson said. However, he added, "It is easy for Peter to be deflected from the path of service onto the path of, well, let's go where the money is and let's go where the power is and the like."

Hoagland also seemed to have an uncanny knack for getting his name in the paper. Johnson said that "lots of other legislators" —including himself—believed Hoagland enjoyed a "special relationship" with the state's dominant journal, the *Omaha World-Herald*, where his father was once a vice president. Hoagland "profited from that relationship in carrying legislation that that newspaper crusaded for," Johnson alleged.

Hoagland's toolbox was impressive. But running for Congress is a very different affair from running for the Unicameral. In the past, he'd campaigned door to door to connect with voters directly and impress them with his sincerity, his lack of pretensions. But the congressional electorate was much larger. He'd have to speak with a different voice, one substantially bigger, if not necessarily louder. But back then Hoagland was weak on TV and addressing large groups. When nervous, he had "this terrible blinking problem," said an aide. And his cautious, fact-heavy speeches went down "like a Sominex pill."

In an early press conference, Hoagland stumbled on a routine question from a local TV reporter: "Can you win if you don't debate [Zorinsky]?" A seasoned campaigner would have slipped this jab by switching on a stock response, like "The people of Omaha lose if she doesn't debate." Hoagland, to his credit, didn't do that. However, he said . . . well . . . nothing! . . . for a disturbingly long time. He just batted his eyelashes in the dead air of the newscast for several embarrassing beats. Then he winced and repeated the question, as if it were craftily nuanced. Finally, his face suffused with pain, he confessed: "I think . . . I don't really have an answer for that now." It was the kind of candor that causes wailing and gnashing of teeth at campaign headquarters.

Still, Hoagland managed to plant doubts about his opponent's *gravitas.* Her platinum-blond hair worn poodle-style and high-pitched voice might have played into his strategy. But so did she. At first, no one said much when she ducked Hoagland's nagging debate challenges. But when Zorinsky literally fled the room after Hoagland showed up for a previously scheduled joint appearance, reporters began to suspect she was not simply above debating, but afraid of it. Around Groundhog Day, one editorial cartoon showed Cece hiding down a hole, quaking in fear of Hoagland's looming shadow.

Hoagland seemed to be gaining in spite of his lackluster campaign style. So reserved was this candidate that he was skittish about appearing in shirtsleeves at a sweltering midafternoon rally, protesting to aides that it didn't seem "appropriate" not to wear a suit. He was also reluctant to "go negative" and air critical ads about his opponent. But on this he gave in too, especially after Zorinsky botched a TV interview, confusing, among other things, the multi*billion*-dollar budget deficit with the multi*trillion*-dollar national debt.

Gary Caruso called Hoagland's new "comparative" TV spot "nitroglycerin" in a cassette. It opened with quick-cutting fright icons—Muammar Qaddafi's sinister scowl; a string of panic headlines. Then, a gravid warning: "It's a tough world out there." Viewers were asked if they could truly afford, in such evil times, to elect a person to Congress who *doesn't even know the difference between the debt and the deficit!*

These fearsome tidings seemed to work, as fearsome tidings so often do in campaigns. A week before the primary, Zorinsky was only ten points up and sinking fast. "She was in free-fall," Caruso said.

Three days before the vote, Hoagland shared an outdoor platform with Jesse Jackson, in town stumping for the Nebraska presidential primary. Jackson looked and sounded like an old-time Nebraska populist, in his feedlot cap, blue jeans, and windbreaker, raging against agribusiness and the greedy rich.

Jackson's appeal was keyed to the ears of an earlier Nebraska, springboard for perhaps the biggest mass political uprising the nation has ever seen, the Populist movement. It was right here on July 4, 1892, that the famous Omaha Platform was adopted. That document spelled out the hopes of common people who wanted to take control of their government away from the rich and powerful banks and corporations that dominated national politics then—and, many would argue, dominate it today.

Some of the Populists' demands, like the issuance of paper money and the direct election of U.S. senators, are mundane realities now, though they sounded distressingly "radical" to nervous guardians of the established order then. Though the Populists had their long-term triumphs, they are known chiefly for the failure of the presidential candidacy of Democrat William Jennings Bryan in 1896. But Populists were after bigger game than just the presidency. They wanted to change the nature of politics. They didn't like policies that were imposed from above on a supine, lethargic, and ill-informed population. They wanted ones that percolated up from below, from the people.

Populist-style anger today is most often focused not on corporate oligarchies of wealth but on, of all places, Congress—the people's branch of government. A few years ago, when Oliver North faced down a joint House-Senate committee and brazenly confessed, "Yes, I lied to the Congress," we made him a cult. Congress, it seems, can't do anything right. Ironically, though we like to elect careful conformists to Congress, we consistently denounce congressmen for not providing "bold" leadership.

When Nebraska populists were unhappy with *their* legislature, they didn't just get cynical, they got busy—abolishing much of it. In 1936, Nebraska, like every other state, possessed a two-house legislature. Anxious for reform, Nebraskans simply lopped off half of it, creating their now famous unicameral (one-chamber) model. Though reformers had solid, sober reasons for pushing their radical remedy, many people quite frankly believed that having "two sets of fools arguing about what to do" is redundant, when one set would do just fine.

Jesse Jackson's Populist-style stump speech was a crowd pleaser, even in today's Omaha, a place not greatly affected by the agricultural recessions that devastated other parts of Nebraska in the 1980s, the kind that nearly wiped out farmers during the Populist era and brought some hard times to Omaha. "We are subsidizing Con-Agra and Carghill and pauperizing the family farmer," Jackson raged to a cheering crowd of mostly white-collar and service workers, who'd probably never lifted a hoe in their lives. Meanwhile, the figure standing meekly behind the rabble-rousing orator was a better symbol of today's prosperous, mostly Republican Omaha: Peter Hoagland, wearing his quotidian blue suit, blue shirt, and red tie, and looking as if he might have come to serve a subpoena.

Jackson whipped the crowd into egalitarian ecstasies, ending on a hopeful howl: *"We won Alaska, look out Nebraska."*

But Jackson's angry populism wasn't enough. He lost the Nebraska primary to the Boston bean-counter, Michael Dukakis. Meanwhile, shy, unassuming Peter Hoagland trounced Cece Zorinsky's last name by eight points.

Hoagland won a lot of respect with his "miracle" primary win. But Zorinsky's obvious weaknesses had been obscured in the glare of her huge early lead. Hoagland wasn't so lucky in the general election. His opponent, Omaha pathologist Jerry Schenken, had raised a lot of money, and cut a dignified figure besides, with his silver-gray hair and meticulous diction. Worst of all, he was a Republican, and Republicans just didn't lose Omaha's congressional seat very often. It had gone Democratic only twice in the last forty-eight years.

Hoagland ran a traditional Democratic campaign, planting doubts about Schenken's commitment to Social Security and Medicare. And he always addressed his opponent as "Dr." Schenken, to stir up any latent resentment of the medical profession. However, on election eve, the doctor was leading the lawyer by three points in the final *Omaha World-Herald* poll. Despite what others said about Hoagland's "special relationship" with the *World-Herald,* the traditionally Republican paper had endorsed Schenken. Hoagland even entertained dark suspicions that the paper's final poll—printed so uncharacteristically close to election day—was an effort to "get" him.

In Hoagland's low-budget motel room, his aides were getting precinct vote results by phone, making the persistent din of the television coverage more irrelevant than usual. So no one was paying much attention when the scene that blossomed on the TV screen matched the one being played out in the flesh directly across the street. Senator-elect Bob Kerrey was in the packed Peony Plaza ballroom, next door to the site of Hoagland's "victory" party, triumphantly addressing his delirious supporters. As usual, Kerrey played the crowd like a maestro. He even *sang*—in mercilessly off-key a cappella—the Australian ballad *"And the Band Played Waltzing Matilda,"* about a soldier who lost his legs in the battle of Gallipoli. Kerrey had lost his own right leg below the knee, shredded by a hand grenade in Vietnam.

Some were reminded of John Kennedy, who sang "Sweet Adeline" at victory rallies. It wasn't the first time Kerrey was compared to JFK—he also has certain Kennedyesque speech patterns, like the "aahs" that caulk his pauses, making one expect heroic couplets to drop from his lips. "We have been selected to lead," he summed up tonight, "and lead we will."

Kerrey had been a favorite here ever since—at the age of thirty-nine—he came from nowhere to win the governorship in 1982. His lively blue eyes and broad brow gave his handsome face a quality of choirboy candor. But people especially liked his cocky, self-ruling streak. Though Nebraska's populism, in the strict sense of the word, was dead and buried, its voters were still fiercely

independent. Kerrey had promised to speak his mind in Washington, and people believed he really would. His name on the ballot
probably explained the 1.2 percent rise in Nebraska voter turnout,
compared to the 3 percent decline nationally.

Kerrey's emotional song coaxed many an eye to tears. Even a
local newswoman blubbered through her live TV wrap-up. And
several misty-eyed Kerrey supporters were heard to avow: "He
will be president someday."

They weren't the only ones saying so. Kerrey was already a
minor "media phenomenon." At his public appearances, grown
women shrieked like teenyboppers at a Prince concert. Kerrey was
a budding "sex symbol" who dated actress Debra Winger. He'd
been the subject of several hyperventilated profiles in the national
press. *Newsweek* gushingly called him "a could-be president with
real crackle." To reporters, Kerrey was a rare animal—a Democrat
with suspiciously liberal leanings who was wildly popular in a
"bastion of conservatism." Kerrey was good on TV, a war hero
who'd won the Medal of Honor, and well known in Iowa, kickoff
point for the presidential primaries—which happens to be right
next door to Nebraska.

Probably no one will ever call Peter Hoagland a media phenomenon. But his chips would not be raked off the table this
night. He had won—though it had taken a while. The vote was so
close Schenken waited until after midnight before conceding. Finally, at around 1:00 A.M., Hoagland delivered his own victory
speech, in a voice shredded by fifteen-hour days pleading for
votes. "I intend to represent all Nebraskans as your congressman," he told the room jammed with the spillover from the
nearby Kerrey gathering. It wasn't exactly *"Waltzing Matilda,"* but
he sounded sincere.

When Hoagland announced his candidacy almost a year before, almost no one would have predicted he'd be standing here
tonight claiming victory. But even in his hour of triumph—though
he was only the third Democrat in forty-eight years to win this seat
—there were those who would rob him of credit. Many were
saying Hoagland owed his narrow win—by only 3,431 votes—to
the outsized turnout of Democrats for Kerrey.

In fact, Kerrey had made several appearances with Hoagland
near the end of the campaign, though some weren't sure how
much "help" it had been. A few days earlier, the two candidates

had made a joint visit to a day-care center. Afterward, emerging from the center, Kerrey joked with reporters, "I brought my kid with me." Just then, Hoagland ambled out—a walking punch line —his ridiculed image lapped up by the nest of hungry lenses and broadcast across Omaha. At least, that's how hypersensitive campaign staff saw it.

But none of that mattered now. Like Kerrey, Hoagland was now a member of that very exclusive club—537 men and women —elected to oversee our superpowerful, tiresomely venal, cash-gnoshing octopus of a federal government. So what if an ever-declining segment of us bothers to vote? Winning's still an honor —isn't it?

Considering the people who'd shown an interest in this seat, Hoagland was easily not the worst choice Omaha might have made. Some of his aides were fond of saying that he would "single-handedly" raise the IQ of Congress. Unfortunately, Congress often appeared to lack not brains, but guts, especially in dealings with pollsters. Hoagland already seemed infatuated with *his* high-priced Washington pollster, whom he described as "brilliant."

Though Hoagland was afloat on a sea of huzzahs at his victory rally, his worries were far from over. The district's strong Republican leanings weren't likely to go away, so his seat might never truly be "safe." He'd have to start begging money soon for his *next* race, even as he tried to crawl out from beneath his debts. Was it worth it?—for a "crappy" job that rated about as much public "esteem" as being an auto mechanic! And how could he claim to "represent" his constituents? As districts went, his was fairly manageable—five counties, seventy-three zip codes, 550,000-plus souls. But in a few months' time, if he was lucky, only a third of them would even be able to tell you his name.

2

A TALE OF TWO STATUES

T he freshman class in the House of Representatives for the one
hundred and first Congress included a few novelties: an actor,
a psychiatrist (the House's first), even a funeral director. But most
of their résumés, like those of every congressional class, were of
the conformist variety compiled by Peter Hoagland. Most of them
were lawyers and businesspeople accustomed to being inside players.

But if the class of '89 was typical, the year was anything but.
Before it was through, Congress would celebrate its bicentennial,
watch a House speaker fall from power, endure a widespread popular revolt against itself, and deal, more or less, with perhaps the
biggest financial blunder—one it was at least partially responsible
for—in its history.

On March 2, 1989, when the House and Senate met jointly to
celebrate the two hundredth anniversary of the first session of
Congress, the nation that observed the bicentennials of 1976 and
1987 with transcontinental fireworks greeted the news with a col-

lective yawn. Senators and House members faithfully represented their constituents, showing about the same level of enthusiasm for the occasion as the folks back home. True, the House chamber was packed. But when you looked closely at the collection of fresh, expectant faces, many did appear rather young to serve in Congress. In fact, a lot of them were congressional staff or interns, who might have been encouraged to attend the ceremony in their bosses' place. It wouldn't do to have distinguished guest speakers addressing a chamber full of empty chairs. Only congressfolk should be subjected to that.

The keynote speaker was historian David McCullough, narrator of a PBS documentary produced in honor of the congressional bicentennial. McCullough's voice-over can be heard on several *American Heritage*-style documentaries. He's a crossover scholar, who tries to make ordinary people understand what it is about those dusty histories that academics find so interesting. On the subject of Congress, he faces a unique challenge. Even scholars seem bored with it.

McCullough said that Congress is one of the most neglected subjects in American historiography. "Our knowledge, our appreciation, of the history of Congress and those who have made history here are curiously, regrettably deficient," he said. Then he listed important books that *have not been written* about Congress. "There are no substantial, up-to-date biographies of Justin Morrill of Vermont, author of the Land Grant College Act; or Jimmy Byrnes . . . or Joe Robinson . . . or Carl Hayden of Arizona, who served longer in the Senate than anybody, forty-one years."

Scholars prefer to view American history from the lofty vantage point of the presidency. Compared to the crowded confusion of Congress, where "there is such a lot of humbug and so much that has been so overwhelmingly boring," said McCullough, the scene at the White House "seems clear, orderly, easy to understand."

Scholars who *have* studied Congress tend to emphasize its propensity—and that of the entire national government—to deadlock. Often a species of cataclysm is required before there is enough political steam to get the gears turning. Two of Congress's proudest achievements are the Homestead Act and the Land Grant College Act, both signed into law on the same day in 1862. All it took to get them through was the Civil War—and the departure from Congress of representatives from the rebellious Southern states, who had blocked the measures for years. The same Congress incorporated the Union Pacific Railroad and abolished slavery in the territories. Unfortunately, the pilots of our ship of state only seem to worry about icebergs after the lifeboats are on the water.

It's easy to get annoyed with Washington's persistent paralysis, to curse corrupt and/or incompetent politicians in a system that fails to function. The deadlocks, however, bespeak not a system that isn't working, but one that's working exactly as designed.

"With the possible exception of the Bible," wrote historian Walter Russell Mead, "no document in the United States is so widely revered and so poorly understood as the Constitution." Twentieth-century Americans tend to view it as simply a democratic instrument, and to explain the government's plodding ways as problems of democracy, which is said to be inherently inefficient. But the Founding Fathers had a somewhat more nuanced view of democracy. And the jalopy-like running style of the government they created isn't caused by democracy so much as by antidemocratic, or antimajoritarian, mechanisms built into the design.

A pair of statues in Washington symbolize the confusion on these matters. The Jefferson Memorial, a circular domed shrine on the shore of the Tidal Basin, is one of the city's more popular attractions. On balmy evenings, many a footsore tourist has passed through the colonnade surrounding the twenty-five-foot-tall statue and experienced something like an epiphany. The place is open on four sides, and Jefferson appears to be musing over the placid water lined with cherry trees. When a soft breeze is blowing, especially when the cherry blossoms are out, the words etched on the interior walls begin to seduce, words like "Laws and institutions must go hand in hand with the progress of the human mind."

Of all the Founding Fathers, Jefferson, author of the Declaration of Independence, is probably the most appealing to modern tastes. From his supple pen flowed certain "self-evident" truths that shook the eighteenth century: "That all men are created equal, and are endowed by their creator with certain unalienable rights; that among these are life, liberty and the pursuit of happiness . . ."

Jefferson had faith in the wisdom of "the people," and believed that if Americans' freedom was to survive, power could be lodged nowhere but with them. The idea is now orthodox enough. But in Jefferson's day he was considered a radical—and a potentially dangerous one—even by those with whom he'd made a revolution.

Behind the Treasury Department in downtown Washington stands a monument to another hero of the nation's founding era. The statue of Alexander Hamilton, smudged with downtown soot, is scarcely noticed by the hordes who pass by. He might have preferred it that way. Hamilton was no fan of "the people." In some of his most oft-quoted remarks, he attempted to take their measure:

> The voice of the people has been said to be the voice of God; and however generally this maxim has been quoted and believed, it is not true in fact. The people are turbulent and changing; they seldom judge or determine right.

Millions have paraded past the statue of Jefferson, to pay homage to the ideal of government by the many, not the few. But the Jefferson Memorial rests on national parkland, hallowed soil reserved for monuments and museums, a realm of visions and dreams.

The statue of Alexander Hamilton, on the other hand, stands next door to the White House, at the heart of this most powerful city. Just as Hamilton's statue is closer to the pulse of everyday Washington life, though it elicits nothing like the reverence shown at the shrine on the Tidal Basin, his ideas seem closer to the reality of American power.

There were basically two opposing influences at work in the nation when the Constitution, blueprint for the government, was written. On the one hand, the founders saw the necessity, theoretical, practical, and political, for the new government to derive its authority from the people. On the other hand, the common people as a political force scared them to death.

As a political matter, "the sovereignty of the people" was a powerful concept. State governments might never have voluntarily ceded part of their sovereignty to a new national government. So the founders assumed that sovereignty wasn't theirs to cede. It belonged, they said, to the people, who could empower such governments as they chose, both state and national.

But the founders were very much alive to the potential of "the people," however useful in concept, to become a mob. In Massachusetts, former Revolutionary War soldiers and indebted farmers were preventing courts from sitting and ordering their land and property seized for nonpayment of debts. Many of the former soldiers were also farmers, who believed they'd been poorly treated—given certificates for later redemption on discharge instead of cash. They wanted the state government to issue paper money, which would inflate the currency and make it easier for them to pay their debts. That would mean their creditors would be paid back with less valuable money, something the wealthy classes, politically more influential, were loath to tolerate.

Such insurrections spread beyond Massachusetts. In Rhode Island, debtors took over the legislature and printed paper money. In New Hampshire, several hundred men had surrounded the legislature to demand the issuance of paper currency and the return of taxes. General Henry Knox, a veteran of the Continental Army, wrote to George Washington in 1786 about the threat:

> The people who are the insurgents have never paid any, or but very little taxes. But they see the weakness of government; they feel at once their own poverty, compared with the opulent, and their own force, and they are determined to make use of the latter, in order to remedy the former. Their creed is "That the property of the United States has been protected from the confiscations of Britain by the joint exertions of all, and therefore ought to be the common property of all."

Though Knox paints a black-and-white portrait of the rebels, his estimate of the extent of their threat was shared by many of the nation's leading men, who would soon travel to Philadelphia to draft the Constitution.

There were those at the Philadelphia Convention who believed that to truly erect a government "of the people, by the people, for the people" meant that every free adult (male) would be permitted to vote; that their votes would elect members of a one-house legislature; that amendments to the Constitution would be relatively easy to pass; and that civil liberties would be guaranteed.

But such measures, which might seem to fit the fiery propaganda of the Declaration of Independence, were espoused by only a few among the generally well-heeled participants in debates on the Constitution. The draft they finally settled on called for a legislature of two chambers, the House of Representatives and the Senate, with only the House to be elected directly by the people; a president selected by an electoral college; a system of courts, with judges appointed by the president and confirmed by the Senate; a process whereby amendments would be very difficult to adopt; no Bill of Rights guaranteeing civil liberties; and property qualifications for voting.

The drafters of the Constitution based all governmental authority ultimately in the people. But they had erected a series of "checks and balances," like the requirement that all bills pass both houses of Congress, the presidential veto, and judicial review. While partially meant to restrain officials, these were also roadblocks between the people and the actual exercise of power. The Senate, for instance, was seen as a check on imprudent projects, such as "a rage for paper money," that might hatch in the popularly elected House, as James Madison explained:

> [S]uch an institution may be sometimes necessary as a defence to the people against their own temporary errors and delusions. As the cool and deliberate sense of the community ought, in all governments, ultimately prevail over the views of its rulers; so there are particular moments in public affairs when the people, stimulated by some irregular passion, or some illicit advantage, or misled by the artful misrepresentations of interested men, may call for measures which they themselves will afterwards be the most ready to lament and condemn. In these critical moments, how salutary will be the interference of some temperate and respectable body of citizens, in order to check the misguided career, and to suspend the blow meditated by the people against themselves, until reason, justice, and truth can regain their authority over the public mind?

The founders have been lavishly praised for their "cool realism"—for not believing their own propaganda about "the people." Even Jefferson cheered the new Constitution. "It is a good canvas," he said, "on which some strokes only want retouching."

One of the retouches he and others wanted—a Bill of Rights—was added after ratification.

But in trying to foil a "tyranny of the majority" with their checks and balances, did the founders doom us to permanent gridlock—or worse—at the national level? Did they make it impossible, or at least enormously difficult, to form majorities potent enough to get things done? In *The Idea of a Party System,* historian Richard Hofstadter summarizes criticisms of the Constitution from this point of view. The founders, he said, show

> little fear of minority tyranny or even of minority obstruction . . . the possibility that, since majorities are to be weak and precarious, a large, aggressive minority, though incapable of taking the reins of government, might veto whatever policy it likes, and thus in effect tyrannize over the majority. There is, in short, no protection of the majority against grave deprivations imposed by the minority.

Hofstadter notes that the founders also did not address

> the possibility that a minority interest in the population, by virtue of superior wealth, organization, and influence, can actually come into the firm possession of power against a pluralistic and divided majority.

If the majority seeks some dangerous policy, then the founders' ample provision for checks by minorities—sometimes called "special interests"—seems prudent. But what if the majority favors measures that are in the public interest? How else can the public interest ever be defined save by consulting the will of the majority?

The founders wanted to provide ample opportunities for "mistakes" that majorities might make to be "rectified." Of course, the Senate has been popularly elected since early in the twentieth century. But having a bicameral Congress still makes it easier to block legislation than to pass it, partly by giving special interests more points at which to apply their pressure. And the decentralization of legislative power, in the alphabet soup of administrative agencies—FCC, NRC, CAB, SEC, etc.—give special interests a whole new playing field on which to coerce and obstruct.

3
MR. BOJANGLES

E ven the most disaffected political pilgrim feels a fuzzy sense of
pride at the sight of the U.S. Capitol, its majestic sprawl, its
soaring dome. But just a short distance down Capitol Hill things
go, well, downhill rather drastically at the Rayburn House Office
Building, an imposing H-shaped presence requiring an entire
square block to choke down its megalithic bulk. Since the building's completion in 1963, most of the epithets in the critic's book
of insults have been hurled its way: tactless, impractical, profligate,
forbidding, elephantine, humdrum . . . *chilling!* One critic found
the building "both dull and vulgar, an achievement of sorts." The
House Banking Committee made its home at Rayburn's much-
abused address.

The Rayburn colossus was another flowering of Washington's
beloved neoclassical style. But its dimensions dwarf mere human
scale. Its stairwells could swallow attack submarines, hallways race
to vanishing points, ceilings soar. Rayburn is long on grandeur,
short on function—less than a third of its square footage is de-

voted to workspace—a combination of grossness and inefficiency that seems a distressingly apt symbol of government at work.

Like its host shell, the Banking Committee was in danger of becoming yet another symbol of public sector waste—on a scale never conceived by man nor bureaucrat. The scandal could be spelled out in three little words that would give cold sweats to politicians for many a year: savings and loans.

Hearing room 2128, the Banking Committee's headquarters, is a typical Rayburn barn. Its ceilings grope for glory, reaching almost thirty feet high, and it is as wide as a baseball diamond. But from front to back, the space is shallow, leaving little room for spectators, who are invariably packed in like fish sticks.

With fifty-one members, Banking was the largest standing committee in Congress, a fact which Peter Hoagland found somewhat daunting. The entire Nebraska Unicameral had only forty-nine members, and it was tough enough to get something adopted there. The hearing room had a three-tiered dais to accommodate the outsized membership. This lent a Last Judgment look to proceedings, with witnesses craning up at ascending ranks of lawmakers to focus on the chairman, reigning magisterially on high, in front of floor-to-ceiling windows curtained in regal purple.

The morning's hearing of the Financial Institutions Subcommittee had already begun when Hoagland slipped into the room. His place on the bottom tier of the dais was marked by a plate inscribed with his name: "Mr. Hoagland." His chair, a padded, high-backed, executive-type swivel model, would see him comfortably through the most monotonous of proceedings. A pitcher of ice water sat on his right, to wet his whistle. A microphone sat on his left, to amplify it. Printed copies of the testimony of the day's witnesses—from which they seldom strayed—were stacked on his blotter.

Hoagland rifled through the pile of papers. Though it was only 9:30 in the morning, he already looked wan and tired. The campaign was supposed to be over, but this weary winner didn't seem to believe it. He'd risen early to speak to a gathering downtown of the American Association of Retired Persons, one of many groups clamoring to get a slice of his time. Every lobbyist in the city seemed to want an audience with the new—and as yet mostly uncommitted—vote on Capitol Hill. Hoagland believed he needed support wherever he could find it, to build a base stronger than his three-thousand-plus-vote victory margin. In his first speech back home after the election, he joked to supporters that "there are *only* six hundred and fifty-four days until the next election." And since his new job required him to get acquainted with a host of pending issues in a hurry, the freshman was under pressure to meet . . . and meet.

Hoagland's daily schedule read like a roll call of American interest groups. He met lobbyists from the Marine Engineers Beneficial Association, the National Association of Life Underwriters, the National Education Association, the United States Army, Mothers Against Drunk Driving, the American Association of Retired Persons, the National Recreation and Park Association, the Nebraska Women's Business Association, the Nebraska Soybean Producers. Of course, there were also meetings with the chairman of the board of U.S. West Airlines, the mayor of Lincoln, Nebraska, vice-presidents from Mutual of Omaha and the Independent Bankers Association of America, the president of Nebraska Educational Television. And that was just a portion of one week on his crammed calendar. There were also visits to Veterans Administration hospitals, luncheons with bankers and with local businessmen, speeches to elementary school students, and receptions for the Boilermakers, the Independent Insurance Agents, the Letter Carriers, and just about anyone with the money to hire a hall and fire up a chafing dish of Swedish meatballs.

The sight of a late-arriving congressman in Rayburn 2128 was hardly unusual. However, the fact that he showed up at all *was* unusual. Only a handful of other members were scattered among the ranks of empty chairs. A newcomer to Washington might have been surprised by the sparse attendance at these hearings, meant to root out what went wrong with the nation's near-bankrupt savings and loan industry. The mess looked like it would cost taxpayers over $100 billion—and that was an *optimistic* estimate.

"So much in the hands of so few" was the lament in the headline of *Insight,* a Washington newsletter for bankers. "Only fourteen out of fifty-one members, 27 percent of the House Banking Committee," regularly showed up for the hearings, *Insight* found. Among them were freshmen Jim McDermott and Peter Hoagland.

Members might have ignored the hearings, but the watchful

eyes of interest groups kept the committee in sharp focus. Reporters from financial industry publications—like *Insight*—showed up daily in Rayburn 2128, tracking legislative nuances for their influential clientele. Meanwhile, the popular press was seldom seen.

Perhaps some committee members were too embarrassed to attend the hearings. Judged by the panel's past handling of S&Ls, its understanding of the physics of finance might be said to resemble its surroundings—high and wide, yes, but not very deep. In less than ten years, with decisive aid from the Reagan administration, policies hashed out in this room helped transform a nagging problem into a stupefying squandering of resources.

That the S&L situation was grave had been known in Washington policy circles since the mid-1980s. Of course, the people had been told very little about it, even as late as January 1989, when Peter Hoagland arrived on the Washington scene—though a major political campaign had just ended, a president and Congress had just been elected.

Though politicians didn't talk about S&Ls, they wouldn't simply go away after the elections, unlike voters. The cost of a "solution" was mounting by $1 billion a month or more. So it was no surprise when George Bush, within two weeks of assuming the presidency, proposed a plan to bail out hundreds of insolvent savings banks. No surprise to Washington insiders, anyway. To the rest of us, it was quite a shock, especially the price tag, which, depending on who you asked, ranged from $90 billion to $500 billion and counting. That's serious money, even in the age of the multitrillion-dollar national debt. It far exceeds what the government spends per year—per decade!—on education or environmental protection, both of which the public would like a lot more of. What was all this money being spent *for?* What happened? The Banking Committee's hearings on Bush's bailout bill promised to address these and other pressing questions—even if few were listening to the answers.

A parade of official witnesses had already testified before the committee's empty chairs. After their opening statements, members were given five minutes for questions, in order of seniority. Hoagland, the lowest-ranking Democrat, was usually among the last to get a crack. He could hardly be expected to play a major role in shaping the complex legislation. But colleagues and staff agreed that his questions showed a "good grasp of the issues."

Many openly praised his intelligence. Members of Congress are notorious for their shameless flattery. But no doubt some of the compliments were sincere. Some members availed themselves of lobbyists who wrote out "astute" questions for them to ask of witnesses—not to mention amendments to legislation, even whole speeches. Hoagland also consulted with lobbyists about questions to put to witnesses. But he seemed quite able to phrase such queries in his own words, and to pronounce the words correctly. Some of his more senior colleagues had trouble doing that.

The witnesses reviewed the causes of the calamity. With great solemnity, and even some breast-beating, they agreed it ought never to be permitted to recur. A man sat quietly at the end of the witness table, his face buried in a funnel, the muscles of his jaw working nonstop. He was pronouncing every word of the proceedings for a tape recorder. His employers would produce a transcript of the tape—the record—and sell it back to the committee at over $4 per page. Often the committee generated hundreds of pages in a day.

As the hearings droned on, it seemed that the creation of an official record was all they were about. There was little skepticism voiced about the proposed bailout, either by committee members or in the press. That was peculiar, since the plan was "designed by the same closed fraternity responsible for the crash of the old system," according to Jim Hightower, the populist Texas agriculture commissioner.

What flashes of controversy there were surrounded the question of funding: who was going to pay? The financial wizards in the Bush administration had come up with some very clever schemes to minimize the political "hit" on the president.

The administration claimed that under its plan the S&L industry would pay the entire $50 billion then considered sufficient to fund the bailout. But the industry was broke. How could it possibly pay? Well, the $50 billion would be borrowed by a so-called nongovernment entity, conveniently created by this legislation, the Resolution Funding Corporation (REFCORP). S&Ls would be responsible for paying back the *principal*. The administration argued that since the $50 billion principal would technically not be a government obligation, there was no reason to add that amount to the budget deficit, ballooning what Bush had promised to cut.

The obligation of the government—i.e., the taxpayers—was

merely to pay the interest on the $50 billion principal. Over the thirty years planned for the transaction, the sum of the interest paid by taxpayers would be in the neighborhood of *$115 billion,* at then current rates.

A few of the witnesses denounced the plan as an elaborate ruse to give Bush "political cover." They recommended paying for the bailout immediately—not over thirty years—to save over $115 billion in interest costs. That clearly would have been cheaper, unless you were a politician who had promised "no new taxes" and lower deficits, as Bush had. Paying for the bailout up front meant higher taxes and higher deficits. The administration was also criticized for underestimating the cost of the bailout, which almost every independent expert said would run much higher than $50 billion, perhaps two or three times as much. If the principal doubled or trebled, so would the mammoth interest cost.

The administration's position on funding the bailout appeared weak, not to say craven. How could it possibly defend a scheme whose only virtue seemed to be that it benefited the president politically? That task fell to the director of the Office of Management and Budget, Richard Darman, slated to appear before the committee. When it came to the fine art of flummoxing congressmen, the man had no peer.

The sleepy hearing room came alive when a "heavyweight" witness like Darman was due. Empty chairs behind the witness table filled with lobbyists and bureaucrats. Media crews flooded the room with wires and lights, so camera operators could kneel before the witness table and harvest sound bites. With all the attention, even seldom seen committee members were drawn to their chairs on the dais. But little of what was talked about here today would be judged sensational enough to make the evening news.

Darman effected a surprising "presence" in the hearing room for a short, pudgy guy. It was his mystique. The government's budget had become so impossibly huge, its financial arrangements so absurdly complex, that people built careers around mastering tiny segments of them. But Darman, it was said, had a map of the whole baffling labyrinth, somewhere behind that annoying smirk of his.

Darman's fluency with mind-fogging budgetary concepts was generally enough to steamroll the standard plodding politico or journalist. Though several committee members challenged him about the administration's funding scheme, like some budgetary Mr. Bojangles, he danced around their objections.

Chalmers Wylie, a slow-talking man with a long, equine face and a rather impressive pompadour, was the committee's ranking Republican. Wylie wondered why we weren't avoiding the huge interest tab by paying for the bailout entirely in 1989. Even if such a plan meant borrowing $50 billion for a shorter term, say two years, wouldn't that be cheaper?

Wylie was talking about acting responsibly: facing debts and paying them off. But Darman patiently replied that to do so would be perceived as "irresponsible" by Wall Street, since it would involve "loading" the $50 billion into the 1989 budget, creating a deficit figure in violation of the Gramm-Rudman deficit-reduction law. This law set limits on how high the deficit could go in a given year. Though it was routinely breached, Darman argued that to do so now would tax Wall Street's patience to the limit. "We would be saying to anyone in financial markets, 'There is absolutely no discipline here, none,' " he said. Consequently, to run up a huge interest tab was more "disciplined" than facing our debts and paying them off at a much cheaper rate. Wylie's five minutes expired, and Darman's peculiar notions of "discipline" and "responsibility" went unchallenged.

Carroll Hubbard, a jowly Democrat from Kentucky, seemed unimpressed with the budget director's looking-glass-world logic. Wouldn't it be cheaper, he reiterated, to borrow the $50 billion over a short term rather than over thirty years?

One way the government borrows money is to sell U.S. Treasury bills, notes, and bonds to investors. At the time, two-year notes, at 9.8 percent, were paying out a *higher* interest rate than thirty-year bonds, at 9.29 percent. Thus "it is obviously cheaper to finance long," Darman said.

This argument seemed to satisfy Hubbard. But thirty-year bonds were only "cheaper" in the narrow sense of lower interest rates. The real factor to consider, obviously, was how long the money would be borrowed. Paying off the money after two years —though at higher rates—would have cost only around $10 billion in interest fees, not the $115 billion in the administration's proposal. Alas, Congressman Hubbard failed to make this obvious argument.

Congressman John LaFalce of Buffalo, New York, was a very ordinary-looking fellow: short, stocky, bespectacled. But he had a "reputation." Words like "blunt," "abrasive," and "intense" were used to describe his legislative style. LaFalce wasn't shy about picking fights if he thought he was right, as he did today, for instance.

LaFalce was in favor of raising taxes to pay off the entire $50 billion over two or three years—without borrowing! In the last year of the Debt Decade, that was radical thinking indeed.

LaFalce wielded a two-pronged fork. Governments, he said, had long recognized that borrowing with bond issues is only prudent when the money is spent on capital improvements—buildings, roads, airports, etc.—that increase the capacity of the community to produce. Then the interest costs of bond issues are justified. But bonding is considered too costly a way to pay for standard government operations and maintenance. "Much less should you bond to fill a hole" like the S&L mess.

LaFalce had another gripe about the administration's thirty-year-payoff scheme. It would mean immorally sloughing the debts of this generation off on our children.

The mention of children seemed to smite something in Darman. "I don't applaud this at all, I regret it," he said, eyes downcast. Nevertheless, he opposed LaFalce's plan. Why? "We are routinely being fiscally irresponsible," he said, "and leaving a large debt for future generations to pay." It was rather cold comfort.

Finally, it was Hoagland's turn to ask questions. While his more senior colleagues could peer down at Darman from their lofty perches, Hoagland's bottom-tier seat put him on almost the same level as the witness—but only symbolically. When it came to actual clout, this legislative pup was leagues below the mighty OMB director. But Hoagland didn't shrink from his duty. With apologies for being "repetitious," he caressingly asked Darman why his elaborate scheme for financing the bailout would be any more reassuring to Wall Street than a more straightforward approach.

Darman was unfailingly polite, but from time to time he permitted a certain contempt for the slow-witted congressional animal to creep over his features. "Apparently," he said, with a mild roll of the eyes, "I cannot answer this question to your satisfaction, because I don't really know how to answer any more clearly than the way in which I have already tried."

With a labored display of "patience," Darman summarized his arguments for the inquisitive freshman. Hoagland refused to be cowed. "I understand the nuances," he softly insisted. "But from the point of view of somebody observing the process in the Midwest . . . they are just going to see this as an elaborate sleight-of-hand. . . ."

Darman was a master at devising arguments. He reached into his bag and quickly pulled out not one but two more for Hoagland's benefit. His first was based on, of all things, Senate rules of procedure. He said that the Senate, unlike the House, permitted amendments to legislation to be offered on the floor. Hence, once senators saw an exception to Gramm-Rudman for the purposes of this legislation, they would rush into the breach with all manner of amendments, stripping out other categories of spending from the discipline of the deficit-reduction law. Soon, Gramm-Rudman's "limits" would apply to nothing.

Secondly, Darman said, there was an astonishing degree of support for the administration's plan from the "community of interest." This support, so hard to come by, so indispensable, must not be risked by changing the fundamental cast of the bill.

Of course, the Senate might have been able to restrain itself from offering any amendments of the kind Darman claimed to fear. And the support of the "community of interest" obviously included the savings and loan industry. Why shouldn't the industry support a plan that so encumbered the taxpayer while letting it off nearly scot-free?

When Darman finished, Hoagland smiled. "That was a pretty good argument," he said. Meanwhile, the chairman had handed a note to a female staffer, who now delivered it to Hoagland. It was a yellow slip of paper, illustrated with the face of a stopwatch that had ticked down five minutes, above a message in bold letters: "Your time has expired."

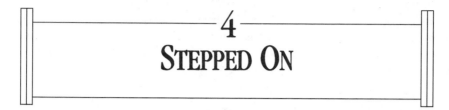

4
STEPPED ON

In number 1415, Longworth House Office Building, Anne Buntain picked up the telephone for perhaps the hundredth time that day. "Congressman Peter Hoagland's office," she said in a lilting voice. "Good afternoon." Anne was twenty-three years old and very pretty in the wholesome, Midwestern manner: flowing wheat-colored hair, sunny smile, big eyes that met yours with no questions asked.

Though Anne might not have been thrilled to hear it, her unflagging high spirits were the stuff that great receptionists are made of. The business of representing the folks back home does not stop with congressmen. Anne was a living symbol of Nebraska's heartland geniality. Or maybe she only seemed like one, nested among so many other symbols. Her desk bordered a small vestibule with a loveseat for visitors, just beyond the door to Hoagland's office. Attached to the desk was a magazine rack jammed with Nebraskiana of every type—maps, guides, propaganda tracts—listing the various things, organic and otherwise,

that symbolized that great sovereign state. The state bird of Nebraska is the meadowlark, the state tree is the cottonwood, the
state flower is goldenrod ("Enough," you may say, but there was
much more), the state insect is the honeybee, the state rock is the
prairie agate, and the state mammal is the whitetail deer. There's
also a state gemstone, fossil, grass, even an official *soil* of Nebraska,
the beloved "typic arguistolls," whatever that may be.

The official tree of Washington, D.C., should perhaps be the
coca tree. One 1989 study concluded that "people in the Washington region may spend as much on cocaine as they do on food and
drink ($8 billion vs. $8.2 billion)."

But cocaine would probably not be a good official substance
of Washington. For that, we should look to something liquid, as in
assets. The three richest communities in the nation, and five of the
top seven, are located in the D.C. metropolitan area.

Of course, the whole point of Washington is that *everything* is
official. It's the official city of the whole blinking country. Appropriately, its fields and boulevards are overgrown with symbolical
furniture—obelisks, equestrian generals, classic revival shrines.

Washington and many of the people in it are supposed to
stand for things. If sometimes the people forget just what, the city
stands for things in spite of them. Waste, for instance: the federal
government spends $1.2 million a year on paper clips alone. Or
perhaps pettiness: John Keker, a federal prosecutor in the Iran-
Contra case, said status-conscious Washington is "like high school"
because "everyone is either in or out," according to an item in *The
Washington Post*. He was also quoted as comparing the city to
places in South Africa because of its "totally segregated" character.

Political comedian Mark Russell says disillusioned Americans
are viewing Washington more and more as a national joke, and
that his humor is no longer just for insiders. "It doesn't matter
where I am," he said. But there are limits to how much even
Washington can entertain. In 1989, three new television series
based in D.C.—one about a freshman congressman—folded
quickly because of "the viewing public's lack of interest in the
nation's capital," wrote TV critic John Carmody.

Of late Washington, mother of laws, has symbolized lawless-
ness. Its high homicide rate earned it the well-publicized nickname
"Murder Capital." That slowed the tourist flow somewhat. But

millions of Americans, despite their "lack of interest" in Washington, continue to make the pilgrimage to its museums and monuments every year.

All of Washington's monuments make for a goodly supply of breathtaking vistas. None, sadly, were visible from the windows of Peter Hoagland's new office. It was a cramped two-room suite in the rear of the Longworth House Office Building, with a not at all uplifting view of the rickety Capitol Hill power plant and its belching smokestacks.

When Hoagland brought his family to the office for a tour, the kids couldn't understand why they weren't "at Congress." There was no dome on the building like the one they'd seen in books. Just this scruffy office, a chaos of stray wires, tatty carpets, scratched woodwork, and halls strewn with furniture like so much jetsam. When the office lottery had been held, Hoagland got near the bottom of the barrel, as freshmen do. These crowded quarters couldn't fit an entire staff, so he was given an annex—three flights up—a long walk to the copy machine. But none of it fazed him or his staff. They were just glad to be here.

By mid-March, the staff had made many improvements since those early, gritty days in Congress. Mail was no longer spilling from huge orange sacks strewn about the office. Now there was a system to log and sort it—sort of. And the gaping emptiness of the bookshelves had been filled with a handsome edition of the U.S. Code—fully 175 neatly arranged volumes, courtesy of the government.

Hoagland was a frugal sort, and he balked at ordering an edition of the code embossed with his name in gold letters—too expensive. He even thought it was a waste of taxpayers' money for him to have a personal set of the basic, stripped-down edition of the code—he would just as soon use the law library. But the House supplies office delivered one anyway. Hoagland also resisted buying flags to stand guard on either side of his office door. Nearly every other congressperson hoisted a pair—one from the home state, one red-white-and-blue Old Glory. But Hoagland viewed this as another bit of frippery he could do without.

Hoagland's flaglessness was of a piece with his unassuming manner, much admired by his staff. Though self-aggrandizement was part of every politician's job, it ran against Hoagland's grain.

According to staff members, when leaving phone messages, he didn't like to identify himself as a congressman, doubtless cutting down on his callbacks in a title-conscious town. He was also uncomfortable wearing the gold eagle lapel pin given to House members, for identification around Capitol Hill, or so it was said. Hoagland found wearing the thing "like bragging about the fact that you are a member of Congress." With rare asperity, he observed that "some hot dogs wear their pins all the time."

Anne used to work for a colleague of Hoagland's in the Unicameral. She leaped at the chance for employment in the new congressman's Washington office. "He's just such a nice person," she said. Her comment summed up the staff's feelings about a man who unfailingly ended phone calls to them with a sincere "thank you" and who often sounded apologetic when asking them to perform some ordinary task.

While Hoagland may have been unpretentious, his idealism sometimes put him on a different wavelength. For example, a copy of *The Power Game,* a seven-hundred-plus-page tome about "how Washington works," lay open on the floor under Anne's chair. Hoagland had recommended that everyone on his very busy staff read the thing. Anne got about a third of the way through before "I was told we didn't *have* to," she said.

Hoagland's staff viewed him as something of an eccentric, though a lovable one. He seemed fairly abstentious. He used no tobacco, watched his (and sometimes others') caffeine intake and drank "at social events." His only apparent addiction was to soup —he couldn't seem to get enough of it. And while he didn't say "Gee Winnikers," like Jimmy Stewart in *Mr. Smith Goes to Washington,* he did say "Gee whiz" quite a lot.

Hoagland's management of his first House floor speech still had some of his aides shaking their heads. Hoagland was introducing legislation in the House that had been placed in the Senate hopper by Nebraska's senior senator, James Exon. The bill would grant federal "scenic river" protection to Nebraska's Niobrara River. Owners of land bordering the river were agitating against the measure, since "protecting" the river meant they couldn't develop their property (or rape the wilderness, depending on your point of view).

The bill held little risk for Hoagland, however, since the Niobrara flows across northwest and north-central Nebraska—nary a drop wets the soil of the 2nd District. If the measure registered at all with his constituents, they would understand that he was simply acting on his much-voiced concern for our natural environment.

On February 2, only the eighth day Congress actually sat in session, Hoagland reserved House floor time to make a speech in support of the Niobrara bill. John Minter was one of two aides who walked across Independence Avenue to the Capitol with Hoagland prior to his speech. John thought the Niobrara bill was a perfect ice-breaker for a freshman. Environmental issues were much on the public mind of late, the bill was "noncontroversial" (in Omaha), "constructive," and, best of all, "not costly."

It looked as if Hoagland merely had to show up and make his speech to reap headlines in the *World-Herald*—maybe even TV time that evening. But on the walk over, he nonchalantly told John and press secretary Gail Handleman of a "courtesy" phone call he'd just placed, to Virginia Smith. That's *the Honorable* Virginia Smith, Republican representative from Nebraska's 3rd District, which encompasses most of the land area of the state, *including the stretch traversed by the Niobrara!* John and Gail rolled their eyes at one another. Their well-meaning boss had alerted the one person in Washington who might spoil his coming-out party.

Hoagland's aides sat in the Members' Gallery to watch his maiden address. He looked nervous, sitting in the well of the chamber, fumbling with a map of the river they'd given him to display on an easel as he spoke. The House was conducting "one-minutes," when any member could gain the floor to make a speech. John and Gail were worried that Virginia Smith would burst in and steal Hoagland's thunder.

And that's precisely what happened. When Hoagland called Smith's office, she was in a Senate hearing room waiting to testify on pending legislation. Alerted by her staff of Hoagland's planned speech, the spry seventy-seven-year-old abruptly quit the committee room and marched all the way across Capitol Hill to the House chamber, to upstage her junior colleague. She secured floor time before Hoagland and launched a speech denouncing the legislation even before he could propose it.

Mrs. Smith looked a bit like a speaker at a ladies' garden club, with her blue hair swept back off her face, high-necked dress, and owlish spectacles. She was a diehard conservative, and champion of the cattle ranchers in her district. It was said that "she speaks for meat." She did not, however, speak for rivers. She consistently supported intrusive "water projects" and other environmentalist anathemas.

"A significant number of the local leaders and local landowners in my district are opposed to this scenic river designation," Mrs. Smith complained in her fussy, schoolmarmish manner. "I will not be supporting this legislation unless there is a consensus among the local people in my district."

The House floor was only sparsely peopled, as usual, so almost no one paid any attention to Mrs. Smith. But the Nebraska press corps had been flacked by Hoagland's staff about his maiden speech. They were expected to be watching closely. The show they were getting was not what Hoagland's media team had in mind.

When Hoagland finally rose to address the nearly empty House, his speech must have seemed anticlimactic to the hometown press, perhaps even to himself. He delivered it in his standard shy, soft-spoken style. But he bravely navigated tongue-trippers like "seven separate ecological, paleontological, and geological ecozones." And he warned that "without the protective easements this bill would provide . . . the tranquillity and peace of the Niobrara River Valley . . . will undoubtedly give way to neon signs, motels, and condominiums."

As Smith's district encompassed the very bed of the river under discussion, her objections would certainly carry some weight. However, no one thought they'd be decisive. After all, both of Nebraska's senators supported the bill. The governor and the state's other House member, both Republicans, endorsed it "in concept." So much for the long view. On the near horizon, Smith's preemptive strike looked like it might just step on Hoagland's headlines.

The evening *World-Herald* confirmed the fears of Hoagland's staff, trumpeting, SMITH OPPOSES SCENIC RIVER BILL. While the article elaborately explained Hoagland's efforts to secure House passage of the measure, he was shut out of the all-important name-recognition-enhancing headline—a dubious reward for his courtesy.

Getting left out of a headline might not seem like a big deal to most of us. But some on Hoagland's team were disappointed—

one staffer in particular seemed downright traumatized. That's because a simple rule applies to freshmen, especially those who won by a whisker: Keep a high profile back in the district—make the homefolk think you're the only one in Congress doing anything. Another ironclad rule, often contradictory, also applied, despite recent claims to the contrary: While you come on like a lion at home, you are to behave like a little lamb in Washington, and keep your mouth shut.

For the average person, whose ideas of life in Congress come from, say, *Mr. Smith Goes to Washington,* that might seem like a backwards strategy. Most people would probably like their representative to give Washington a piece of his mind when he got there—as Jefferson Smith, played by Jimmy Stewart, did in the movie. But Washington's power elite doesn't exactly appreciate it when real-life Mr. Smiths come to town. Hell, it didn't even like the movie.

When Mr. Smith discovers the political machine's well-crafted graft, he risks ruin to face down corrupt politicians, the press, even his own angry constituents, in a lonely filibuster. In the end, Smith's simple virtue triumphs; integrity is restored to our democratic institutions. The Library of Congress, unshy of hyperbole, has named *Mr. Smith* one of the twenty-five best films of all time. That citation reflects the movie's popularity now. But back in 1939 when it premiered in Washington, officials were screaming for the head of its director, Frank Capra. They thought the film gave aid and comfort to our Axis enemies with its portrait of American democracy gone wrong. "I took the worst shellacking of my professional life," Capra wrote. Some Hollywood producers were so worried about a congressional crackdown on the industry that they offered Columbia pictures $2 million to can the film.

Columbia stood its ground and released the picture, to widespread critical acclaim. Ironically, a polemic played out in letters pages at the time that resembled the recent controversy over flag burning. One side was appalled at the film's affront to the dignity of what Americans hold most sacred. The other side said the right to make such affronts is what we hold most sacred.

Nowadays, one might risk getting roughed up by rednecks if he burned a print of *Mr. Smith.* But the film's initial reception by official Washington might stand as an instructive metaphor for any would-be Mr. Smiths in the corridors of power.

Real-life Mr. Smiths have had a hard time getting to Washington in the first place. According to an account in *Honest Graft* by *Wall Street Journal* reporter Brooks Jackson, Democrat David Martin turned his 1986 North Carolina congressional race into a crusade for good government. Martin wanted to end the insidious practice of congressional candidates accepting campaign money from special interests with a legislative agenda. Washington lobbyists took note, flooding Martin's opponent with cash in an attempt to bury the reformer. The campaign committee of Martin's own party even withheld full funding, so displeased was it with his reformist message. Martin lost.

Hoagland wasn't likely to launch a reform crusade anytime soon. Though he'd flirted with rebelliousness in his life, he was hardly a born rouser of the rabble. His parents were both bona fide members of the ruling class, and young Peter had something of a princely childhood.

5

FREE MEDIA

Peter Hoagland looks like his great-grandfather on his mother's side, Joseph Franklin Carpenter, a tall, willowy man whose deep-set eyes seemed ablaze with dreams. Around 1905, Joseph convinced his five brothers, also his business partners, to build a huge poured-concrete warehouse for their paper company in downtown Omaha. It was a risky investment on what would become the first structure of its kind west of the Mississippi.

Ever since Omaha was chosen by Abraham Lincoln to be the eastern terminus of the transcontinental railroad, there were opportunities aplenty for enterprising capitalists to make a buck. By the 1880s, with the railroad laying its bed across the plains and the Homestead Act awarding generous acres of rich soil to settlers, the entire state of Nebraska seemed a land of promise. Its population more than doubled in just a decade, from 452,000 to 1,062,000.

Even after drought and depression wilted farm profits in the 1890s and people began fleeing the state, Omaha still thrived. It

was the last outfitting station for intrepid westward trekkers. And
as the West blossomed, Omaha watered it with wholesale goods,
supplying farmers and cattlemen with bricks, carriages, flour, and
all things manufactured or processed. The rail terminus became a
way station for livestock ranchers. A meatpacking industry grew,
which boasted the third-biggest stockyards network in the nation.
At one point, the city was said to shelter "more pigs than people."

But a few years later, when the lurching cycle of economic
boom and bust had temporarily bottomed out, Joseph Carpenter
lost faith. In a black mood mirroring the dire news of the day, he
convinced himself the business would be crushed under the
weight of debts assumed to finance the warehouse, a structure that
now seemed quite extravagant. One day, Joseph's youngest son
found him dead, his inert hand wrapped around a pistol.

But the bleak vision that drove Joseph to suicide was a mi-
rage. The Carpenter Paper Company thrived, eventually becoming "one of the largest paper wholesalers in the nation," according
to a 1980 report prepared by the Omaha City Planning Department. Meanwhile, another local businessman was making good.
George A. Hoagland, who'd started the Hoagland Lumber Company in 1850, was reaping a fortune on sales of railroad ties to the
Union Pacific line.

When Laurence Hoagland, grandson of the Hoagland Lumber king, married Naomi Carpenter, granddaughter of the
founder of Carpenter Paper, it might have appeared to be an ideal
"merger" of lumber's supply with paper's demand. But the family
said Hoagland Lumber never did any business with Carpenter Paper. The former was eventually sold, and Laurence Hoagland
went to work for the paper company as a vice-president.

Peter Hoagland was born November 17, 1941, the second of
Laurance and Naomi's three children. The family lived in a close-
knit upper-class section of west-central Omaha. Among their
neighbors on those serene, richly arbored streets were the presidents of the bank, the railroad, the newspaper. Naomi Carpenter
Hoagland was a registered Colonial Dame. And the Hoaglands'
closest friends always seemed to be Republicans, preferably of the
rock-ribbed variety, as were Peter and his older brother, Laurence. (The politics of Jane, his younger sister, are not spoken of.)

The Hoaglands' lavish Tudor-style home—an exact replica of
one in England—was cared for by a small domestic staff, and

young Peter grew amid the accouterments of the comfortable. He took tennis lessons at the club and went to camp every summer. He wasn't at all rebellious. His worst bit of "monkey business," recalls his mother, was stealing a candy bar, when he was around eight. Otherwise, the boy was "almost too good."

But something happened to young Republican Peter after he went away to college—a sort of political metamorphosis.

It probably hadn't occurred yet when he finished Stanford, where he graduated with distinction in International Affairs. As an undergrad, Hoagland was already a budding trustee of the established order, serving on a committee that meted out discipline to fellow students.

After college, Hoagland spent a summer interning in the Washington office of Nebraska Senator Roman Hruska, scoping out the Capitol, locus of his boyhood dreams. Hruska later won fifteen minutes of fame in defense of Richard Nixon's nomination of the lackluster judge Harold Carswell for a vacancy on the Supreme Court. To the embarrassment of Nebraskans, Hruska argued that mediocre people deserve representation on the court too. Hoagland mostly answered correspondence for his patron, though he remembers waiting in the senate chamber for Hruska to deliver a speech he'd written, only to be disappointed when the senator never delivered it. In a picture taken with Hruska back then, a close-cropped, perfectly groomed Hoagland looks like the quarterback in some fifties teen flick, standing respectfully next to his chortling, potato-faced senator.

At the end of the summer, Hoagland began a stint in the Army, mostly stationed in Washington. He was in from 1963 to 1965—"wartime," as he later put it on campaign brochures. Hoagland had been in ROTC since high school, and won a cushy assignment as a plainclothes operative for the Army's "intelligence" division. Again an enforcer of conformity, he lived off-base in a Georgetown apartment, running background checks on candidates for security clearances. He also briefly clerked in a nearby bookstore. Part of his training included "black bag" techniques—how to pick locks to break into a subject's home—which he said he never used. He was eventually ordered to quit the bookshop. Some of its titles were deemed too "subversive."

The change in Hoagland seems to have begun during his years in Washington. He got a close-up look at the effect on the city of John F. Kennedy, and his ideas of energetic, activist government. Hoagland was impressed with what he viewed to be Kennedy's approach to problem-solving, a search for pragmatic answers that were based not in ideology but in philosophy, in a disinterested quest for intellectual truth.

After the Army, Hoagland was accepted at both Harvard and Yale law schools. He picked Yale because its program emphasized law "as an instrument of social change." But there wasn't much change socially for Hoagland in New Haven, despite any intellectual broadening he experienced there. His friends were still of the same privileged background.

One of Hoagland's Yale brethren, Mike Walsh, currently the Omaha-based chairman of the Union Pacific Railroad, recalled many talks about career plans among his classmates. One big question was often mulled: whether to go "back home" or pursue riches in the wider world. Going "back home" was a euphemism. It didn't mean settling down to enjoy the simple life, but planting roots to nourish a later run for Congress.

The students were mentally pinning their colors on a map of the United States. A few besides Hoagland, including John Spratt of South Carolina and David Skaggs of Colorado, later won seats in Congress, always something of a postgraduate school for elite Ivy League universities. Harvard's graduates wind up in Congress so routinely that the school regularly offers a course on running for office. Of the 535 men and women in the 101st Congress, forty-eight attended Harvard, twenty-two studied at Yale, and five have degrees from both.

After graduating from law school, Hoagland worked for ten months in a Washington law firm. Then he clerked for a year in the office of a federal judge, enjoying its atmosphere of legal intellectualism.

After his clerkship ended, Hoagland signed on as a lawyer for the District of Columbia office of the public defender. It was an ideal laboratory for him. D.C.'s public defender's office was unique in the nation. Since the District is federal property, all its criminal cases are federal cases. And since federal courts pay court-appointed attorneys well to represent indigent, lawyerless clients, there was no dearth of experienced local lawyers volunteering to take their cases. So the D.C. public defender's office not only was the best-funded legal aid bureau in the country, it also had one of the lightest caseloads. Hoagland got more trial experience than he ever could in a corporate firm, without dealing with the scarce resources and huge backlogs that usually plague legal aid lawyers. Though he made considerable financial sacrifices to work for the public defender's office once again, he viewed the problems of the deprived from a relatively comfortable perspective.

At the public defender's office, Hoagland met the woman he would marry, Barbara Erickson, a self-described "blue-collar kid" from New Jersey with a leftish outlook. As the turbulent sixties cooled into the committed seventies, Hoagland was moving in the earnest atmosphere of liberal "bleeders," and his metamorphosis was completed.

On the surface, the young tool of the ruling class seemed to bloom into an enlightened instrument of progressive change. At the office, he looked like something out of *Mod Squad,* wearing longish hair, sideburns, and what Barbara describes as "these ties," wide, flowery things he bought in England. He rode a motorcycle to work and ran rivers in a kayak on occasional weekends. During the week, he tried to change the world.

But under Hoagland's wide ties still beat the careful heart of a born conformist. He enjoyed his work, but never got emotionally involved with clients, the way, for instance, Barbara did. For him, cases were intellectual exercises, learning experiences. When he visited clients in jail, he never noticed the expressive graffiti smeared on the dank walls. He rode a motorcycle—a scooter really—mostly because it got good gas mileage. He didn't tell his parents about it. That wasn't all he kept from them.

In September 1973, Peter and Barbara were married in Washington. Soon it was "back home" to Omaha for the newlyweds, where they moved in with his folks. Hoagland quickly took steps to get his political career off the ground. He cut his hair, put on a conservative suit, and took a job in a law firm. But some of the changes in him appear to have stuck.

Peter and Barbara began doing volunteer work for a congressional candidate—a Democrat. But they kept trips to campaign headquarters secret from Peter's deeply Republican parents, using the excuse that they were "going to a movie." Barbara could scarcely believe what she was seeing. "This person is thirty-four years old and he doesn't tell his mother what party he's in," she recalls thinking.

Soon the inevitable happened. Naomi Hoagland confronted her son with an ugly "rumor" going around that he was—a *Democrat!* "To hear Barbara tell it, Mrs. Hoagland said 'Democrat' the way someone else would say 'drug addict,'" Hoagland was nudged out of the closet. He later enjoyed telling audiences that his father, fond of cursing Franklin Roosevelt at the family table, couldn't decide which was worse, his son's being a lawyer or a Democrat.

Hoagland's switch was partly philosophical, and, his wife suggests, partly practical. Being a Democrat might not matter much in Nebraska's largely nonpartisan politics. But in Congress, if and when Hoagland got there, it just might. "It was clear the Democrats were going to have the power" in Congress, Barbara said.

But perhaps Mother knows best. Naomi Hoagland is certain that Watergate—and Richard Nixon's resignation in 1974—was the real reason for her son's disillusionment with the party of Lincoln. If so, he wasn't alone. Republicans across the country were voted out of office in '74. A budding politician was bound to be impressed.

Hoagland quickly found his niche amid the general post-Watergate reform euphoria. In 1975, he mounted a Common Cause–inspired ballot-initiative campaign in Nebraska for "sunshine" laws, to require open hearings in the statehouse and financial disclosure for officials. When his petitions filled quickly, the legislature was roused into action, passing a tough new ethics law. It was seen as a victory for Hoagland, whose star was on the rise.

In 1978, Hoagland won a seat in the Unicameral on his first try, from his upper-middle-class district of west Omaha. His brochures from those days show him tossing a football, Camelot-style, in an oxford shirt.

Hoagland joined with other newly elected state senators to shake up the legislative establishment. On issues like health care cost containment, water quality, and education, when senior members blocked action in committees they controlled, this "new breed," as they were called, held their own unofficial hearings and invited experts to testify. The old bulls were furious. But the youngsters got things done. For example, with their help, a landmark health care cost containment bill was passed in 1979.

Hoagland earned a reputation for candor and directness in

the statehouse. "You always know where he stands on an issue" was one lobbyist's oft-echoed comment. But he also began to seem a little like a political chameleon.

As the reformist seventies surrendered to the reactionary eighties, Hoagland rode the wave. He still worked on education and environmental issues. But he seemed to put more energy into high-profile campaigns for stiffer penalties against drunk drivers and to outlaw slot machine gambling. Hoagland thought both bills were the right thing to do and good for Nebraska, but championing such relatively noncontroversial issues looked like cheap headline-grabbing to some.

If Hoagland appeared a little cautious during his early days in Washington, it was partly due to lessons learned in the Unicameral. After the new breed revolted, their elders sought revenge. Hoagland found his progress blocked on committees. He waited years for a chairmanship that should have come his way much sooner. Jim Crounse, his current staff chief, who was with him in Lincoln during the rebellion, summed up how he and Hoagland felt about it now. "We learned not to do it again," he said.

Hoagland was going to do things by the book this time.

As of January 3, 1989, each member of the House of Representatives was entitled to $431,760 in "clerk-hire" money for staff salaries. A further $146,388, on average, would cover office rental and equipment, travel, and miscellaneous items. This figure, significantly, did not include the cash value of the frank, considerable for a typical legislator, which defrayed postage costs.

On paper, the congressional office budget could be viewed as a fairly modest stipend to support research and coalition-building for legislative solutions to our nation's vexing problems. But some see in it the makings of a taxpayer-financed PR machine which can be used to wage a "constant campaign." In any case, Hoagland's first step was to hire an administrative assistant, the top staff slot, to manage it all. Hoagland hired Jim Crounse, his staff chief from the early days in Lincoln, who'd since become a professional campaign consultant, most recently employed by the Democratic Congressional Campaign Committee in Washington, electioneering arm of House Democrats. While Jim was with the DCCC, he had advised the Hoagland campaign "on my own time," he said. During the primary, when the party's own rules dictated neutrality for party employees, Cece Zorinsky had objected to Jim's role in the Hoagland camp. But party leaders, not known for enforcing their rules, didn't make an issue of it.

As second in command, Hoagland hired another political operative, Gary Caruso, manager of his primary campaign, as communications director. He was the official chief "spin doctor" in relations with the media. One full-time media aide was the norm in the House. Hoagland hired Gail Handleman, officially as a "Legislative Aide," but unofficially she seemed to do an awful lot of work on "media." Between Jim, Gary, and Gail, the media was "flacked" routinely—alerted to possible stories about Hoagland. Freshmen weren't expected to accomplish much, but Hoagland wouldn't mind seeming as if he were by getting in the news as much as possible. This used to be called "publicity." Now politicians refer to it as "free media." Gary was something of a free-media genius. Jim, meanwhile, specialized in "direct mail," the use of sophisticated postal marketing techniques to win friends and influence voters.

Of the $431,760 Hoagland was allotted for staff salaries, exactly none was spent on hiring people with Washington policy or legislative expertise. To help with the Banking Committee he hired an "intelligent generalist" who had no experience in banking issues.

Jim Crounse was a genial thirty-seven-year-old with a roly-polyish build and a bushy mustache. He was the first to admit that he didn't have much experience running an office and probably didn't have the temperament for it. He considered himself too laid-back about organizational details. But somewhere in Jim's job description you expected to find a sentence like "Maintain an acute state of anxiety about the political ramifications of all things." When it came to managing Hoagland's public image, Jim suddenly turned into a detail man.

The day the *World-Herald*'s Niobrara story was published, Jim actually phoned the paper to request a change in the headline for the next edition. After some haggling, he got a change, though not exactly what he wanted. Hoagland's name still didn't appear in the headline, but it was switched from SMITH OPPOSES SCENIC-RIVER BILL to BACKERS OPTIMISTIC ON SCENIC-RIVER BILL.

Right from the start, Jim guarded Hoagland's public image exactly like a man who owned a stake in it. During an early trip to Washington after the election, Hoagland was denied entry at the

door of the Capitol by a security guard. The congressman-elect
wasn't carrying the right ID. Nicole Simmons, a *World-Herald* reporter, was with Hoagland. She wrote a story mistakenly stating
that he'd been barred on his "first" visit to the Capitol. Actually,
another guard had let him pass without fuss earlier that day. In any
case, one might well ask, who cared? But Jim wasn't amused. He
thought the story made Hoagland look silly. "It was inaccurate!"
he insisted.

Jim locked horns with Simmons again soon. On the afternoon
Hoagland was sworn in, his office was jammed with revelers from
Nebraska. In the midst of the jollity, someone pointed to the television, aglow with C-Span's coverage of House floor proceedings.
All the congressfolk were crowded into the chamber voting on
something. But wait a minute! Hoagland was a congressman now,
and *he* wasn't voting.

Oops! He'd missed a vote—on his first day!

The roll call was on a Republican nuisance motion, doomed
from the start, to send House rules back to committee. It was
purely procedural, the sort of thing the press overlooks all the
time. But standing right behind Hoagland as he watched his colleagues voting, and the clock running out, was Nicole Simmons.
Of course she wrote for the evening paper that Hoagland "missed
his *first* opportunity to vote."

Missing votes was a touchy area for Hoagland. During his last
term in the Unicameral, his legal work had kept him away from
the legislature fairly often, and he had faced sharp campaign criticism for excessive absenteeism. A representative who fails to vote
fails to represent in the most basic way.

Simmons's story only mentioned the missed vote, buried in
the sixth paragraph, with not a word about Hoagland's prior absenteeism. But to hear Jim tell it, banner headlines were screaming
HOAGLAND MISSES FIRST VOTE. He was livid. He called Simmons
to point out that her facts were wrong again, Hoagland had actually missed his *third* vote, not his first.

Jim's jitters were hardly unusual in this age of the political
"attack video." He wasn't reacting so much to what Simmons had
actually written but to how it might be amplified out of all propor-
tion in a thirty-second TV spot by an opponent in the next campaign. After all, the election was *only* some six hundred days away.
To answer attacks on the missed "first" vote might cost tens of

thousands of dollars in TV time, the true price, in Jim's mind, of Simmons's slip-up. He didn't seem to think a story that said "Hoagland misses vote on *first day*" might be just as open to mischievous publicity.

Jim's protectiveness was understandable. If Hoagland lost this job, where did that leave him? Besides, the two went back a long way. Jim said his boss was "like an older brother" to him.

When Jim was twenty-five and still a law student at Creighton University, he filed as a candidate for one of Omaha's seats in the Unicameral. Soon he got a phone call from a soft-spoken guy named Hoagland. Jim recognized the name. It was on the primary ballot with his own. But he'd never met the fellow. Hoagland didn't exactly make a winning first impression. In his caressing way, he asked Jim to drop out of the race and support *him!*

Jim says people always get this story wrong. "He was running against *me!* I filed first."

Jim found Hoagland's offer insulting and stayed in the race. But Hoagland spent some serious money, handily winning a slot on the ballot for the general election. Suddenly, an alliance with the man didn't seem so outrageous. The two met over dinner—it was supposed to be Hoagland's treat but he forgot his wallet—and Jim agreed to help elect his former opponent to the Unicameral. They've been partners, more or less, ever since.

Hoagland was always something of an issues nerd. His blood raced to the arcana of groundwater and health care cost containment. But Crounse was a news freak and "political junkie." At seventeen, he'd memorized, for no particular reason, the names of every U.S. senator, though he "wasn't much with trigonometry."

While Hoagland's staff seemed to carry on his campaign from the D.C. office, he took care of legislative matters, often with minimal involvement from them. On most issues, "he's his own LA," said John Minter, another former DCCC employee who was nominally Hoagland's LA (legislative assistant) on some of those very issues. Meanwhile, among John's early tasks was the forging of Hoagland's signature on hundreds of "personal" computer-generated letters to constituents.

One day, Hoagland's banking aide, Nancy Nagel, was asked by Jim—and very nicely—to keep him and Gary informed of what the boss was up to in the Banking Committee. Hoagland himself was very hard to pin down for a briefing. Nancy, assuming the information was needed for press releases, bridled a bit. "I can't read your journalistic priorities," she snapped.

Hoagland's wife, Barbara, on the other hand, could read them. Early in the year, at Barbara's insistence, Hoagland didn't tell his staff that she was pregnant. "They would have sent out a press release," said Barbara. (They eventually found out, months later, and they *were* tempted.)

At the DCCC, Jim had been taught that the ideal congressional office combined legislative and PR activities as much as possible. That meant finding an issue to work on in Washington that could be milked for media back home. Jim and Gary thought they had an ace in the hole: the scandal at Omaha's Franklin Credit Union.

Omahans tend to believe the best about people. So no eyebrows were raised when Larry King, a local black businessman, was showing signs of some very high living. Signs such as the diamond rings sprouting like fungi from his stumpy fingers, the $65,000 wristwatch, the Corvettes, the Mercedeses, the chartered Learjet whisking him to New York, Los Angeles, Jamaica, the rented limos carting him to the Plaza, the Ritz, or his $5,000-per-month palazzo in Washington, D.C. King must have seemed like one of Omaha's thriftiest bon vivants, for he managed it all, and much more, on the meager salary of $16,200, paid him for running the local Franklin Community Credit Union—running it into the ground, as it turned out.

But who could suspect Larry King of till-dipping? Several local brahmins were on Franklin's board of advisers. And the credit union was a model of community self-help, a spring of hope watering the eventual reflowering of impoverished north Omaha. It made poor families' savings work for their own community— not just enrich uptown bankers—through lending to neighborhood and minority-run enterprises, whose loan applications ritually rot in the in-boxes of uptown banks.

King gave lip service to Republican mantras, like "A hand up is not a hand out," easily wooing national party leaders. He was groomed for greatness, a man to lead blacks back to the party of Lincoln. He became vice-chairman of the National Black Republican Council. A passable baritone, he sang the national anthem at the 1984 Republican National Convention, and he hosted a hoe-

down at the 1988 enclave, which featured those grand old partiers
Ronald and Nancy Reagan. King picked up the $100,000 tab.

But just a few days before the '88 election, Franklin was
raided by waves of dark-suited federal agents, who accused King
of embezzling over $30 million. There were many red faces
among the Omaha—and Republican Party—elite. Blushing most
scarlet, perhaps, was Harold Andersen, publisher of the *Omaha
World Herald.* He was a member of Franklin's advisory board and
had run building-fund drives to finance the construction of addi-
tions to the credit union. One was a sanctuary for King, in which a
brass bed was installed, where the hope of north Omaha allegedly
stretched out his burly three hundred plus pounds for midday
cocaine-stoked trysts with call boys and prostitutes.

Gossip was rampant in Omaha. There were whispers that a
high-level cover-up had shielded King. Rumors flew that prominent citizens might be sucked under in the whirlpool of scandal.

The House Banking Committee had jurisdiction over federally insured credit unions like Franklin. But when committee assignments were being made, a seat on Banking might have seemed
like the last place Hoagland would be comfortable. He'd never
had much interest in high finance. His millionaire brother Laurie
was the family's investment guru.

Hoagland's interests in environmental protection and education might have suited him better for the Interior Affairs or Education and Labor committees. But Banking *was* handling the year's
biggest piece of legislation. And it was among the more powerful
committees, after obvious heavyweights like Energy and Commerce and Ways and Means, on which open seats were rare. Banking members, like the members of other powerhouse panels,
attracted lucrative attention from lobbyists when it came time to
pony up campaign contributions.

Freshmen were allowed to serve on only one major committee. Despite Hoagland's lack of interest in financial matters, he
chose to enter the race for one of the three open seats on Banking.
He said he wanted in on the year's main action—the S&L legislation. But getting a seat on Banking would also permit him to play
a role in the mushrooming, media-intensive Franklin affair back in
Omaha.

Hoagland relied on regional comity for help to win the seat.
Dan Glickman was a veteran congressman from Kansas, the place

permanently wedded to Nebraska by a hyphen in accounts of Civil War history. Glickman was a member of the Steering and Policy Committee, the Democratic Party organ that makes committee assignments. He argued before that panel that Hoagland belonged on Banking because Omaha was a regional financial center, and its representative deserved a voice.

Jim McDermott, the psychiatrist freshman from Seattle, won the first of the Banking vacancies with the backing of then Majority Leader Tom Foley, also of Washington State. Richard Neal, the freshman from Springfield, Massachusetts, got the second slot with help from his state's delegation, which had *two* members on Steering and Policy. But the contest for the third and last slot was close. Hoagland and another freshman were tied, both one vote shy of winning, on three separate ballots. Then, as Hoagland heard the story, John Mack, chief aide to House Speaker Jim Wright, left the committee on the delicate errand of summoning his boss from the lavatory to break the tie on the next ballot. When a new tally was finished, Hoagland emerged a one-vote winner. Those present assumed the speaker himself had put him over the top. Perhaps those visits Hoagland and Crounse had paid to Mack after the election had paid off.

6
LEGISLATIVE ATMOSPHERE

S everal very overweight men piled into Hoagland's inner sanc-
tum, his office-within-the-office, for a spot of lobbying. After
they quickly filled available seating, a few found places against the
wall to lean, arms crossed. Their dress was casual—slacks and polo
shirts stretched over important paunches—but their mood seemed
edgy.

Hoagland swung his chair away from his desk to face them.
Many congressfolk conducted business from behind their desks,
staring down visitors across the powerful expanse of their blotters.
Such muscular furniture language wasn't for Hoagland. He faced
his desk democratically to the wall, so no artificial barriers came
between him and his guests. But certain barriers are immune even
to enlightened interior decorating.

This group was a delegation from the Omaha Chapter of Associated Builders and Contractors. During Hoagland's fall campaign they backed Schenken "in a big way," he said. Now the
tables, speaking of redecorating, had turned.

Hoagland withheld his usual boyish smile as the group's spokesman searched for an icebreaker. Many lobbying styles are practiced on Capitol Hill, involving varying degrees of discretion. This group seemed to opt for the lowest possible degree, eschewing subtlety altogether.

Organizations of a certain stripe commonly visited Congress in herds, to symbolize voting strength. But these bulls seemed to charge past symbolism to veiled threats. "We have two hundred and forty contractors throughout the state," the spokesman said, adding that many were in the Omaha area. One could easily have interpreted these words, and the gruff tones they were delivered in, as being in the nature of a warning, but Hoagland did not seem to feel that was the case.

Like many out-of-town groups that visit Congress, these men were big on pins and other chestware. Their busy shirtfronts sprouted American flag pins, Nebraska silhouette pins, name tags ("DICK: Associated Builders and Contractors"), even blue ribbons, as if they'd finally been appreciated by the judges at the county fair.

Hoagland listened, silent and expressionless, as the leader finished and other members of the group piped up with their concerns. "Double-breasting," grunted one man, suggesting this was not something he was fond of. It was said to occur when a contractor operated both a union and a nonunion shop out of the same offices, and channeled work to the nonunion shop as a means of breaking or lessening the influence of the union.

"Line-item veto," mumbled another man, almost inaudibly, "what do you think?" Hoagland didn't think much of giving the president the power to veto sections of a bill without vetoing the entire bill. But before he got a chance to say so, another man blurted out: "Minimum wage!" The builders were against the proposed hike. Again, Hoagland was on the other side of the issue.

But none of the other builders kept the minimum-wage ball in the air. A few were admiring the nest of photographs of Hoagland with other politicians, which hung above the conference table. Pictures were sent to members all the time from the official photographers on Capitol Hill and at the White House. The centerpiece of Hoagland's collection showed him sharing an unsynchronized handshake with George Bush, who was, regrettably, looking away when the shutter snapped.

Though Hoagland hadn't been given much chance to speak, the group's leader expressed the hope that "a dialogue" might be established between the builders and their congressman. They wanted Hoagland to use them as "a resource." They left a package, as do nearly all lobbyists worthy of the name, containing a breakdown of issues, and "our logic."

Hoagland's response, when he could finally give it, was cool. He didn't have time to study their issues right now, but he would look into them. He suggested that they call him. He probably couldn't have been much nastier if he tried.

Mercifully, the buzzers sounded that signaled a vote in progress. Hoagland had to rush off to the floor.

Votes were often annoying interruptions. It took ten or twenty minutes or more to walk to the House floor, figure out the issue being voted on, make up your mind, vote, and come back. After all that, it was hard, if not impossible, to refocus on what you'd been doing.

But votes could also be lifeboats to freedom. At times, when Hoagland was closeted with some lobbyist, he seemed to breathe easier when he heard the telltale high-pitched squall in the area of his right kidney—his beeper. He would calmly lift it from his jacket pocket and place it where his guests, impressed by the "insider" ambience, could hear. The beeper's tiny speaker crackled, and a wave of static washed up a jagged male voice: "This is the House Democratic Cloakroom . . . members have fifteen minutes to record their votes."

Going to the floor wasn't always an escape. When Hoagland's schedule was jammed with lobbyists—which seemed to be always—they were often stacked up in the waiting room like so many DC-10s. Hoagland sometimes had to "meet" with them on the fly, walking to the floor or some other appointment. This is a standard way of doing business on workaholic Capitol Hill. Movable meetings are sometimes written in on a member's daily schedule.

Once Hoagland rushed off to vote with a pair of ambitious young men in pinstripes who represented Merrill Lynch from the Wall Street law firm of Seward Kissell. At Independence Avenue, the group waited for the light before crossing to the Capitol, its ivory dome looming. One of the lobbyists focused serious eyes on Hoagland. In a voice raised to compete with midday traffic, the lobbyist launched into a quick lesson for the congressman on the complex topic of brokered deposits. These were a principal cause, or so many believed, of the savings and loan meltdown. Naturally, this pair wanted to *protect* brokered deposits from congressional curbs.

After the light changed, the lobbyist summed up as they crossed. "So, that's brokered deposits," he said to a seemingly baffled Hoagland. "Pretty clear, huh?" Hoagland's as polite as they come, but even he couldn't choke back laughter. He cordially suggested the pair "send something" to explain their position.

Hoagland finally shed his lobbyists and hustled into the ground-floor revolving door on the east front of the Capitol marked "Members and Staff Only." In the marble lobby, a Capitol policeman stepped up, as if to block his way. Hoagland wasn't wearing his lapel pin. "I'm a congressman," he said, less shyly than usual. The nearby elevator exploded in mock applause. Above it, a "Member's Only" sign glowed, as always during votes. "Make 'em learn who you are," a voice roared from the elevator, causing much laughter within, as Hoagland stepped aboard.

If Congress seems like a circus sometimes, the House chamber is at least a three-ringer: part cathedral, part commodities trading pit, and part low-rent comedy club.

When the chamber isn't crowded, it has a somber, high-church feel. Soft sunshine filters through the skylight, bathing the white marble of the altarlike speaker's rostrum in a warm glow. On either side of the rostrum hang gilt-framed portraits of secular saints. On the left is George Washington, his wooden teeth hidden behind a stiff grimace, resting a guardian's hand on a copy of the Constitution. Opposite the Father of Our Country is a dapper gent who may qualify as its Godfather, French general the Marquis de Lafayette. His nation's last-minute aid was the midwifery that saw us through our revolutionary birth traumas.

Ringing the three-story-high chamber are relief images of the Lawgivers of the Ages: Hammurabi, Innocent III, and Napoleon, among others. Each is in profile, except a copiously bearded Moses in the back of the hall, staring fixedly forward. If the heat of *his* gaze doesn't make you feel the weight of your responsibilities, engraved on the front wall is this prayer from Daniel Webster:

Let Us Develope The Resources Of Our Land, Call Forth
Its Powers, Build Up Its Institutions, Promote All Its
Great Interests, And See Whether We Also In Our Day
And Generation May Not Perform Something Worthy
To Be Remembered.

In this rich environment, visitors can almost hear echoes of
the epoch-shaping oratory of bygone days, when Cicero and De-
mosthenes were still models for those who would persuade an
audience with words. But these days, if guests happen to drop by
when the House is in session, they might be disappointed to find
only a small gang of lawyers who have apparently overdosed on
Robert's Rules of Order.

Generally, only members from committees with jurisdiction
over a bill bother to debate it. The flow of their "expert" remarks
is often clogged by statistics, or specimens of Washington's peculiar argot, its "sequesters" and "grandfathered non-bank banks."
A member of the British House of Commons, Gordon Brown,
called our House "boring" compared to the stately anarchy of his.
"It's more technical," he said.

Spectators almost always outnumber legislators on the floor,
though they probably can't make much sense of what is being said,
if their blank stares tell anything. At one time, debates not only
filled the galleries with scions of Washington society, but brought
attentive crowds of lawmakers to their seats in the chamber. Of
course, in those days members only *had* seats in the chamber.
There were no congressional office complexes. The cloakrooms
were places to hang coats. Nowadays, with most members off in
committees or their own domains, debates are conducted by a
handful, fulminating by the hour before row upon row of empty
chairs.

Is *anyone* listening?

Naturally, the official reporter of the House catches every
word on his stenotype machine—for the *Congressional Record.* But
those words aren't necessarily the last word. Before the *Record* is
printed, transcripts of the day's proceedings are sent to members,
so they can edit out any embarrassments—unseemly candor, gram-
matical errors, or whatever—that may have leaked into their remarks. Editors at the *Record* also give it a scrubbing.

While what is said on the floor sometimes doesn't make it into the *Record,* what is never said often does. Members are allowed to submit written statements—"extensions of remarks"—for printing. These read like speeches delivered on the floor, complete with addresses to the chair ("Mr. Speaker . . ."). Only their smaller typeface tip the reader that they were never spoken at all.

Sometimes the censors let things slip by in "extensions" that might not have gotten into the *Record* otherwise. William Dannemeyer, the archconservative from California, submitted a racy extension about a pet hate of his: homosexuality.

"Militant homosexuals," Dannemeyer wrote, do not want Americans to learn of their heinous habits. "They do not want you to know that the average homosexual has homosexual sex two or three times per week." Dannemeyer wasn't shy about revealing the rites of the gay demimonde, with references to such exotic practices as "rimming," "fisting," "handballing," and the widespread use of "vegetables" and even "light bulbs" as erotic aids. The stodgy pages of the *Record* had never seen the likes before. Naturally, some were outraged. What Dannemeyer wrote "would not be published in a family newspaper," said Andy Jacobs, an Indiana Democrat, according to one published report, which said he tried to have the pages expunged from the permanent record.

If members pay any attention to events as they unfold on the floor, they generally do *not* do it the old-fashioned way, by sitting in the chamber and listening. They do it the American way—by watching TV. Throughout the day, tubes all over Capitol Hill glow with C-Span's coverage of House and Senate floor proceedings. But members with schedules anything near as packed as Hoagland's seldom have time to sit back and watch. Their staffs have even less free time. So sets are left to drone in the background, like video Muzak, pumping legislative "atmosphere" to every corner of Congress.

Of course, the presence of TV cameras in the chamber affects what is said, rewarding with exposure on network news speakers who spice their remarks with outtakeable sound bites, and punishing with oblivion any purveyors of elaborate, well-reasoned arguments that TV can't digest.

One of the 101st Congress's sound-bite artists was James Traficant of Youngstown, Ohio. The sleepy chamber perked up when he swaggered to the podium, a most uncongressional-looking figure, dressed in cowboy boots and—yes—bell-bottom pants! His tie was loosened, his hair askew, and there was rowdy gleam in his eyes.

Traficant's idiom was the one-minute speech—make that the one-minute barroom tirade. A populist who believed his "rust belt" constituents had been forgotten by Washington, Traficant almost daily strode to the well to launch verbal warheads at the powers that be. He eschewed the foamy preambles that normally padded House floor speeches. In a broadside aimed at the proposed Stealth bomber, the Pentagon's hyperexpensive aircraft ($500–$800 million apiece) that much resembled the comic-book Batplane, Traficant roared, "What's next? A hundred-billion-dollar Batmobile?"

That line, like many of Traficant's, became a network news sound bite. But his spotty notoriety won little respect from peers, who couldn't forgive his crudity. They would chuckle condescendingly as he strutted away from the podium and the House snapped back to its normal torpor.

Something like the old-time excitement returns to the chamber when it is time for a vote. Lawmakers, who have perhaps been relaxing in the leather armchairs of the cloakrooms, now pour noisily onto the floor, clapping colleagues on the back, administering stabbing punches in the arm.

Hoagland wasn't altogether at ease with such male-bonding rituals. He even winced when labor union allies addressed him as Pete. But he understood the friendly mauling as compensation for the disputes of a properly functioning legislature.

The carpeting in the House chamber was chosen to protect flesh-pressing politicians. Its pattern—gaudy flame-red rosettes bordered in blue and white—duplicates the floor of the original House chamber. But like all good modern things, it is also functional. Its "static-free" fabric prevents lawmakers from passing along anything shocking with their tribal handshakes and backslaps. Despite the carpeting, there was static between Republicans and Democrats in the House these days. It was visible even in little things.

The main business of the day was a vote on a bill that would raise the minimum wage for the first time in over eight years. Republicans and Democrats agreed that it ought to be raised. It was getting embarrassing. After all, Congress had just tried to get *itself* a whopping raise—from $89,500 to $145,000—though few members had supported the raise publicly. The only divisive issue was, how much should the minimum go up? A Republican amendment, to create a subminimum six-month "training wage" for "new hires" and a lower raise overall, was defeated. A Democratic amendment, which retained the bill's higher raise and included a compromise training wage—for a person's first job only—passed. Hoagland had trundled back and forth to the floor all day, voting down with the Republican amendment, up with the Democratic amendment. The only remaining business was a vote on the bill itself.

"The question is on passage of the bill," announced the speaker pro tem. "All those in favor, signify by saying 'aye,' those opposed, 'no.' "

As usual right before a vote, a few dozen conservative Republicans had collected on the floor. They outnumbered Democrats in the chamber by at least four to one. The thin ranks of Democrats could muster only a splintered, listless chirp of an "aye" for their alternative. It was no contest. The Republicans positively drowned them in a throaty chorus of "NO!"

Democrats, however, were in the majority. The gavel was in their hands. "In the opinion of the chair," said the speaker pro tem, "the ayes have it."

Clustered around the minority bill manager's table, a clutch of Republicans laughed loudly, though not without bitterness. Their side would almost surely lose the roll-call vote to follow, which would summon the whole membership back to the floor, including all those Democrats. But some believed the chair's refusal even to grant the obvious—that they'd outshouted the Democrats—was just one more example, however slight, of the majority party's "abuse of power."

It was only natural that House Republicans, in the minority for so long, would eventually develop a chip on their collective shoulder. But these days, they were emphatically irked by the bare-knuckled style of Speaker Jim Wright, House Democrat in chief. His office was the source, at least potentially, of great power. To tap it required an understanding of the arcane rules of the House and a strong will. Wright had both.

The majority party "organizes" the House and controls all

committee chairmanships. That's a good deal of power in itself. But control of the Rules Committee, which it also has, is where the real clout lies. Though any committee can send legislation to the floor, most bills have to pass through Rules first. Its members decide the length of time bills can be debated, whether amendments can be offered, even which amendments will be "in order" and subject to a vote. There is simply no greater power in a legislative body.

Wright had at times used Rules skillfully—some would say fiendishly. When President Reagan vetoed a bill to reinstate the "Fairness Doctrine"—which required broadcasters to provide equal time to opponents of views aired on their stations—Wright reportedly used the Rules Committee to tack the doctrine onto an unrelated piece of legislation, which had strong bipartisan support. When Republicans screamed, Wright tightened the screws. He reportedly had Rules attach another rider to the same bill, killing a cost-of-living pay raise for members of Congress that Republicans had been denouncing far and wide. Hence, Republican votes against the bill would seem like hypocritical votes *for* the pay raise.

Republicans waxed indignant about such tactics. But who could doubt they'd do likewise if their party regained control? During the New Deal era, even when they weren't in the majority, Republicans on the Rules Committee routinely joined forces with conservative Southern Democrats to stop civil rights bills from coming to the floor. Nowadays, Budget Director Richard Darman was famous for using procedural acumen to further political ends.

But Republicans were unlikely to regain majority status anytime soon. In frustration, some adopted guerrilla tactics. For instance, they demanded "surprise" recorded votes on noncontroversial items—down to the formerly rote daily approval of the House journal—to catch Democrats away from the chamber and infect their records with missed votes. Meanwhile, Georgia Republican Newt Gingrich, a "movement" conservative, filed charges against Wright with the Ethics Committee, claiming the speaker had violated various House rules. The institution's sacred gentility was curdling.

Congressman Murphy, of Pennsylvania, rose to address the chair after the voice vote on the minimum-wage bill. "Mr.

Speaker, on that I demand the yeas and nays," he said, invoking any member's right to call for a recorded vote.

One of the great rituals of representative government now began again. Two buzzers sounded in every hallway and office on the House side of the Capitol, warning members who might have misplaced their beepers that a recorded vote was in progress.

Inside the chamber, lights were dimmed. A scoreboard was projected on the sidewalls, displaying time remaining out of the fifteen minutes alotted for balloting "by electronic device," along with the number of "yay," "nay," or merely "present" votes. Representatives again poured noisily into the chamber, inserting computer-punched vote cards into machines in the backs of chairs. On the wall behind the Press Gallery, the name of each member, formerly invisible, was illuminated from behind, making an enormous scorecard. Green or red lights blinked on beside names, signifying votes for or against the bill.

From time to time, members glimpsed up at the score. A green light went on next to Hoagland's name. He believed a minimum wage hike was long overdue. Besides, unions had supported him, and this was an important issue for them.

Since "whips" from both parties polled their membership, the outcome of most votes was known in advance. As expected, the bill passed comfortably, 248 to 171. But even when no real drama surrounded a vote, electricity was in the air. Something seemed very right about governing a country like this, with open debates, competitively.

Viewed from outside the chamber, unfortunately, the process didn't seem to be working so well—at least, not this year.

Even before Congress began work in 1989, the public wasn't very happy with it. According to polls, Ronald Reagan had convinced people that Congress was responsible for the nation's stupendous deficits. But when Congress returned after the 1988 elections, members had something besides tending to the fiscal crisis on their minds: securing a fat pay raise. It was as if the institution had hung a "kick me" sign on its back. Lawmakers in both parties privately supported the healthy 51 percent boost, but a public outcry forced them to vote it down.

The episode did nothing to increase people's sagging faith in Congress, especially, it seemed, in its "liberal" members. In a letter to President Bush, copies of which were sent to members of

Congress, this mood found characteristic, if somewhat caricatured,
expression.

> Dear Mr. President . . .
> . . . You should stop trying to pacify these *crybaby liber-
> als* in Congress. Let us get some honest conservatives to
> run for Congress in 1990 and tell the people the truth.
> . . . We have had a *liberal Congress* for forty years, they
> are the cause of our national debt and our national defi-
> cit. They, the liberal Congress, are responsible for Amer-
> ican abortion, the most dastardly *crime* known to man.
> Only Joe Stalin and Adolph Hitler belong with the abor-
> tion group. Maybe I should include China. . . . The
> good people in America will not support any one who
> looks like a liberal, who acts like a liberal, or smells like a
> liberal. . . .

In the early 1980s, Congress had indeed acquiesced to Reagan's program of huge tax cuts—mostly for the wealthiest Americans—combined with enormous increases in military spending.
Many Democrats blamed those policies for the tripling of the national debt, the persistent yearly deficits, of the Reagan years. Reagan's own Office of Management and Budget director, David
Stockman, admitted as much. In *The Triumph of Politics,* he wrote
about the reasons why some—though far from all—Democrats objected to Reagan's tax cuts. "They thought they would create intolerable, permanent deficits," Stockman wrote, "and they were
right."

Many Democrats believed Republicans were playing an irresponsible game with the nation. They'd been winning the presidency by campaigning against taxes—indeed against
"Washington" and "government." But the actual tax cuts they
supported were a windfall for the rich. "The vast majority of
American families . . . are paying a *higher* share of their incomes
in overall federal taxes than they did ten years ago," wrote Robert
McIntyre, director of Citizens for Tax Justice, in 1988.

Many Democrats supported raising taxes, especially on the
wealthy, to balance the budget. But Bush had swept into the
White House on a "no new taxes" pledge. He insisted that "fat"
must be cut out of government to reduce the deficit. His call for
cuts instead of taxes was very popular. But he refused to trim the
grossly inflated military budget. And it was unclear what more

could be slashed from the domestic budget, already emasculated
during the Reagan years.

In the 1990 budget, the money allotted for "domestic discre-
tionary spending"—programs that the government was not already committed to pay for—was exceeded for the first time by the
over $170 billion paid in *interest* on the national debt. Meanwhile,
Stockman himself admitted that the deficit had nothing to do with
"overspending." He blamed it on "the nation's decimated revenue base"—in other words, undertaxing.

Congressional Democrats feared that if they proposed higher
taxes—even just for the wealthy—to reduce the deficit, the news
media would glibly portray them as "tax-and-spend liberals." Instead, they chose to wait until the president saw for himself the
inevitability of new taxes. Meanwhile, Bush proposed yet another
tax *cut*—in the rate paid on capital gains. It seemed to many Democrats like one more giveaway to the wealthy, who of course had
more capital to make gains on in the first place.

But Republicans didn't oppose *all* tax increases. In the early
1980s, Social Security taxes had been raised to create huge surpluses in the system, to cover the cost of benefits in later years
when the tax base would shrink. But those surpluses were "borrowed" to reduce the size of the budget deficit—one of many
gimmicks, like putting the S&L bailout "off budget," that hid the
deficit's actual size.

New increases in Social Security taxes were scheduled to take
effect in 1990. These "regressive" taxes hit lower- and middle-
income Americans hardest, since they weren't collected on por-
tions of a person's income over $42,000. But the Bush administra-
tion—despite the president's "no new taxes" pledge—did not
object to the Social Security tax hike. After all, it would further
inflate the trust fund surplus—over $150 billion in 1989—and
further reduce the *apparent* size of the deficit.

Using the surpluses to reduce the deficit meant, in effect, asking lower- and middle-income Americans to bear the burden of
current government expenses—not to fund their retirement. It
had once been an article of faith that government expenses should
be paid by revenues from progressive taxation, that those who
could afford to pay more should do so. Every advanced industrial
nation applied this principle, including the United States during its
decades of greatest prosperity—until the 1980s.

House Speaker Jim Wright reportedly favored returning to a more progressive tax system. But in early 1989, his support in the House plunged. Wright's actions during the pay-raise episode seriously eroded his power base. He managed to alienate not just Republicans, but his own party.

Congress had crafted a quiet way to get its boost. Lawmakers had created a salary commission to recommend to the president raises for members of Congress and senior government officials. President Reagan, in one of his last official acts, approved the commission's recommendations and sent them back to Congress. If both the House and Senate didn't vote to reject the raise, it was to take effect automatically.

But the public pressure, stirred up by Ralph Nader, among others, was too much for the Senate, which voted the raise down. House members were furious. They said the Senate was decorated with wall-to-wall millionaires who really didn't need the money. Worse, they suspected the Senate of cynically shifting the heat of the public's fury onto the House. Now if the House blocked a vote, the Senate would get the money anyway, but none of the blame.

House members wanted Wright to hang tough and block a vote in their chamber, which would have saved the raise, since both houses had to vote it down to kill it. But for once the news media had public attention riveted on an issue. Wright refused to block a vote, stripping political cover from House members. When they had to go on record and vote for the raise if they wanted it, it was incinerated 380–48. Wright was scorned in the House for giving in to public pressure. He became an untouchable overnight in his own party's caucus.

While the "salary grab" further tarnished Congress, Bush's standing in the country steadily improved. When Hoagland spoke to an elementary school class back home, he mentioned that he would have preferred Democrat Michael Dukakis to have been elected president, instead of Bush. "BOOO!" said the gentle sons and daughters of Omaha, according to an account in a local newspaper. The children's reaction reflected as any political scientist will tell you, the feelings of their voting-age parents. Hoagland was quick to apply the pacifier. He and George Bush agreed "on many more things than we disagree on," he said.

Hoagland walked a tightrope on the pay issue. He told local

reporters he was against the "excessive" raise and sponsored a bill
to kill it—one of dozens thrown in the hopper for that purpose.
But in the same interviews he invariably mentioned how much
higher his cost of living was going to be in Washington. The mortgage on the $400,000 house Hoagland eventually bought in
Maryland was "well-over" his current congressional take-home
pay, he later said. And he commuted to work on the bus and
subway every day.

While Hoagland was denouncing the raise, he offered the
balm of praise to his colleagues in their darkest hour. An article in
the *National Journal,* a policy magazine widely read in Washington,
quoted the freshman from Nebraska at length:

> "Congress, back in Nebraska, has a reputation for being
> a squalid, self-serving institution," he said. "I was really
> very surprised . . . at the uniformly high quality of the
> members. My impression is that the House is a mer-
> itocracy. Members are smart, personable, and well-moti-
> vated. That's not the way it looks from Nebraska."

This was one freshman who seemed to grasp early how to win
friends and influence congresspeople.

During the minimum-wage vote, Hoagland worked the chamber,
flashing his guileless smile and shaking hands. Though he had
crow's-feet around the eyes like any forty-seven-year-old, his shy-
ness and quiet enthusiasm made him seem almost "too young to
be a congressman," as one colleague remarked.

Hoagland's background in the Unicameral had taught him
that a big part of his job was getting to know other members. It
normally took 218 votes—a majority—to get anything done
around here. Loners didn't get far. Hoagland even studied his new
colleagues for homework. After floor sessions, he looked up members he'd met in *The Almanac of American Politics* a biographical
almanac.

There were thirty-two other newcomers to the House's "meritocracy" this year. Already, Hoagland was a minor standout in his
class. Politically speaking, no place is more visible than the
roughly eleven by fourteen inches "above the fold" on the front
page of the *Washington Post.* The watchful eyes of the powerful
gaze there each morning, secretly hoping, or dreading, to find

their own faces staring back. On December 27, 1988, Peter Hoagland's picture made it above the fold in the *Post*—at least, his forehead did—alongside the headline "A Congressman-Elect Finds Constituents' Demands Won't Wait."

Hoagland's case was offered as a peek at the plight of a poor freshman, nagged by demanding constituents even before he took office. The story made Hoagland's face and name at least vaguely familiar in Washington, and he got a double hit of publicity when the *Omaha World-Herald* reprinted an abridged version.

On the floor, Hoagland seemed to be making himself at home, darting all over to introduce himself. Some freshmen without his experience didn't seem quite so in the swing of things. Richard Neal sat alone amid rows of empty chairs, a lost look in his eyes. Before he came to Congress, he had been the mayor of Springfield, Massachusetts, the place he now represented. In those days, local politics had revolved around him. Now even his staff, who'd worked for his powerful predecessor, had more legislative experience than he did.

But Neal's political base perhaps gave him more luxury to contemplate his new life. Unlike Hoagland, he'd swept into office with 80 percent of the vote. It looked as if he actually *could* keep his seat as long as he wanted.

As for Hoagland, if you asked him about polls, a cloud of worry darkened his brow. The *World-Herald*'s first post-election poll in February gave him a mere 38 percent "approval" rating. That was down from the 50 percent vote that barely won him the election. Being in office was supposed to make his numbers rise.

Hoagland needed a way to connect with his district, to bond his name to its congressional seat. The Franklin fiasco presumably gave him an excuse to strut his stuff, and perhaps get some great media doing it.

Hoagland had recently visited Bob Fenner, regional counsel of the National Credit Union Administration. He hoped the two could "find a way for him to respond" to the Franklin mess, said Fenner. They came up with an amendment that Hoagland would try to attach to the S&L bailout bill, which would require credit unions to have audits at least once a year. Franklin had gone years without one.

Of course, the NCUA already had the power to order an outside audit of any federally insured credit union. In fact, many criticized the agency for not acting in the Franklin matter, despite ample—and flagrant—warning signs. Besides, requiring future audits wouldn't bring back the millions stolen by Larry King, though it might prevent similar tragedies elsewhere.

Hoagland had already begun lobbying Banking Committee colleagues to win support for his amendment. He told them that NCUA regulators might have had an easier time auditing a politically well-connected place like Franklin if they had been *required* to.

"It sounds rational," one Banking member, Paul Kanjorski, had replied, a tone of surprise in his voice, as if rationality were the last thing he'd expected to hear. Kanjorski then ended the meeting by energetically slapping Hoagland on the back. "You're doing a *terrific* job," he said. "We're very proud of you."

Whom had he meant by "we" exactly? Party sachems? Democrats on Banking? Right-thinking people? Hoagland smiled bashfully and slapped Kanjorski's back in return, but hesitantly, as if he were swatting a spider.

7

UNTHINKABLE

O utside the window of Longworth 1415, the twin smokestacks of the power plant pumped a woolly nebula into the late-afternoon haze. On the ledge inside, Hoagland's fax machine beeped, then began spitting out electronically reconstituted clippings from the evening edition of the *Omaha World-Herald.*

Hoagland's district staff clipped stories and transmitted them to Washington at least twice a day, after the morning and evening editions came out. Long-distance phone rates made this a particularly expensive way to read the hometown press. But the D.C. office craved the news, and couldn't wait for the paper to come in the mail. They needed to stay up to date on what was happening in the district, and perhaps wanted to check whether the press had taken their bait and put Hoagland's name in print. The district office even faxed updates from the sports and obituary pages.

Gary Caruso hovered impatiently over the fax machine. He was waiting to send Hoagland's statement on the afternoon's minimum-wage vote out to Omaha TV and radio stations. As communications director, Gary wrote many press releases. The office kept a steady stream of them flowing to Omaha. Naturally, releases went out only on positions Hoagland wanted to call attention to. Reporters didn't seem to mind. Often they just took what they were given. Gary estimated that at least 60 percent of Hoagland's coverage was based on press releases and other pump-priming done by the office media team.

When the hometown media weren't reacting to some "feed" from Hoagland's office, they were generally satisfied with whatever quotes they could pry from him to plug into "reaction" stories about events in Washington. Reaction stories were generally about splashy subjects that were getting big play on national TV, and over which Hoagland's current influence was about nil.

But on issues close to the bone, there was often little probing. Gary was amazed that no local reporter had ever asked Hoagland where he got all the money he loaned to his campaign. Perhaps he had saved it all up from his law practice, as he said. To borrow such money from oneself was perfectly legal. But no one ever even asked.

The *World-Herald* had apparently decided not to bother covering Hoagland in the upcoming Banking Committee markups of the savings and loan bailout bill, one of the biggest in years, though the paper had two reporters in Washington, and two other area legislators, Doug Bereuter and Jim Leach, were also on the committee. Gary said the editors had decided the subject was "too complicated" and to rely on wire stories. As for Hoagland's role in the markups, they would be forced to rely on what he chose to tell.

Hoagland's staffers indulged their own partisan urges when they wrote his press releases. Issuing them was a way for them to leap into the political fray. Gary had recently written a release about a proposal by the treasury secretary, Nicholas Brady, to deal with the Third World's massive debt. Brady asked U.S. banks to "forgive" part of their unpaid loans to poor countries. Under his proposal, the World Bank and International Monetary Fund would pick up the slack. Both institutions were "heavily supported by U.S. taxpayer money," Gary wrote.

Brady's plan struck Gary as a subsidy of Japanese multinational banks—to which much of the debt was owed—paid for by American taxpayers. "They must be dancing in yen in Tokyo," he wrote within quotation marks, followed by the words "Hoagland stated." Then on the last lines of the release, Gary put a bit of bombast in Hoagland's mouth: "It's time for the United States to stop being a financial cookie jar for the rest of the world."

Gary knew he'd gone too far this time. "Peter's not going to like it," he predicted. Sure enough, after reading it, Hoagland frowned. "I don't think so," he gently said. "It doesn't sound like me." But making Hoagland sound not quite so much like Hoagland was one of the tasks Gary had assigned himself after he was hired to manage the primary campaign. The first time he heard his candidate make a speech, he wanted to cry—from boredom.

Gary quickly wrote a new stump speech for Hoagland, a partisan tub-thumper attacking the wasted opportunities of the Reagan years. He then coached the candidate about delivery, reminding him to avoid rocking back and forth on his heels as he spoke and further lulling audiences into slumber. Many who heard the new speech agreed it was among the finest Hoagland ever made, said Gary, though one observer remarked, "It was fine . . . but it wasn't Peter."

Gary, a native of Massapequa, Long Island, wore a perennial smirk under his thin black mustache. He added a dose of New York cynicism to the optimistic Mid-western ethos of the office. Though only thirty-two, he'd already seen politics at the highest levels as a trip-advance man in Jimmy Carter's White House and for Senator John Glenn's presidential campaign. Though not as trim as he was in college, where he played lacrosse and rugby, he still carried himself with a hint of the athlete's swagger. That Hoagland permitted Gary to tinker with his speaking style was a mark of respect for the man's experience.

Gary recalls working for the White House as "something I really loved." The job took him to forty-eight states, where he met governors, mayors, and captains of industry. Though he was a college dropout (he later graduated), these dignitaries treated him "like royalty" because he represented the White House.

Gary didn't like to think of politics as "just another business." He worked only for politicians he respected. Carter and Glenn had met high standards. "Washington reporters will tell you Carter was the most intelligent president in this century," he said. And Gary was downright worshipful about Glenn. "I thought this guy was *God* . . . [the] most unassuming, kind, caring man." Gary saw in Hoagland qualities he'd admired in Carter and Glenn: intelligence, lack of pretensions.

But Gary wasn't awed by many politicians. He was particularly critical of his new employer. Not Hoagland so much as the United States Congress.

Gary had been disgusted by the doubletalk surrounding the pay-raise affair. When it was believed Wright would block a floor vote and provide "cover," Gary had seen members in Longworth's hallways give one another thumbs-up signs, gleefully predicting they'd get the money. Later, he saw some of the same members denouncing the raise on the House floor. "They're such hypocrites," he said.

Gary liked and respected Hoagland, but viewed his own job as a step down from his former heights—perhaps several steps. After watching aggressive national reporters sparring with Glenn and Carter, he viewed relations with the more cooperative hometown media as less exciting. Besides, a House freshman was a political nowhere man, too insecure to do much more than keep on campaigning. "There's no challenge," Gary said of his new job.

As Gary fed Hoagland's purported words about the minimum-wage vote to the fax machine, the black-and-white portable TV near him was tuned to CNN. The newscaster speed-talked a report on the vote. Then chunky presidential spokesman Marlin Fitzwater bobbed into view, snarling threats of a Bush veto. The president thought the bill was still too rough on business. So much for compromises.

Gary might have been frustrated in his job, but like so many congressional aides, he was a "news junkie." For such people, Capitol Hill was a regular shooting gallery. He was so hooked that his day "began" with CBS's *Nightwatch,* a news-talk show airing in the small hours. Later, he watched the sunrise news, then *Good Morning America,* followed perhaps by a dollop of *Donahue.* And there was always CNN to see him through a dry spell.

Gary got his serious media fixes at work. The office received daily stacks of clippings from papers across the nation. They were also linked to computer news retrieval services, Lexus, Nexus, you name it. Gary could often be found happily fishing in the AP "Datastream" for breaking wire stories. Then there were racks bulging with (complimentary) subscriptions to almost all major national papers and magazines. And TVs were everywhere, tuned to C-Span or CNN. Besides this windfall, Gary's job called for frequent chats with reporters, national and local, who, as a class, are notorious dealers in political gossip—the pure stuff.

Hoagland didn't have time to review today's press release. He had to rush to the airport for his flight back to Omaha, where he was spending the upcoming Easter recess. (By the end of March, Congress had already taken thirty days off, out of a possible sixty working days.) When Gary finished faxing Hoagland's release to Omaha newsrooms, he quickly phoned the district office. Someone had to meet Hoagland at the plane, before any reporters got to him, and tell him precisely what he'd said in that statement of his.

Just around the corner from Longworth is the Democratic Club, housed in a squat, nondescript stone-and-glass vessel. Judging by the building's appearance, one wouldn't suspect anything significant happens inside. Among the neighborhood's neoclassical behemoths, it has all the splendor of a branch bank in a shopping center. One of its functions is similar. It is a place where money changes hands—in the form of campaign contributions.

The entrance hall of the club is lined with portraits from the Democratic pantheon: JFK, tanned and manly on the deck of his yacht; LBJ, in loose khakis, looking ready for a Texas turkey shoot; Harry (the haberdasher) Truman, wearing a business suit and slippery smile. The wood-paneled bar on the ground floor is comfortable, almost cozy. But most of the banquet rooms upstairs are ordinary, functional, with stain-resistant carpets and rollaway bars.

One evening, a week before the minimum-wage vote, Hoagland dropped by a fundraiser at the Democratic Club for Rep. Tom McMillen of Maryland, a Banking Committee colleague. Years earlier, a much-younger McMillen had made the cover of *Sports Illustrated.* At the time, he was a beanpole in short pants and floppy brown bangs, and the most sought-after high school basketball player in the nation. After a successful career in the NBA, only his towering six-foot-eleven frame made him a standout in Congress, where his silver-gray hair, expensive charcoal suit, and red "power tie" blended right in.

"There are a lot of ex-jocks in politics because of the competition," Gary, a former college jock himself, said. "It's like a Super

Bowl every election year." There are other similarities between politics and big-time sports. Money greases the gears of both. But in athletics, money chases talent—the ability to win on the playing field. In politics, money often *is* the ability to win.

Hoagland put off mingling and attacked a table set with chafing dishes of scallops wrapped in bacon, stuffed baked potatoes, crab cakes, and other like fare. After a stop at the open bar—for a club soda—he was ready to go. There were many other members of Congress in the room, and the usual mix of lobbyists with lapel stickers that named their employers: Bell South, McDonnell Douglas, AFL-CIO, et cetera.

Hoagland, according to his wife, was never much at mixing it up with the boys. "He sorta thinks he's the type who can chum around with the guys at the B-Ball game, but he isn't," said Barbara. Once he asked McMillen, "Were you really in the pros," unaware of the man's superjock past. But members appreciated it when other members came to their fundraisers, the higher-ranking the better.

McMillen was probably happy tonight to see the strapping chairman of the tax-writing (and tax-break-dispensing) Ways and Means Committee, Dan Rostenkowski, muscling up to the bar. Such heavyweights add an aura of "clout" to an affair, which is bound to please the assembled lobbyists. They write checks (up to $2,000 under current law) for the hosts of gatherings like this one. No one believes they are just paying for the food. And powerful members like "Rosty," with lots of padding in their campaign bankrolls, often put a little something in the plate themselves.

If a lobbyist is disappointed often enough by a member's legislative behavior, he quickly drops that member from his gift list. Without the money, members can hardly afford to pay for the expensive television ads and direct-mail blitzes that establish their "presence" in the district during campaigns. In fact, those things *are* their campaigns, for the most part. Even worse, if a lobbyist stops giving a member money, he will very likely start donating to the member's opponent, in the hope of recruiting another "friend" to Congress. This arguably makes pleasing lobbyists more important than pleasing voters, if only because lobbyists pay attention to what congressfolk do in a way voters seldom can.

McMillen, a celebrity outside politics, *might* have survived without checks from lobbyists. Then again, he might not. He didn't seem to be taking any chances. His soiree netted a cool $85,000.

After eight o'clock, when the crowd was thinning, Hoagland sat slumped in a chair against the wall, club soda in hand, staring into space. His schedule listed every fundraiser he was invited to, amounting to several each week, often more than one a night. No one could go to all of them. But he'd seen enough. They might have looked like parties, but fundraisers weren't fun. Night after night, sometimes two or three times a night, members drag themselves to the same banquet rooms, to claw at the same hors d'oeuvres and force small talk with the same lobbyists, the same colleagues.

One of Hoagland's aides, John Minter, said that his boss had a habit of blurting out opinions that seemed to come from nowhere. He admitted to being baffled by these outbursts, asking himself, "Where does he get these sudden passions?"

Tonight, it was clear that something other than the grind of the political party circuit was getting Hoagland down. He seemed to be nursing some rather basic doubts. Wearing a look of perplexed pain, he suddenly wondered aloud, "Do the laws passed by Congress actually improve the nation, or just make things worse?" Coming from a man who'd been calling Congress a "meritocracy," this seemed like a surprising turnabout.

Of course, there were very good reasons for doubting Congress. Few believed it was accomplishing much "worthy to be remembered" this year. In fact, congressfolk probably preferred to forget these past few months.

First there was the public humiliation of the pay-raise episode. Then the Senate's refusal to confirm John Tower as defense secretary, after several days of embarrassing debates about his, and the Senate's, drinking habits. Throughout, the question before the "world's greatest deliberative body" seemed to be "How many martinis can dance on the head of an H-bomb?" It was not the Senate's finest hour. And no sooner had the Senate hung Tower out to dry than the House Ethics Committee began investigating the speaker, which threatened to be the biggest distraction of all.

Some work was getting done, but when you looked at bills coming to the floor, many had a disturbing quality: they were redos of past congressional mistakes, or what looked a lot like mistakes. Just the previous year, Congress had passed the Medicare Catastrophic Coverage Act, to shield elderly and disabled citizens from the astronomical bills that accompany serious illnesses. But the law's higher Medicare premiums infuriated certain factions of the elderly—wealthy, politically active factions. Now many members vowed to amend, or even repeal, the legislation.

Congress was also under intense pressure from business lobbyists to repeal "Section 89," a part of the "tax reform" legislation of 1986, intended to prevent discrimination in employee benefit plans. Employers were screaming that the bill's reporting requirements were overly complicated and "burdensome." Now Section 89 also looked as if it would die young. Then there was the savings and loan rescue. That particular redo would actually be the *fourth* attempt in less than a decade to deal with the crisis. Misbegotten efforts were also launched in 1980, '82, and '87.

And of course, there was the budget. Throughout the eighties, whenever it was mentioned, the word "crisis" never seemed far away. Every politician promised to bring the deficit—not to mention the debt—"under control." Yet this year, the president and Congress were conniving yet again on ways to put off the inevitable reckoning. Bush fudged figures in his fiscal 1990 budget proposal, which said the deficit would be "only" $100 billion. Putting the billions needed for the S&L bailout "off budget" was just one of many gimmicks used to reach this optimistic estimate. With such gimmicks stripped away, the actual deficit looked like it would exceed $250 billion. Despite some carping, Congress went along with the president's transparent ruse.

Many believed that politicians' insatiable appetite for campaign money was a big reason why Washington seemed so reluctant to solve long-term problems. The savings and loan disaster was a painful illustration of the point.

In the late seventies and early eighties, it first became clear that many S&Ls were failing. Some believe that Washington could have solved the problem then by forcing weak S&Ls to close. That would have required the Federal Savings and Loan Insurance Corporation (FSLIC) to spend most of the billions it had collected in premiums from S&Ls. But it wouldn't have cost taxpayers anything.

But that plan reportedly didn't sit well with lobbyists from the U.S. League of Savings Institutions, who gave millions to candidates—for presidency and Congress—in the eighties. Seemingly loath to offend their benefactors, our officials never seriously considered the obvious solution to the S&L problem. Instead, they adopted the much riskier plan, favored by the league, which helped bring on the catastrophe that will cost taxpayers dearly.

That is often the way contributors wield influence. Most politicians don't sell votes outright. But the pressure to get money makes lawmakers reluctant to offer proposals they know their benefactors won't like. This mind-set has a perverse effect, spelled out by *Wall Street Journal* reporter Brooks Jackson in his book *Honest Graft.* When politicians seek solutions to problems, often "the obvious becomes unthinkable," Jackson wrote.

Hoagland had always been a supporter of campaign finance reform, and currently favored a system of public financing for congressional campaigns. It seemed like a natural. The way the government is structured already gives special interests certain built-in advantages over the pluralistic and divided majority of the population. Why should they be permitted, even encouraged, to blatantly manipulate the political system for their own ends with strategic infusions of cash? Why shouldn't public money be used to buy back our government? Even if you believe politicians when they say campaign contributions don't influence their decisions, the huge chunks of time they spend raising money certainly doesn't make them better public servants.

There is another nondescript building just around the corner from the Democratic Club where Hoagland also spent a lot of his time. It houses the headquarters of the Democratic National Committee and the DCCC. Lawmakers take turns occupying the boxy offices at the DCCC to make phone calls to political action committees, or PACs, to ask for campaign money. Anyone can form a PAC and make contributions to congressfolk. But most are run by businesses and unions with a legislative agenda.

It was against the law for Hoagland or his staff to perform campaign work in his congressional offices—perish the thought. So he often took time out of a busy day, ducked over to the DCCC, and made his calls. Quite often. He was currently raising money for four different races: to pay off debts from the primary and general elections in 1988, and to launch both anew in 1990. Most of the Hoagland campaign's debts were owed to Hoagland himself. If he ever wanted to see that money again, he had to make those obnoxious calls and raise cash to pay the debts off. It was an

excellent, if somewhat perverse, incentive. A secretary at the
DCCC said Hoagland should get the "telephoner of the year"
award.

Most fundraising is done from PACs specifically set up to donate to politicians. The process is quite routine—like ordering
towels from a catalog. On a typical call to a PAC run by Massachusetts bankers, Hoagland was put through to the secretary in charge
of solicitations. Would one of their lobbyists be at his upcoming
fundraiser? The secretary asked the congressman to fax an invita-
tion, then said, "Could you spell your name for me?"

But the very routineness of most fundraising tends to disguise
what is, at bottom, a highly questionable system. Politicians, including Hoagland, insist that special interests that donate to them
do so merely out of a desire to promote "good government." But
even they don't seem to believe that. When Hoagland was making
calls one day, he purposely didn't place any to PACs "whose legislative interests don't coincide with any of the committees I'm on."

Fundraising from special interests is tedious, degrading, and
ethically suspect. But while Congress enacted partial public financing for presidential campaigns, it has failed to do so for its own
elections, or to do anything else about campaign finance reform.
For instance, Hoagland's reliance on money raised from special
interests to reimburse himself was perfectly legal and proper.

Lawmakers excuse their inaction by arguing that the public
doesn't support public financing, that people deeply resent Congress and would rebel at the thought of underwriting its costly
electioneering. Public financing for congressional campaigns
would probably cost $200–$300 million per election. A substantial sum, yes, but in our $1 trillion annual budget (a thousand
times a thousand million), milk money. One proponent of public
financing put the cost in perspective by noting that the Pentagon
spends $150 million every year on military bands.

Private interests are only too glad to pony up the paltry millions in contributions it costs them to rent our political system.
Some spend more on advertising. Meanwhile, the public is paying
for congressional campaigns already. The blizzards of newsletters
and other unsolicited mail lawmakers send to constituents during
election years, which former Senator Pete Wilson candidly described as "thinly veiled campaign literature," cost taxpayers well
over $100 million in 1988. Add the cost of staff salaries and office

space devoted to campaigning (illegal but routinely done), and the tab probably doubles. And of course there are also the *indirect* costs of the current system, the hundreds of billions, perhaps over a trillion, it will cost for the S&L "solutions" of the early eighties. And that is just the price of one misbegotten policy.

But lawmakers have good, if selfish, reasons for preferring the status quo. Special interests, seeking to buy influence, don't waste money on losing causes. They pump rivers of cash to incumbent officeholders. Challengers get only a trickle. That makes their odds of winning almost nil. In 1988, 99 percent of incumbents won reelection. When such things happen in other countries, we deny that free elections have taken place.

Under the current system, Hoagland was almost guaranteed to raise a lot more money than any challengers for his seat, barring some unforeseen political earthquake or scandal. But if public financing took effect, he would face challengers with nearly equal resources every time he ran. He might learn to love those fund-raising calls yet.

But Hoagland, slouched in his chair, wasn't loving his job tonight. Did he still want to be a congressman? "I'm not so sure I do," he groaned. Normally, Hoagland's outlook about things political was very optimistic, almost complacent. "I believe good triumphs in the end," he once said. For instance, because public financing was "the right way to go," he viewed it as all but inevitable. So where had tonight's dark clouds come from?

John Minter said Hoagland had a "LIFO" memory. The acronym denotes a method of bookkeeping, "last in, first out." John noticed that Hoagland was often as impressionable as a pillow. He would espouse the opinion of the last person he'd spoken to, especially if it was someone he respected. Such was John's explanation for those "sudden passions."

Hoagland said he'd been talking with "former members" about the failings of Congress. Though he wouldn't say which "former members," he'd met recently on business with John Cavanaugh, who happened to be the last Democrat to represent Nebraska's 2nd Congressional District. Cavanaugh was also a man whom Hoagland deeply respected, as did much of Omaha.

After serving only two terms in the House, Cavanaugh quit in 1980. He was only thirty-five, handsome, blue-eyed, strawberry-blond, popular. A long career seemed his for the asking. But he wanted to spend time with his family. Congressmen didn't get to do much of that. Perhaps now, through Hoagland, some of Cavanaugh's other complaints about Congress were being aired.

Tonight, Hoagland talked about his family, too. They were still living in Omaha at this point and the kids didn't understand why he was never home. Hoagland's malaise probably wasn't helped by the tense atmosphere that had overtaken his office of late. Some of his staffers, Jim, Gary, John, were miffed because he didn't consult with them. He seemed dissatisfied with their work. Sometimes he even asked them to consult other, more experienced Hill staffers to get a read on an issue. "What I really need is a good, smart lawyer," Hoagland said, someone to help parse the substance of issues, not just their politics. He seemed to view his own staff as too political.

He certainly trusted them when they told him to look at the camera when the red light was on, and to avoid tilting his head to the right when speaking in public, not to mention certain political poses they might have counseled. But when he was in a mood to be a congressman rather than a candidate, he seemed to resent being "handled." He tended to go it alone.

For instance, Hoagland didn't consult his staff about a proposal recently brought to him by John Cavanaugh. Like many ex-members of Congress, Cavanaugh was now a partner in a law firm, and functioned, at least part of the time, as a Washington lobbyist.

Cavanaugh also thought the campaign finance system was overdue for reform. The situation was much worse now than when he left office, just eight years before. He had never had to hold a Washington fundraiser. His campaigns had cost only a little over $100,000, most of which was raised locally. Hoagland had spent $858,000, and had raised much of it out of state.

Cavanaugh now did volunteer work for Common Cause, the public interest lobby, as Hoagland had, and made speeches critical of the campaign finance system. But he played another role. Cavanaugh was associated with the highly respected law firm of Kutak, Rock & Campbell. The firm's lobbying arm gained access to and leverage with congressfolk the way everyone did, with campaign contributions. "I don't have any embarrassment about being for reforming the system and being a participant in the system," Cavanaugh said.

One of Kutak, Rock & Campbell's clients was Mike Yanney, a

wealthy Omaha businessman. When Hoagland went to Yanney for support in 1988, he was turned down. But now Yanney wanted something from Hoagland. Shortly after the election, a PAC controlled by Yanney donated $5,000 to Hoagland's debt-reduction fund. Recently, Cavanaugh had met with the freshman on Yanney's behalf. The Bush S&L bailout bill presented a problem for some savings and loans Yanney had invested in. Cavanaugh thought Hoagland might be able to help.

Hoagland quickly grasped the political benefits that might be his if he helped the influential Yanney. He also thought that the man's policy argument made sense "on the merits." So he agreed to sponsor an amendment to the S&L bill on Yanney's behalf without bothering to consult with anyone on his staff about the possible political ramifications of doing so, which would soon become all too obvious.

8

MOST EXPEDITIOUS,
MOST COMPETENT

When Curt Prins plopped his six-foot-five-inch self into the chair next to Hoagland's desk, one got the impression that he'd learned to make himself comfortable. With an air of ease, he sank back, stretching out long legs that looked like hinged stilts.

In yet another sports-politics overlap, Prins used to referee college basketball games part-time. Now fiftyish, balding, and unlovely, he looked very much like the creature of Congress he was, working full-time as staff director for the Financial Institutions Subcommittee. It was said that Prins actually ran the subcommittee for its chairman, Frank Annunzio of Illinois. That made him, at least potentially, among the more powerful staff members in Congress.

Hoagland sat quietly as his leggy guest initiated small talk. Prins was astonished by how fast the S&L bailout bill was moving through Congress. "It's like wartime legislation," he said, shifting eyeglasses on the bridge of his bulbous nose.

Sometimes Prins liked to make himself very comfortable on
the job. But these days, that wasn't easy. The subcommittee was
currently very busy. It was a big bill, with lots of paperwork. Prins
fondly recalled more tranquil times, when he was able to stretch
out on his office couch and sleep for hours. He seemed to consider
it a good day when he could do that.

As Prins went on about the slumberous old days, Hoagland
stole what looked like a baffled glance at Nancy Nagel, his legislative assistant for Banking, who was sitting in. Nancy was a "gener-
alist" with no prior experience of banking issues, or of powerful
staff members, for that matter. She seemed as nonplussed as Hoagland.

The subcommittee was about to begin markups, when legislation was reviewed section by section and amendments were considered. Prins brought up Hoagland's amendment concerning
credit union audits. "I didn't wanna open your presents before
Christmas morning," he said with gruff sweetness, "but your
amendment's gonna pass."

Hoagland permitted himself a shy smile.

"It's a good amendment," Prins gravely enthused. "You've
worked hard on it, and you've been a good, loyal member of the
committee."

The word "loyal" landed in the conversation with a kind of
thud. Prins now seemed to speak not for himself, but for Annunzio. Hoagland quietly took note, wondering what was up.

"It's not by chance that you've been picked for certain
things," Prins said. He was referring to Hoagland's appointment
to the subcommittee's "examination and review" task force, which
was evaluating S&L auditing and oversight. "Some people were
picked for tasks, some people were picked for rewards." Prins
implied that Hoagland belonged in the "rewardee" category.

Hoagland's presence at subcommittee hearings hadn't gone
unnoticed. "I don't recall that you've missed a minute," Prins said.
"You've been with Mr. Annunzio every minute." Though that
was not quite true, Hoagland's attendance record had been exem-
plary, especially compared to that of his generally absent colleagues. And Hoagland wasn't just there for decoration. "You've
asked very good questions," Prins said.

Annunzio was not known as a subtle legislative tactician.
Prins seemed intent on proving it, with his frank talk of "loyalty"

and "rewards." Was he merely buttering up a new vote in town, or did he want something?

"The big leaders down here are not the famous ones you see on television," Prins said. "You start showing the other members how smart you are, you'll get killed around here." Prins had already praised Hoagland's mental acuity, so he obviously hadn't meant "smart" as in "intelligent," but as in "smart ass"—a person who bucked the system. Real power was wielded, he seemed to suggest, by those who quietly did favors, scratched backs, cut deals.

Even at this early stage, Hoagland did seem to be adept at playing the game. He'd already persuaded Congressman Carroll Hubbard, chairman of Banking's Oversight and Investigations Subcommittee, to bring his panel out to Omaha later in the year for a public hearing on the Franklin Credit Union. That would undoubtedly generate a lot of "media" for Hoagland, perhaps even some useful information for the good citizens of Omaha. But when Hoagland heard Prins describing him as a budding master of the inside game, he said it made him feel uncomfortable.

Prins finally got around to the little matter that had brought him. Annunzio was offering an amendment to the S&L bill concerning the "qualified thrift lender" or QTL test. Savings and loans could borrow funds from regional federal home loan banks at below-market interest rates if they proved that at least 60 percent of their loans went for home mortgages. Annunzio wanted to "raise" the standard to 80 percent, purportedly to keep S&Ls away from risky investments and get them back in the business of mortgage lending. But his amendment looked as if it would actually water down the current standard. It would permit S&Ls to count such things as consumer, small business, and education loans as home mortgages. Furthermore, it would allow them to count home loans to low-income borrowers *twice.* These loopholes made the supposed 80 percent standard more like 40 percent, or even lower than the current 60 percent test. In other words, in the name of forcing S&Ls to make *more* home loans to qualify for cheap money, the amendment looked like it would actually permit them to make *less.* To some, it smelled like a gift to the S&L lobby, with which Annunzio was said to have close relations.

"Everybody else is going along," Prins said, "and the chairman would sure like your support." When Hoagland kept silent,

Prins offered another rationale. "It's a press-release amendment,"
he said. "Pro-housing."

Prins showed more team spirit when he noted, with disap-
proval, that the Senate Banking Committee was going over the
S&L bill in closed-door sessions. He praised the House's—i.e. his
own subcommittee's—handling of the legislation, where open
hearings would be followed by open markups.

But just a minute or so later, and without any prodding, Prins
completely reversed himself. He now seemed to feel that open,
public proceedings were a nuisance. In the old days of back-room
brokering, "you could do whatever you wanted," he said. Now
members were constantly being watched in their committee
rooms. Only not by any "public." They were watched by lobbyists. Prins threw his head back and scoffed. "I've never seen 'the
public' in here. Maybe some homeless people who've come in out
of the rain. But not 'the public.'"

He was absolutely right. During markups, hearing rooms
were lousy with lobbyists. Who else but them, and the wealthy and
powerful interests they served, could afford the time and expense
of bird-dogging Congress? Their presence made members uneasy.
Several of Hoagland's colleagues had admitted as much to him. It
was as if the eyes of Money itself were always on them.

Frank Annunzio seemed to be reaching for something grandiose
to set the tone for his subcommittee's markups of the Financial
Institutions Reform, Recovery and Enforcement Act, or FIRREA
(fie-ree-ah) as everyone called it. Unlike the recent hearings on
the same bill, these markups were a hot ticket. Lobbyists in expensive suits, some with cellular phones peeking from their pockets,
were stuffed in the tightly bunched chairs of the spectators' section. On hand also were dour delegations from several government agencies, FDIC, FSLIC, the comptroller of the currency, the
Treasury Department, among others. Even the press section was
packed.

Rayburn 2128 was so jammed that an overflow room was
opened upstairs, where a loudspeaker was set up to carry the audio
portion of the proceedings. Attendance at markups, unlike at hearings, was all but mandatory. After all, when you got right down to
it, hearings were just well-intentioned talk. But the talk at markups
became the language of law.

Just what the final language of the S&L legislation would be was still in doubt. Committee members were swarmed by lobbyists waving amendments they wanted introduced. Hill staff often referred to lobbyists as "slime," as in "There's slime waiting to see you"—according to Nancy Nagel, who said she didn't apply the term herself. Of course, more than a few lobbyists were former Capitol Hill staff, and many now on staffs coveted the lucre that came with lobbying.

Already, 165 amendments had been filed, many drafted by "slime" and sponsored by committee members. Some sought to water down proposals in the Bush bill that S&L owners believed were unfair. The owners objected to the bill's increases in deposit insurance premiums for S&Ls (which would make them higher than the ones paid by banks), its stiffer capital standards, and its new regulatory structure, which would take away the Federal Home Loan Bank Board's "independence" and put it in the Treasury Department.

But after the S&L horror story of the eighties, the thrift industry didn't have nearly the credibility it once had had on Capitol Hill. Many lawmakers were angered by the S&Ls galling reluctance to take their medicine, despite the fact that taxpayers were being asked to cough up tens or hundreds of billions to bail them out.

But the S&L lobby seemed to know no shame. At the same time that it was bristling at the prospect of regulations similar to those applying to banks, the lobby asked permission to use the same insurance fund logo on the windows of S&Ls that banks used. Why? Because the banks' FDIC logo *had a better reputation* than their notorious FSLIC brand. *What brass!* was the conclusion of some members, who listened to such pleas in disbelief.

Some even said there really was no reason to have an S&L industry anymore, and if this bill proved its undoing, so what? But others argued that in taming the "go-go boys" who infested the S&L industry in the eighties, the government shouldn't penalize the operators of old-fashioned, sound, healthy, home-mortgage-writing thrifts. They also claimed that many of the new regulations were merely a gift to the banking industry, to give it a long-sought competitive edge over S&Ls. Rep. Stan Parris of Virginia characterized the pending confrontations in the markups as "two elephants fighting on the grass." The S&L industry was one elephant, the banking industry the other, "and the taxpayers are the grass."

The S&L markup was even more crowded than most, since the bill was a response to "the biggest financial catastrophe since the Great Depression," as more than one member had said. Frank Annunzio, not known as a gifted orator, did his best to rise to the occasion. Recalling Winston Churchill's famous speech after the Battle of Britain, when he described England's victory as "the end of the beginning" of World War II, Annunzio called what the subcommittee was about to do for the S&L crisis "the beginning of the beginning." Redundant, overreaching, and vague, it was vintage congressional rhetoric.

Some experts thought the S&L bailout might more likely mark the beginning of the end—of American economic might. Bush's people were doing their best to lowball the bailout's cost. They still claimed that $50 billion would be enough to liquidate insolvent S&Ls. But that number was openly ridiculed by financial experts, and even by some committee members. For one thing, no one was sure how many S&Ls were insolvent. Were there four hundred? Six hundred? And how large were their assets—$350 billion, $500 billion? Estimates were revised constantly. But one thing seemed clear—$50 billion was just a down payment to awaken from this nightmare. With our ballooning national debt and its astronomical interest costs steadily devouring the fisc, some believed the bailout might finally nudge us into the economic abyss.

Annunzio wrapped up his long opening statement with a promise to try to meet the president's timetable and produce a bill "within forty-five days." But that was impossible. The deadline was only two weeks away, and the bill still had to go to the full committee, after which it would be referred to four other committees before it reached the floor. Nevertheless, Annunzio employed a version of the scare estimates that others would use in the hours and days to come, to prod members into quicker action. Every month the S&L problem festered, he said, the industry lost an additional $1.6 billion, which would have to be paid by taxpayers. "These are not normal times," he concluded.

The seventy-three-year-old Annunzio had made his bones in Mayor Richard Daley's Chicago, and was a typical alumnus of machine politics: short, bald, jowly, unsubtle. But not being a

Churchill has never stopped a congressman—especially one with a little power—from winning the praise of his colleagues. Wherever two or more legislators are gathered, the honeyed words are sure to flow.

After Annunzio finished, other members were given the chance to speak. As usual on such occasions, few could resist the temptation. Henry Gonzalez, chairman of the full Banking Committee, summarized amendments he would offer, then kicked off the morning's festival of flattery. From his seat on the third tier, he looked up at Annunzio and commended the subcommittee chairman for being "most expeditious, most competent, hardworking and diligent" in organizing these proceedings. Douglas Barnard, a high-ranking Democrat, praised "the orderly and excellent way" Annunzio's staff had functioned. Chalmers Wylie had kind words for President Bush, who had acted "boldly" in addressing this crisis. Another Republican, Toby Roth, judged Annunzio "most expeditious, most fair."

One lower-ranking Republican was another ex-jock in politics, the gentleman from Kentucky, Jim Bunning. He had won fame as a fireballing right-handed pitcher for the Philadelphia Phillies. But today he took the prize for left-handed compliments, telling Annunzio: "You didn't lie, you kept your word," about the announced markup date.

When the speeches were finally over, the subcommittee began debating amendments to the bill and putting them to a vote. Lobbyists watched closely, holding scoresheets supplied by the subcommittee in their laps, which listed the names and office phone numbers of all members, next to boxes for "aye" "nay," and "proxy" votes. Lobbyists used these to track who voted with them and who might need a bit more persuading.

Until the previous November, when Fernand St. Germain was chairman of the Banking Committee (and the Financial Institutions Subcommittee), lobbyists for the savings and loan industry probably hadn't had to resort to such painstaking tactics. St. Germain was what is known in the papers as a "staunch friend" of the industry. It was said that he made sure S&Ls got what they wanted in the way of legislation. Industry lobbyists contributed $149,200 to his campaigns between 1984 and 1988.

St. Germain had been defeated in the last election, in perhaps the only district where savings and loans were an issue. All that remained of him at today's proceedings was his sad portrait in oils hanging on the wall, along with those of other departed chairmen. Not only was the nation better off without St. Germain, so was Hoagland. The former chairman was notorious for making decisions and cutting deals on legislation privately, without hearings or discussions, and ramming his work through the committee. Both Gonzalez and Annunzio believed in doing things out in the open. Thanks to them, Hoagland would, right off, get a chance to watch a major piece of legislation torn down and rebuilt before his eyes. Meanwhile, in a very poky legislative season, a freshmen on another committee might have been cutting his teeth on a commemorative for National Meat Appreciation Day.

The S&L bill was more than three hundred pages long and maddeningly complex. Even the Bush administration, which had submitted the thing, didn't appear to understand it, or in any case still seemed to be discovering subtle ambiguities in its starchy legalese. Bush's people were submitting amendments to their own bill two or three times a week.

Despite the bulk and complexity of the bill, Hoagland dove into his work, clearing out his office when the stack of amendments arrived from the committee so he could be alone to study them. At first, he wanted to read them all, but had to be satisfied with trying to master the most important ones.

Weeks before, Hoagland had telephoned his older brother, Laurence, an investment manager who lived in St. Louis and was the acknowledged family "genius," to get some background on the S&L problem. With Laurie's expert help, Hoagland had hoped to come up with some "plausible solutions" to present in Rayburn 2128. Unfortunately, solving the S&L mess was like trying to "solve" an earthquake. But unlike an earthquake, this was no act of God. This you could blame on people, probably people in Washington. But you couldn't blame Hoagland. He hadn't been there.

If you've seen the movie *It's a Wonderful Life* (and who could avoid it?), you witnessed what was perhaps the first bailout of a savings and loan. It happened during the upbeat love-thy-neighbor ending, when everyone in town gave money to George Bailey (Jimmy Stewart), president of the local building and loan (same as an S&L), so he could pay what he owed the ruthless local banker, whom he still had the grace to address as *Mr.* Potter. Yes, life sure is wonderful in this film, even in the colorized version, and bailing out the Baileys made everyone feel just terrific. But no matter how you colorize the offscreen savings and loan saga, it inspires little more than disgust.

In the old days, S&Ls operated in a cozy, government-regulated universe, taking deposits of long-term savers, paying low interest, and making home mortgage loans at slightly higher rates than they paid.* In spirit, they were not unlike George Bailey's dowdy building and loan.

But in the late seventies, the racy new world of instant electronic funds transfers and high-yield money markets enticed depositors away from their sleepy S&Ls, whose interest rates were capped by government regulation. The caps were designed to prevent rate wars from destabilizing the banking system. But they made it impossible for S&Ls to compete in an era of high inflation. When the rates S&Ls could pay fell below the inflation rate, their depositors actually lost money by "saving" with them.

When the industry cried for help, Congress lifted the caps. S&Ls created money markets of their own, winning back a lot of the deposits they'd lost. But they were still hammered by the interest-rate "spread." S&Ls were holding lots of fixed-rate thirty-year mortgages earning as little as 6 percent. But they were forced to pay out much higher rates—12 or 13 percent—to lure depositors. The spread all but leveled the industry. Its net worth plummeted from $32.2 billion in 1980 to just $3.7 billion in 1982.

The next act in the tragedy was the most ironic. In 1982, when Ronald Reagan and his "free-market" economics were enthroned in Washington, S&Ls might have been well served indeed by a stiff dose of the marketplace medicine Reagan loved to preach about. Inflation had finally been curbed. The "magic of the marketplace" meant deposit interest rates would soon fall too. If the industry had been content to let the spell work, it might have come all the way back to life.

But the chalice of the marketplace left a bitter taste. Many

---

* This discussion of the history of the S&L crisis is informed throughout by the following books and articles: *Inside Job,* by Stephen Pizzo, Mary Fricker, and Paul Muolo (McGraw-Hill, 1989); "The Looting Decade," by Robert Sherrill, in *The Nation,* November 19, 1990; "How the Cleaver Family Destroyed Our S&Ls," by James Bennet, in *The Washington Monthly,* September 1990; "Chronicle of a Debacle Foretold," by L. J. Davis, in *Harpers,* September 1990.

institutions were too badly damaged by the spread to recover. Those could, and probably should, have been permitted to die. Their depositors would have been reimbursed by the Federal Savings and Loan Insurance Company (FSLIC), whose fund was built by fees collected from savings and loans. It would have been a multibillion-dollar loss for the fund. But no taxpayer "bailout" would have been necessary.

However, the industry's leaders reportedly would have none of that. Instead of permitting sickly S&Ls simply to die of natural, free-market causes, they wanted to help those institutions "grow out of their problems," so owners could recoup their investments. Somehow, the financially strapped industry found enough money to shower on politicians—presidential candidates and members of Congress alike—paving the way for their strategy in the halls of power. For once, the industry had invested wisely. Congress and the Reagan administration cooperated enthusiastically in the early eighties to help failed S&Ls. The plan was to "deregulate" S&Ls, then a very trendy policy in the think tanks. Though deregulation was sanctioned by the best minds in Washington, applied to S&Ls it was little more than ideology masquerading as economics and represented nothing less than the repeal of common sense.

Ever since the thirties, when federal deposit insurance was created to guard the banking system against "runs," regulations had been in place in government-insured financial institutions, to keep owners from "speculating with other people's money," in Franklin Roosevelt's words. The existence of deposit insurance meant that the taxpayer stood behind every bank deposit and would make good on it should the bank fail. If bankers (or S&L owners) weren't reined in by regulations, it was believed, nothing would stop them from imprudently speculating with their deposits, since they knew that while they could keep any "profits," the insurance fund, and ultimately the taxpayers, would absorb the losses.

In the early eighties, when imprudent speculation was back in style, going by the name of "entrepreneurship," regulations put in place to protect the insurance fund—and taxpayers—were repealed one by one. As a result, S&Ls that were failing, and plainly lacked adequate capital to do business under "old-fashioned" rules, were now encouraged to solicit government-insured deposits and try their luck at "growing."

Getting the cash deposits with which to invest was made easier by loosened regulations on such things as brokered deposits, chunks of money from pension funds and institutional investors. S&Ls used to be limited to holding only 5 percent of their deposits in such "hot money." Now, there was no limit.

Brokered money sought high returns, so S&Ls entered into frenzied interest-rate wars to get it. Paying out high rates for their deposits meant that they had to seek high returns on the investments they put those deposits in, which of course also involved higher risks. But what the hell, it wasn't their money. And the people that made the deposits weren't worried that their S&Ls might be taking too many risks. After all, new regulations had also increased the coverage of government deposit insurance—from $40,000 to $100,000 per account—injecting even more hot money into the system.

Running an S&L or bank is fraught with temptation to begin with. On the one hand, your vaults are brimming with cash deposits. But all that green is entered on your books as *liabilities,* since you must pay it back on demand—with interest. There's always a temptation to loan the money out to the first warm biped who asks for it. After all, loans are *assets*—they're owed to you—and the interest paid on them is *income.*

Formerly, S&Ls had been restricted to making low-risk loans, such as home mortgages. New, looser regulations allowed high-risk commercial real estate loans, for condo and shopping mall construction projects, even outside an S&L's community, where risks were impossible to assess. Such high-risk, high-yield activities were seen as ways for "sick" S&Ls to get well again.

Banks were traditionally allowed to make these higher-risk loans. But their owners also had to keep a higher percentage of "tangible capital," i.e., stocks and other instruments that could be readily turned into cash, to back up loans should they fail. In other words, owners risked losing a good chunk of *their own money* if investments went bad.

Thanks to the deregulators in Washington, S&Ls weren't required to keep much capital at all in reserve to back up their loans. That was partly the point of S&L deregulation in the first place. Since many S&Ls didn't have enough capital, they would have been forced out of business if required to get it. To avoid such a dire outcome, they were actually allowed to count *intangible* assets,

like "goodwill"—the "value" of the S&L's customer base and reputation in the community—as *cash!* Of course, if the S&L went
bust, depositors could hardly be paid off with "goodwill." The
money, we repeat, came from federal deposit insurance. So despite all the talk in Washington of heroic "entrepreneurship,"
those swashbuckling free-marketeers were really gambling with
government "house money." Heads they win, tails we lose.

Shortsighted as they were, the new regulations *might* have
worked if a lot of steady George Baileys were running S&Ls. But
deregulation relaxed the standards for S&L ownership too. In the
dowdy old days, most federally chartered S&Ls were mutual as-
sociations, owned by their depositors. Others were joint-stock
companies. A group of at least four hundred stockholders was
required to charter an S&L, and a clear community need for the
institution had to be shown, to keep out sharks simply looking to
play fast and lose with other people's money.

But the new rules encouraged single owners with "entrepreneurial skills" to open S&Ls, regardless of a community's
need. Along with federal deposit insurance, it was just the right
temptation to lure all the wrong people into the business,
slimeballs who would make George Bailey's nemesis, old man
Potter, seem positively philanthropic.

Many of the new breed of S&L owners came into the business
primed to believe that the traditional prudence of bankers was for
sissies. Some quickly grew impatient with the milk of interest income and went for the whole cow of ownership, which was also
now legal. S&Ls owners invested in all manner of exotica, including tanning beds, windmill farms, hot-tub spas, a buffalo sperm
bank, and a kitty litter mine.

And if owners wanted to live well while waiting for their
investments to pay off, they took out big loans themselves—
$50,000, $100,000, $500,000, a million. Who could stop them?
And they spent business funds on European chefs, gold and silver
chess sets, leather toilet seats, receptions where lion and antelope
meat were served, and new cars (one S&L exec bought five in one
day for his family), among other entrepreneurial necessities.

"Goodwill" made things really convenient if you were not
only a gambler who liked to live well but a thief besides. Since you
had little of your own money down, you gladly viewed the measly
capital you put up as a cover charge for stealing millions of your

own institution's deposits. The way you did it, of course, depended on your entrepreneurial "ingenuity." You might have enlisted the aid of other crooked S&L owners. You gave millions in unsecured loans to them, and they returned the favor. Of course, no one had to worry about paying anything back. Or you might have made loans to developers for a handsome kickback. Or loans to a company you had interests in. The opportunities for safe and profitable fraud in this brave new world of finance were limitless.

The total losses from all bank holdups in a given year seldom tops around $30 million. Some white-collar swindlers got away with more than that from *one S&L*. Armed bank robbers almost always go to jail for a long time. But most S&L scam artists haven't been caught, and if the past is any guide, probably won't be prosecuted if they are caught, and probably won't do much time if they're convicted. As of 1989, the average sentence for a convicted S&L embezzler was three years.

The new "anything goes" regime might yet have worked if Reagan administration regulators—the cops on the beat—could have grasped that now was the time for *tighter* supervision of S&Ls. Instead, Reagan cut the staffs of supervisors and examiners. Meanwhile, federal auditors who remained on the job were not auditing, examiners weren't examining, and when they happened to trip over flagrant abuses, prosecutors weren't prosecuting. And it was all *not being done* as a matter of *policy!* To do such things would be "regulation," wouldn't it? It would interfere with that old marketplace magic, which, as anyone not addled with ideology knows, has always involved some chicanery and downright criminality. When S&L violations couldn't be ignored, "enforcement" often amounted to a surly letter from the feds, with no follow-up.

As if the watered-down regulations at the national level weren't bad enough, state legislatures followed Washington's lead and deregulated S&L's with state charters—many of which were also federally insured. States often made regulations even looser than at the national level, particularly in Texas and California, where a high percentage of S&L failures eventually occurred. Why were state legislators so anxious to get in on the deregulation action? Some say that they, too, wanted to bank some of those free-flowing S&L industry campaign contributions.

The upshot of S&L deregulation was that hundreds of formerly "sick" S&Ls not only didn't get well, they lost even bigger piles of government-insured money than ever. And they were joined by hundreds more failed institutions. When Congress hunkered down to debate the Bush bailout plan in early 1989, no one knew the extent of the government's losses. Was it $50 billion, $100 billion, $200 billion, half a trillion? Whatever the amount, everyone seemed to agree on one thing: the taxpayers would pay. But before taxpayers were aware enough to ask who was to blame, "bipartisanship" blossomed conveniently in the corridors of power in early 1989. No one pointed fingers, since everyone had blood on his hands.

Democrats in Congress had interfered with the investigation of individual cases of S&L fraud—the famous Keating Five affair being just one example—by intimidating regulators.

Meanwhile, Republicans in the Reagan administration appear to have interfered with the investigation of *all* cases of S&L fraud, since they believed such things amounted to "regulation." Don Regan, Reagan's treasury secretary, reportedly tried to pressure out of office the only man in Washington who seemed willing to see the truth: Ed Gray, chairman of the Federal Home Loan Bank Board, chief regulator of S&Ls. For years, Gray had been pleading with the administration for more examiners and with Congress for tighter regulation of S&Ls. When Gray's term expired, Reagan appointed M. Danny Wall to replace him, a man considered a good friend of the S&L industry, and who had helped create much of the deregulation legislation of the early eighties as staff director of the Senate Banking Committee.

Wall ran what looked like a political coverup in 1988. As S&Ls tumbled like dominoes across the land, he repeatedly underestimated the cost of the burgeoning failure, assuring pliant reporters that no taxpayer bailout would be needed. Almost immediately after the election, Wall changed his tune, when Reagan was safely back on the ranch and Bush was in the White House. Democrats acquiesced in the cover-up, by not raising the S&L issue in their campaigns (with some exceptions). They too were returned to power in Congress. Did this represent the proper functioning of a two-party system, or brazen, cynical collusion?

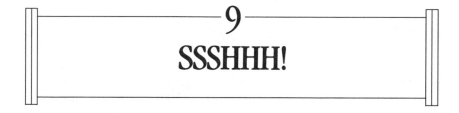

9
SSSHHH!

For someone who had been in office less than three months, Peter Hoagland was looking pretty good. Late in March, shortly before markups began, Hoagland attended a meeting in the book-stuffed office of Congressman David Price with lobbyists from the Federal Deposit Insurance Corporation. Price and Hoagland had agreed to sponsor an amendment that was on the FDIC's wish list for the S&L bill.

It looked like an adroit move on Hoagland's part. Though Price, a Democrat from North Carolina, was only in his second term, he already had a reputation as a "serious" student of policy, not a bad reputation to have.

Price, a plain-looking man of solemn mien, was about as "substantive" as they come in Washington. Formerly a professor of political science at Duke, where his academic specialty was Congress, he'd written numerous articles and even a couple of books about the place. Adding to his aura of *gravitas* was his background as a Yale Divinity School graduate and lay Baptist preacher.

Many had high hopes that Price, with his scholarly detachment, would remain above *mere* politics. But during his first term,
weeks before election day, he voted against a gun control bill
apparently under pressure from the National Rifle Association.
That wouldn't have seemed so craven had he not been one of the
bill's cosponsors.

If Price had proved that professors can be politicians too, he
also impressed colleagues with how rapidly he adapted to the practical business of legislating. During his first session, his bill to force
banks to disclose the terms of home equity loans became law—
quite an achievement for a rookie.

Now, along with Hoagland, Price seemed to have found another policy screw that needed tightening. Their amendment to
preserve the FDIC chairman's political "independence" and raise
the cap on the agency's borrowing authority was well received and
looked like it would pass in subcommittee without a fight.

Hoagland wasn't shy about plunging into the thick of the
action on the S&L bill, and seemed to be winning points for it.
Early in April, the banking industry newsletter *Insight* contained
this laudatory item: "Certain congressmen will have emerged as
having heavily influenced subcommittee and full committee thinking, among them . . . David Price and Peter Hoagland, who
mastered technical arguments to make the case for a more independent FDIC."

Hoagland also lobbied for his credit union amendment—
which had turned into a rather sizable overhaul of existing law—
and he was looking very much like an alert, active, up-and-coming
legislator. But he was still a new kid, and sometimes it showed.

In the meeting with FDIC lobbyists, the name of the infamous
Federal Home Loan Bank Board chairman, Danny Wall, happened
to come up. Hoagland chose this opportunity to make one of his
extraplanetary "where did *that* come from" remarks of his.

"I've heard Wall did a fine job," he said.

At first, the lobbyists squinted at him in puzzlement, as if they
weren't sure their faculties were functioning. Maybe he was just
joking. But Hoagland, sitting there in his relentless baggy blue
suit, his voice vibrating with guileless heartland enthusiasm, had
sounded very sincere.

One of the lobbyists, a blondish, conservatively suited woman
in her mid-thirties, finally decided that he wasn't kidding. "Well,

yes," she said, "he got *you all* off the hook." By "you all" she meant, of course, "you congresspeople." In Washington just now, Hoagland's praise of Danny Wall was akin to hailing Bob Haldeman, Richard Nixon's infamous henchman, for his fine job covering up Watergate.

The problem in the S&L industry all along had been what to do about the increasing numbers of failed thrifts. At first, closing them and paying off their depositors wasn't an appealing alternative, since it would cost the industry dearly in various ways. Later, as the ranks of sick thrifts mushroomed, it was no longer even an option. The losses in S&Ls, if they had to be liquidated, would have far exceeded the insurance fund.

In the early and middle eighties, the bank board needed a way to keep from closing thrifts that were failing and putting heavier and heavier demands on its lighter and lighter insurance fund. It devised an ingenious strategy—at least it was considered so at the time. Instead of closing sick S&Ls, it decided to merge them with healthy ones. But incentives had to be offered to get a healthy S&L to swallow a sick one, whose assets weren't worth as much as its books said they were.

For one thing, the bank board computed the difference between the lower actual value of a sick S&L's assets and their higher book value, and offered this to prospective buyers in a form that was equivalent to cash, at least to them. Healthy S&Ls were permitted to count this difference between the real and book values of assets acquired in mergers with sick thrifts as part of their core capital requirement—the amount of money they had to keep in reserve in order to legally do business at all. That meant the owners had to put up less of their own money to meet capital requirements. Their new form of capital was known as "goodwill."

Goodwill was not a wholly new concept. It has long been used to account for the difference between the sale price of a given business and its lower book value. Goodwill was said to take into account intangibles, like a business's customer base and reputation in a community, its value as a going concern.

But an S&L was not an ordinary business. Unlike others that counted goodwill on their books, S&Ls were backed up by government insurance. If they failed, their goodwill would be worth naught to the insurance fund, or to the taxpayers who ultimately stood behind it. And goodwill wasn't the only form of phony capital dreamed up by the regulators. In sum, by 1987, 45 percent of the thrift industry's net worth was "goodwill" or other forms of fictive capital. That meant it was only 55 percent capitalized, which was very thin ice.

By 1988, it was clear that the goodwill deals were not doing the trick. Thrifts were still dying like rabid animals, after frantic speculative fits. And even regulators were nervous about how much fictive capital was in the system. So were the owners of healthy S&Ls, who were no longer coming to the table to cut deals with the bank board for sick thrifts. But the bank board had to keep cutting deals. It couldn't afford—either financially or politically—simply to close down sick thrifts and pay their depositors.

For one thing, the insurance fund was nearly dry. If the bank board didn't find buyers for sick thrifts, it would have to go to Congress for more money, and the whole sorry condition of the insurance fund and the industry might emerge as an issue in the '88 election. That could well hurt George Bush, whose Republican administration had been responsible for overseeing savings and loans—regulating them—though it had touted "deregulation" with religious zeal. It could also hurt Democrats, who'd had a hammy hand or two in deregulation themselves, and who'd sometimes interfered with what little regulation there was remaining. Politicians who'd gotten wind of the odoriferous dealings at the bank board were not at all eager to investigate.

Nevertheless, to hide the rotten fruits of deregulation was a big job, but the new chairman of the bank board, Danny Wall, seemed up to it. He gave the press and Congress estimates of the extent of the hole in the insurance fund that seemed outrageously low to many at the time, and which have since appeared to some as downright lies. Congress clearly should have, and probably did, know better. The press, in this case acting more like a stenographer to the powerful rather than a "watchdog," accepted for the most part what it was told by officials concerning S&Ls.

Wall also refined the practice of cutting deals to unload sick thrifts. Since goodwill alone wasn't bringing in buyers for them, he came up with other pot sweeteners. Buyers were given guaranteed returns on assets, guaranteed limits to losses, millions in tax breaks, and waivers from capital standards, if they bought sick thrifts. As if that weren't enough, they were also given FSLIC notes worth billions to provide them with an "income stream."

It was more like a river. FSLIC was technically out of money, but it was now virtually minting the stuff to pad its deals. For instance, financier Robert Bass of Fort Worth bought the insolvent American Savings and Loan of Stockton, California. For $350 million in cash, he was given $2 billion in subsidies from the bank board, including $500 million in FSLIC notes, as well as generous tax breaks, which, while they didn't cost FSLIC a dime, cost taxpayers millions. But at least Bass put *some* money down. Other buyers got huge assistance agreements without putting down a cent.

In December, after the election, with Ronald Reagan on his way back to the ranch, George Bush contemplating his new address on Pennsylvania Avenue, and Congress home for Christmas, Wall really went to work. To take advantage of tax breaks that were set to expire at the end of the year, he cut a flurry of supergenerous "midnight deals." All told, on his own say-so, Wall had obligated the federal government—without hearings, debates, markups, votes, in short, without the approval of Congress—to spend over $70 billion. (At the time it was believed he spent *only* $40 billion, but that number has since been revised.) Since Bush had asked for only $50 billion in initial outlays for the entire S&L bailout, it looked as if Wall had completed his own bailout while Congress was home for Christmas.

Peter Hoagland had a dilemma.

The bailout bill under consideration in the banking committee would do away with "goodwill" and other phony money and make S&Ls come up with cash to meet their capital requirements within two years. But the bill would not take away the pot-sweeteners—tax breaks, FSLIC notes, etc.—awarded to buyers of thrifts in 1988. Danny Wall's generous giveaways, many of which went to wealthy, well-connected financiers, like former Treasury Secretary William Simon and corporate raider Ronald Perelman, would be made good by the government.

The owners of Commercial Federal Savings and Loan of Omaha were angry. They were not well-connected financiers, just the operators of a 102-year-old institution that had long been conservatively managed. In 1987, they'd taken over the faltering Empire Savings and Loan of Denver, Colorado, at the bank board's behest. Since Empire was in a deep hole, with assets worth much less than their book value, the bank board permitted Commercial Federal to book $200 million in goodwill capital, to be written off gradually over thirteen years. Now the S&L bill said it had to be written off in two years. That would be very expensive.

Commercial Federal's owners naturally came calling on their congressman, who just happened to sit on the Banking Committee. "A deal is a deal," they argued. The argument was echoed by S&L owners and lobbyists in the offices of nearly every Banking Committee member, and of many other members besides.

Hoagland was torn. He favored the bill's stiffer capital requirements. The industry could no longer be allowed to make investments without putting its owners' cash at risk, not the money of innocent taxpayers. Doling out goodwill in the first place now looked like a huge mistake. He didn't think that mistake should dictate current policy.

But on the other hand, Hoagland couldn't deny that Commercial Federal had a good case. The government had offered it a deal, it had gone along in good faith, and now the government was trying to renege.

As a freshman, Hoagland could be expected to be politically neurotic and hypersensitive to the needs of his district. Perhaps complicating things, one of Commercial Federal's executives, and its lobbyist on this very issue, was Don Schinzel. He was the father of Dave Schinzel, Hoagland's own aide, to whom he was probably closest.

But Don Schinzel, typical of your genial Omahans, was not one for high-pressure tactics, or for trying to cash in on his son's position. While he believed in the rightness of his cause, he also understood that Hoagland was in "a tough spot."

When Sherry Ettleson got to the Rayburn Building at 7:15 one morning, a straggly line of bike messengers in tights, T-shirts, and sunglasses stretched from the still-locked front door all the way around the corner. It looked like a Bon Jovi concert was scheduled, not markups on the S&L bill.

Ettleson was a lawyer for Congress Watch, a public interest lobby created by Ralph Nader in the seventies. She was typical of her breed: young, idealistic, hardworking, underpaid. Since the markups had been infested with well-greased financial industry lobbyists, she had arrived early to get a good seat.

The proceedings were to begin at 9:00. As the hour approached, Ettleson learned why seats had been so hard to come by. Limosines and taxicabs choked the horseshoe-shaped driveway, disgorging phalanxes of pinstripe-suited, Gucci-shod lobbyists. Gradually, groups of up to ten lobbyists took the places of the messengers, whom they'd hired for $10 to $30 an hour. Some had been waiting all night. Eventually, Ettleson found herself at the back of a much-swollen line. When the doors opened, she was lucky to get a seat.

Ettleson, a wide-eyed and wispy creature, was hard pressed to compete with the expense-account-bloated financial industry lobbyists. At twenty-seven, she was just a few years out of law school and had been on the job only a couple of weeks before the markups began. That gave her a lot of catching up to do on an unusually big, complex bill. Besides, her organization, like all Nader-affiliated enterprises, didn't make campaign contributions.

For their clout, Nader's groups relied on hard work, the sainted status of their founder, and strategic outpourings of good old-fashioned public outrage. But that had been unexpectedly hard to come by on this bill. When it came to issues like the existence of alternatives to the hugely expensive funding plan, the public was in the dark.

Taking their cue from besieged members of Congress, the media had treated the "goodwill" issue as the centerpiece of the bill. But this and other S&L issues involved mind-gumming concepts that, it was widely believed, most people would be unable to understand, assuming they weren't too bored to care. Consequently, even when the press grasped what was happening, its coverage of this epochal undertaking was exiled to the business pages. Meanwhile, television pretty much ignored the bailout bill completely, agog over the much more telegenic drama of Jim Wright's embattled speakership.

As told in the nation's business pages, the story of the markups revolved around whether or not the S&L lobby would "win" by fighting off stiffer regulations, or "lose" and be forced to swallow them. But before the hearings had even begun, the S&L lobby had already won, since a taxpayer-funded bailout had become the only thinkable policy. That it penalized the middle class and the poor, who had little role in the mess, was viewed as regrettable.

As a result, perhaps the only issue the public really cared about and could understand—who should pay—was discussed by nobody. Well, not exactly *nobody*. Ralph Nader had a lot to say on the subject, but Congress and the news media treated him like nobody.

"Average citizens neither caused nor benefited from the policies" that led to the S&L disaster, Nader told a crowded Washington press conference. "The full cost of the bailout should be borne by those who benefited from the deregulation of the Roaring Eighties: financial institutions, the wealthy, and corporations that continue to avoid their fair share of taxes."

No great, or even not-so-great, national debate ensued about these proposals, since few heard of them. Nader's press conference was virtually blacked out. Among major newspapers, only the *Wall Street Journal* ran a story. Network news shows were silent (the *McNeil-Lehrer Newshour* did a thirty-second piece).

Though Nader was no public official, he had reason to believe his opinions might be newsworthy. Only days earlier, his virtually single-handed campaign to galvanize the nation against the congressional pay raise had won on the House floor, buoyed by a shrill popular protest. And opinion polls routinely showed the public to be sympathetic to his views. One poll, published in the *National Journal* around the time the Bush S&L bill was introduced, said 70 percent of respondents wanted to know more, on a given issue, about what Ralph Nader had to say.

It might have seemed odd that the media were ignoring Nader's bailout funding proposal so soon after his hugely successful anti-pay-raise crusade. But on Capitol Hill, Nader was shunned precisely because of his outspoken opposition to the boost, which both houses of Congress voted down. Though "shunned" perhaps isn't strong enough. Freshman Jim McDermott threatened to throw a reporter out of his office if he brought up Nader's name again. And during a Banking Committee markup, Doug Bereuter of Nebraska voted against a consumer-oriented amendment not with a simple "no," but by declaiming, with some fury, "I am voting *against Ralph Nader.*"

Frank Annunzio was proud of his subcommittee. At the end of hearings, he routinely announced: "You have been meeting be-

fore the largest subcommittee in the history of Congress. It is
larger than some of the standing committees."

That it was. But during markups, the largest subcommittee in
congressional history looked more like a cattle auction. Lobbyists
not only packed Rayburn 2128, they were six deep in the hallways
outside. When members and staff dared to step out of the hearing
room, they were hailed, pawed at, grabbed by the arm, and otherwise implored to sponsor amendments.

A lot of lobbyists had approached Hoagland this way, and he
was tempted to offer some of their amendments. Nancy said that a
couple of times she had to stop Hoagland from offering such
amendments, when she didn't think there was enough time to
study them carefully.

But the frenzied pace only enhanced the persuasiveness of
lobbyists. With little time for study, Hoagland sometimes felt
forced to rely on them to interpret the complex bill. He asked one
bank lobbyist to evaluate "the regulatory part" for him. "It
doesn't make a whole lot of sense to me," Hoagland admitted.

Nancy was in much the same fix. She was only twenty-six,
with little Washington experience, and none on the Hill, when
Hoagland hired her. Doing a member's committee work carried a
certain cachet among Hill types. She was surprised when Hoagland asked her to do his. "I got a better job than I wanted," she
said.

Nancy's dark hair, flowing in unruly waves to her shoulders,
and her large, limpid brown eyes emphasized a detached casual-
ness in her manner, somewhat out-of-place in the driven atmosphere of Congress. She praised Hoagland for not pressuring her
the way members commonly do staffs. Stories of abuse were all
around.

One that was told in the Hoagland camp concerned an aide to
the late Nebraska Senator Ed Zorinsky who accompanied him to a
party after work. Both were dressed in business suits. When they
arrived and learned it was a "black tie" function, Zorinsky flew
into a rage and fired his aide on the spot for not warning him.
Such petulance was inconceivable with Hoagland. "He's just such
a sweetheart," Nancy said.

Hard as she was trying, Nancy admitted there were "huge
gaps" in her understanding of the bill. Nothing in her liberal arts
training had prepared her for the reams of deadening regulatory
jargon that now crossed her desk. Any help she could get making

sense of it was quite welcome. When a lobbyist handed her a dreary memo that clarified "bank powers," her features relaxed as if he'd given her a good neck rub.

As expected, the Price-Hoagland amendment passed easily, on a voice vote. The Bush bill was going to put the S&L insurance fund into the much more trustworthy hands of the FDIC. But it was also going to take away the political independence of the FDIC chairman, currently William Seidman, a popular figure on Capitol Hill. Many members didn't think he should serve only at the pleasure of the president. Besides that, the bill was going to cap the amount of notes the FDIC could issue, to prevent future "midnight deals" from occurring in that agency.

The Price-Hoagland amendment preserved the chairman's independence and raised the cap on FDIC borrowing. Since its passage was a "setback" for the Bush administration, it was also noticed. On April 8, the *New York Times* covered it on the front page of its business section: BUSH PLAN ON SAVINGS SET BACK— HOUSE PANEL VOTES TO INSULATE FDIC FROM WHITE HOUSE. Of the sponsors, only Price was quoted.

But Price-Hoagland was mere bureaucratic slap boxing. The sanguinary struggles were to come, between Bush and the banking industry on the one hand and S&Ls on the other. Meanwhile, it was every blade of grass for itself.

According to the almanac *Politics in America,* Frank Annunzio saw himself as a protector of the common man. He once crusaded against, among other things, credit card interest rates, accusing card issuers of "plastic loan-sharking." But his plan to cap the rates had failed, like most of his "little guy" measures. His sincerity was not questioned so much as his stubbornness and unwillingness to compromise.

Annunzio now seemed to have another fixed idea: that savings and loans were the common man's best friend, as opposed to predatory banks. Echoing the argument of S&Ls everywhere, Annunzio sponsored an amendment on capital standards to rescue goodwill, because "a deal is a deal." A few suspected that Annunzio "carried water" for S&Ls. The industry had given him $29,660 in campaign contributions in recent years.

The legislation would have required S&Ls to come up with 3

percent of their assets in tangible capital—cash or financial instruments readily converted to cash. Annunzio's amendment let them off easier, requiring only 1.5 percent tangible capital, and 1.5 percent in a mixture of goodwill and other "phantom" capital. Like Hoagland, subcommittee members had been hearing from the S&Ls back home on this issue. Annunzio's amendment, cosponsored by Republican Stan Parris, was a combination of proposals from fully thirty subcommittee members.

The debate on Annunzio-Parris was by far the most spirited yet. Before a standing-room-only crowd in Rayburn 2128, members made impassioned pleas for fairness to S&Ls on the one hand and fiscal sanity on the other. Doug Barnard, Democrat of Georgia, argued that the bill's too-harsh capital rules subjected "over thirteen hundred institutions to be undercapitalized," and might lead to their ruin.

Full committee chairman Henry Gonzalez was adamantly opposed to watering down the capital rules. "Time after time we have accepted industry arguments that we give them just a little more time, just a little more phony-baloney bookkeeping . . . and everything would be all right," he said. "We did those things and everything is not all right."

The vote was very close. Some roll calls are straight party-line affairs. Democrats vote one way, Republicans another. There are usually deviations from these strict alignments. But on this committee, and on this bill, the deviations were sharp and unpredictable. For instance, on Annunzio-Parris the question was whether the committee would back the more conservative capital standards of a Republican president, or the more liberal rules wanted by S&Ls. Ironically, conservative Republicans and Democrats tended to side with the S&Ls, while liberals tended to favor stricter standards.

Annunzio-Parris passed by a whisker, 24–23. After a bit of agonizing, Hoagland voted against it, reluctantly concluding that the need to clean house in S&Ls outweighed Commercial Federal's legitimate claims. But on two later subcommittee votes, the looser rules of Annunzio-Parris were tightened back up somewhat, with the elimination of two other fictive forms of capital. Hoagland voted to scratch one of them, but on the other, he appeared to make a gesture to his hometown thrift.

The other amendment dealt with "subordinated debt," a

form of debt that Commercial Federal had taken on to buy Empire, and that the bank board had allowed to be counted as capital. Hoagland voted against nixing "subdebt" from the capital mix, though it was eliminated, and handily, by a vote of 28–19. Before the markups began, Hoagland said that sometimes you had to "fall on your sword," and speak or vote for a losing proposition to please lobbyists, or the folks back home—provided your vote didn't do any real damage.

Despite the later setbacks, the S&L lobby had triumphed on the goodwill issue, the first real test of its strength since the abuses of the past decade became public. That had a lot of people worried that the so called "reforms" in the current bill might not amount to much.

On the last day of subcommittee markups, Annunzio took exception to some criticisms of his staff that had been making the rounds. They'd been accused of improperly taking on the tasks of members by working out "backroom" compromises on amendments. "The staff has handled more than thirty thousand pieces of paper during this markup, without a single major mistake," Annunzio announced testily, ignoring the point in heroic style. "The staff has had to go without sleep, it has had to go without meals, and it has had to go without a normal life. But I'll be damned if the staff is going to go without praise and my deep-felt appreciation for a magnificent job."

When Annunzio finished, Chalmers Wylie bellied up to the mike. "Mr. Chairman," he said importantly, "I would associate myself with your remarks." This locution was peculiar to congressfolk, their equivalent of beatniks in a coffeehouse snapping fingers in appreciation of a haiku.

But not many wanted to associate themselves with alternatives to the administration's super-costly plan to use long-term bonds to pay for the bailout. To abandon the bonding approach would have certainly meant a tax increase, in itself enough to send politicians running. But picking a fight over the funding issue almost certainly would have attracted much more attention to the mammoth cost of the bailout, perhaps leading an angry nation to demand to know *who was to blame.* That was a subject Washington didn't want to discuss just now.

Congresswoman Marcy Kaptur learned how sensitive the funding question could be after she brought the matter up in a "one-minute" on the House floor. Kaptur looked younger than her forty-three years, with collar-length blond hair wound in loose curls on her forehead. Her mode of dress fell on the conservative end of the spectrum of congresswomen, tending to flouncy blouses that buttoned primly at the throat.

Kaptur was beginning her seventh year in the House. She sat on the influential Budget Committee, and on the top tier in the Banking Committee, among the panel's heavyweights. But her clout wasn't what it might have been. She had a reputation on Banking as something of a softie. Staff members still chuckled about her failed amendment to require that banks offer savings accounts for children.

Kaptur said that despite Bush's "no new taxes" pledge, his bailout proposal, particularly the heavy interest charges of the deferred payment plan, amounted to "the biggest tax increase in recent memory. . . . the taxpayer is being sent a bill of over $200 billion over the next thirty years." Kaptur favored "an alternative to this tax bill" to make "those who are responsible for this debacle pay for it."

The lady was quickly brought to book when Newt Gingrich, the recently elected House minority whip, rose to reply. Gingrich was a leader of the new breed of radical right-wing Republicans. Like his party colleague and soulmate Lee Atwater, he was a reactionary in progressive packaging. He wore his prematurely gray hair in an early-Beatle-style mop-top. And with an elfin grin on his pudgy face, he lashed Democrats with a mercilessly glib tongue. A sound-bite artist and practiced manipulator of the media, he mounted a one-man campaign to train press attention on Jim Wright's record that laid the groundwork for his charges against the speaker before the Ethics Committee. For that, and countless insults, he was probably the most popular pinup on Democrats' dartboards, someone they loved to loathe, and probably had learned to fear a little.

After calling Kaptur's remarks "entirely appropriate," Gingrich issued a not-so-veiled threat to his colleagues across the aisle. "Democrats who want to make partisan points about the savings and loan problem should be very, very cautious," Gingrich warned. There was lots of evidence, he said, "about . . . how we got into the . . . mess and . . . the role of the House Democratic Party."

Gingrich offered the Democrats a deal, which had seemed

tacitly accepted by both parties until now. "I am prepared to . . . say nothing about any of that," he said. "But if there is going to be any bashing of George Bush and any bashing of the Republican Party, I just want the Democrats to understand that we are fully prepared to talk about how the mess got so big and who was responsible."

What Gingrich was asking, openly, on the floor of the House, was that his Democratic colleagues continue to cooperate in a conspiracy of silence about the S&L fiasco, for the benefit of politicians in both parties. For the most part, in the coming weeks and months, Gingrich got what he wanted.

Hoagland had expressed, however gingerly, skepticism about the bailout funding scheme in his questioning of Darman. But this freshman was accomplished enough in the art of politics to recognize a masterpiece. "It's just so politically convenient," he said of the plan. That was an understatement.

The principal political benefit of Bush's "off-budget" scheme was that it avoided an unpopular tax increase now by incurring hundreds of billions in interest charges later. But it did much more. The plan not only took the $50 billion in immediate bailout borrowing out of the budget deficit, it then *added* that $50 billion to the credit side of the ledger as "collections." So instead of making the near-term deficit swell by $50 billion, Bush's plan would make it *appear* to shrink by $50 billion.

Congressional Democrats weren't about to fight for a radically different funding scheme, to let middle-class and poor taxpayers off the hook for the bailout, and possibly save hundreds of billions of dollars in interest charges besides. Though potentially a popular plan, it was much too risky. The media might paint them as tax maniacs. They might end up alienating the middle class in an attempt to save it.

Even the most liberal of Democrats seemed wary of challenging the basics of Bush's funding plan. Congressman Barney Frank was a consistent scourge of the Republican right. But during Darman's appearance before the Banking Committee, Frank was quite agreeable to the administration's costly plan for long-term borrowing. "I think that when it comes to whether this is short-term, long-term, we ought to leave that to the experts at the Treasury Department," he said.

There *was* an alternative funding plan gaining support among congressional Democrats. It too called for borrowing the bailout money long-term, with those hundreds of billions in interest costs. In other words, it was still "politically convenient."

But the borrowing was to be "on-budget," so that the Treasury could issue the bonds, not some "nongovernment" agency. Since Treasury bonds paid a lower interest rate, this alternative would save $150 million a year, or around $4.5 billion over the thirty-year life of the bailout. It wasn't much, considering the staggering cost of the basic plan, but it was the best the "opposition" party seemed willing to do. The plan had the added political benefit of not permitting Bush to portray $50 billion in deficit spending as a $50 billion credit.

Such nibbling around the edges didn't satisfy the stubborn John LaFalce. The question of whether to make the borrowing on-budget or off-budget "has gotten a lot of debate," he said during subcommittee markups. But it was unimportant. It might have saved $5 or $10 billion over thirty years. But *taxing* to raise the money, instead of borrowing, might have saved $100 to $150 billion or more. "It is not simply the additional dollars, it is almost a moral question," LaFalce said. He thought it was wrong "to say that our children and our grandchildren should pay" for our mistakes, which is what a long-term payment plan meant.

The administration claimed it opposed an on-budget payment plan not for political gain, but because it would violate Gramm-Rudman deficit-spending limits. But LaFalce argued that a pay-as-you-go plan would violate no such limits, since it would spend on the bailout only what was raised in taxes during a given year. It wouldn't increase the deficit at all. But it would increase taxes. That, of course, was why the notion was dead aborning.

LaFalce went through the motions anyway. The Banking Committee did not have jurisdiction to enact a tax plan. That was Ways and Means' jealously watched bailiwick. So LaFalce offered an amendment that would merely commit his colleagues, in principle, to his approach.

Barney Frank, as usual, was blunt. "Although I am not going to vote for it," he said, "it would be the only honest approach to Gramm-Rudman since the foolish bill got passed."

On the voice vote, there was scarcely a peep for LaFalce's "honest approach."

10

CHAIRMAN GONZO

H oagland answered the phone and leaned back in his chair, cradling the receiver. As he locked onto the reporter's voice, his expression was intent but serene at the same time, like a tennis player who knows where the serve is going. Phone interviews were easier. Questioners couldn't see your face if they tripped you up. You could regain your footing. On television you were more exposed.

Listening to the questions, Hoagland saw clearly the kind of portrait his interviewer, a *World-Herald* reporter, was intent on painting, in which he'd be a mere shrub in the scenery. It wouldn't be anything original, of course. Just a "quick and dirty" copy of a larger work that was then luridly flickering on the nation's telescreens. Its subject was a corrupt Congress, whose speaker himself stood accused of malfeasance, and now teetered on the precipice of political doom. What say you, freshman, about that?

On April 17, in a shocking development, the House Ethics Committee, whose whitewashing "investigations" often made it seem more like the House laundromat, said it had found "reason to believe" that Speaker Jim Wright had violated the institution's rules in sixty-nine instances. This finding was roughly equivalent to an indictment, and it was very big news. The *World Herald*'s scribe was preparing a "reaction story" on the subject, canvassing legislators from the Omaha–Council Bluffs area for pertinent quotes.

The reporter guided the congressman to the edge of the abyss, prodding him to utter something "controversial." Meanwhile, Hoagland attempted to lead the discussion back to the green glades of Good Government. To begin with, he gently stated the obvious. "It's clear to me that the charges are serious." His soothing phonespeak, as always, was like the aural massagings of late-night FM jocks.

Would Democrats support the speaker?

Hoagland pondered. He wouldn't denounce Wright. Who knew, the man might survive. "I don't think ethics are partisan," he said, deftly appealing to Nebraskans, whose legislative politics are officially nonpartisan at the state level. Hoagland then dashed the reporter's hopes for a spicy lead, recalling, at length, his own successes in the area of ethics legislation in the Unicameral.

Hoagland valued his courtroom experience as a trial lawyer, where his every word entered "the record" and had to be chosen with care. That was good training for dealing with the media. A lawyer is less likely to slip up and say what's really on his mind.

After the phone call, Hoagland said things about Wright he hadn't told the reporter. But even now, he held himself curiously aloof from opinions. He rarely said "*I* think" when discussing some topic. Rather, he mentioned what he'd *heard* recently about this or that, as if to make his listener a spectator at the lively debate taking place in his mind.

Hoagland now said that he'd "heard" from a very well connected Democratic lawyer that Wright would most probably survive. The ethics charges, this lawyer said, would simply hang there, until they were forgotten. "Sometimes problems just go away," Hoagland said. He didn't say whether he thought Wright *should* survive.

Hoagland's opinion-shyness might have been simply part of his lawyerly makeup. He hadn't read the special prosecutor's brief on Wright yet, so he naturally didn't want to rush to judgment.

But beneath the Solomonlike surface, Hoagland showed flashes of paranoia. One day, he told aides something he'd *heard* from a financial industry lobbyist. "I should be paying higher taxes," the well-paid lobbyist had said. "This country is undertaxed." According to John Minter, Hoagland was amazed that the men could profess any such thing. As John recalled the incident, Hoagland grew silent, as a new motivation for the lobbyist's apostasy seemed to dawn. Maybe he had just been doing a con job, enticing Hoagland to actually *propose* higher taxes, knowing he'd be shot down for it.

The Financial Institutions Subcommittee markups had been punishing. Over four days, the sessions lasted thirty-two mind-fogging, nit-picking, fine-print-examining, eye-watering hours. More than two hundred amendments were presented, each accompanied by a windy speech. Then they were debated, tediously, repetitiously, and either withdrawn, for lack of support, or voted—at last!—up or down. Now that it was all finished, now that the panel had finally approved this enormous and ever-burgeoning bill, all forty-three members of the subcommittee—plus four others—would do it all over again, at the full Banking Committee markups.

Talk about duplication of effort.

The hiatus between subcommittee and full committee markups gave the various opposing factions a chance to catch their breath, plot new strategies, and charge again. Amendments could be offered in full committee that weren't offered in subcommittee. Amendments that were withdrawn in subcommittee could be offered again in full committee. Even amendments *defeated* before could be flogged anew. So the whole tiresome process, of lobbyists accosting members and staffs to hawk their wares, went on as before, maybe more so. But there was one crucial difference. Now the gavel would be in the hands of Henry Gonzalez, new chairman of the full committee.

It was fitting that Gonzalez represented the area of arid Texas scrubland where the legendary Alamo stands. Over the years, he'd often been the last man at the fort, fighting the hopeless battles. His constituents in the Hispanic sections of San Antonio—where he was unbeatable—knew he'd never surrender. Even at seventy-three, Gonzalez still had enough wind to deliver tireless "Special

Orders" harangues on the House floor, on everything from assassinations to the evils of oligarchy.

But populists like Gonzalez didn't find Washington, land of
the done deal, a very welcoming place. He'd long been dismissed
by insiders, who no more liked his polyester suits of yellow and
green than his principled, sourly uncompromising stands.

Gonzalez was an unlikely-looking tribune, with his prune-
shaped bald dome, weathered complexion, and nose like an un-
formed lump of clay. But what he lacked in charisma he made up
for in passion. Almost as soon as Gonzalez was elected to the Texas
senate in 1956, he filibustered the governor's plan to close schools
where forced integration was making some locals uncomfortable.
And on the day, in 1962, when he was sworn in to the House of
Representatives, he already had a bill to repeal the poll tax tucked
in his pocket.

According to *Politics in America,* Gonzalez didn't sell himself
back home as a voice for the Hispanic community. "I have never
sought public office on an ethnic basis," that almanac quoted him
as saying, "and I never will." His concerns were classically populist. He mistrusted concentrations of capital and opposed sweetheart deals for plutocrats, like the government's creation of a
privately operated communications satellite industry, which he
called the "Telstar giveaway." He also favored phasing out the
nuclear power industry, another measure that went down better
outside Washington than inside.

But over the years, some of Gonzalez's principled stands have
come off as little short of clownish. In 1977, he quit the chairmanship of the House Select Committee on Assassinations, empaneled
to look into the Kennedy and King killings, claiming the investigation was pointless, since "vast and powerful forces, including the
country's most sophisticated crime element, won't stand for it."
But the probe had been Gonzalez's idea in the first place. Later, he
waged a lonely—some thought pathetic—crusade to impeach Ronald Reagan, introducing resolutions to that effect in 1983, after
the Grenada invasion, and again in 1987, in the wake of the Iran-
Contra revelations. "Nixon is an Eagle Scout compared to this
guy," he said during the latter effort.

Gonzalez condemned Reagan's "illegal" wars on Grenada
and Nicaragua, and the contempt for Congress—and law—evident
in the Iran-Contra affair. While some of his attacks were clearly

out of the mainstream, there were those—including the World
Court, which found the Nicaragua war to be in violation of international law—who agreed with him. But his eccentric style was
not a winning one.

Gonzalez had a keen intelligence, but like a tumbleweed that
blew off with every gust, he tended to ramble. In his long speeches
on the impeachment resolutions, he ranged far, to his days in the
Texas senate, the secretiveness of the Federal Reserve, interlock-
ing corporate control of the media and banking, and the plight of
the poor in Central America, among other topics. A case, perhaps
a strong one, could be made that these were all related—Gonzalez
certainly believed them to be—but his loose exposition made him
look like a crank.

Gonzalez's lonely crusades, and oft-repeated stories about his
prickly temper, established his "reputation." Once he'd punched a
man for calling him a Communist, and threatened to "pistol-whip"
another for the same offense. You don't have to be an anthropolo-
gist to know that such stuff sells among the tribes of Texas. Nevertheless, the Washington blue-suits kept their distance.

But Gonzalez claimed that often as not, his "extreme" views
were vindicated. In the 96th Congress, for example, he went to
the well frequently, week after week, to warn whoever might be
listening that organized crime had been involved in the murder of
a federal judge in San Antonio. Colleagues thought him daft, but
the feds eventually reopened the case and won five indictments,
and Gonzalez was personally thanked by FBI Director William
Webster for keeping the issue alive.

Despite Gonzalez's gift of prophecy, in early 1989 he was "all
but dismissed in the House as a flake," as *Politics in America* put it.
Many thought he simply wasn't up to the job of chairing the Banking Committee, especially as it was beginning to deal with "the
biggest financial catastrophe since the Great Depression."

But an odd thing happened. By the time full committee markups began, Gonzalez was shaping up as a main ally of Bush's effort
to tighten standards in S&Ls. Many Republicans had deserted the
president in subcommittee markups, allying with conservative
Democrats to pass looser capital rules.

Before the second round of markups began, Gonzalez called a
caucus of committee Democrats. According to an account in *The
Washington Post,* he told them the capital standards issue was "the

litmus test on whether anything has changed" in the S&L industry, that it was "the guts of this whole issue." On the role of his party, he had no doubts. "As Democrats, we had better be able to say, 'When the choice was presented, we sided with the taxpayers.'"

Tim Phillips, a political operative with the Democratic Senatorial Campaign Committee, became Peter Hoagland's campaign manager for the 1988 general election after Gary Caruso had to bow out to fulfill previous commitments. Urbane, ironic, and not a little cynical, Tim was quite unlike Hoagland's other operatives. While they sometimes saw their boss as a bit of an absentminded professor, Tim appreciated the man's skill at playing the inside game. "He doesn't look like he knows what he's doing," Tim said, "but he does. In his own quiet way, he knows exactly what he's doing."

Tim predicted big things for Hoagland. "One day, we're going to look up and see Peter Hoagland in the leadership and wonder, how did he do that?" he said. "It's just his way—he's very effective."

Hoagland had been keeping busy trying to put his imprint on the enormous S&L legislation. His credit union audit amendment had alerted a Banking Committee staffer to some other changes that were needed in the law governing the NCUA. So Hoagland's original measure, with lots of staff help, was growing. By the time it was ready to be offered, when the bill reached the House floor, it had bloomed into a sixteen-page rewrite of NCUA regulations.

Not surprisingly, Hoagland ran into some stiff opposition from credit union lobbyists, who didn't think they needed any new regulations. They even threatened to inform credit unions in Hoagland's district of his plans. Hoagland was furious, according to one witness—after the lobbyist left the room. He promised not to back down in the face of such threats, and didn't. He did agree to eliminate sections of his proposals to win the credit union lobby's support. But that was how deals were done.

The freshman had yet another amendment in the works. It was the one brought to him by his former congressman, John Cavanaugh. It would exempt a pair of S&Ls, controlled by Omaha financier Mike Yanney's America First corporation, from "cross-guarantee" provisions in the bill. Anytime a member introduces an amendment that seems to benefit a small group of people, he is open to charges of pandering to "special interests." But Hoagland believed the Yanney amendment, despite how it might have appeared, would serve the public interest too.

It would also serve Hoagland's interests rather well. He needed to broaden his base in Omaha, where he hadn't gotten much business support in the last campaign. Yanney was a prominent local businessman whose backing could lead others to get behind Hoagland. As far as Hoagland was concerned, the Yanney amendment had "no downside." He planned to introduce the measure in full committee markups, and didn't even bother consulting his staff about it.

While Hoagland was handling the inside game, his staff was flacking the media, dealing with constituent "casework," and dropping blizzards of mail on Omaha. Such techniques contributed to incumbents' 99 percent reelection rate. They seemed to be working for Hoagland too. A *World-Herald* poll in April showed his "job approval" had climbed to a solid 54 percent.

Round Two of the capital standards fight had commenced. Gonzalez announced that he would offer an amendment to stiffen capital requirements in full committee markups. The Bush administration launched an all-out lobbying blitz to support him. Ironically, the man who fought to impeach Ronald Reagan was now one of George Bush's staunchest allies, on this issue anyway.

Hoagland was lobbied in his office by an assistant treasury secretary, and got a phone call from Treasury Secretary Nicholas Brady—and he'd voted *with* the administration in subcommittee. But the issue was crucial. No votes were being taken for granted this time around. A huge chunk of the capital base of the nation's *healthy* S&Ls, some $23 billion, was goodwill—in other words, nonexistent.

Naturally, S&Ls were fighting to the last to keep from having to raise that kind of money. And just as naturally, to the dismay of many, members of Congress were fighting with them. Frank Annunzio sent letters to committee members naming the thrifts in their districts that would fail, or so he claimed, if the Gonzalez amendment was adopted.

Editorial writers weighed in heavily on the side of stiffer capital rules. Their preachy tone angered some. Stan Parris ruefully referred to Gonzalez's measure as "the *Washington Post* capital standards amendment."

Despite the high-octane lobbying, many were convinced that Gonzalez's amendment would fail because it was too unyielding, giving thrifts very little time to raise new capital before the regulators would come bursting in. But during debate on the measure, Democrats Charles Shumer of New York and Bruce Vento of Minnesota offered an amendment to the Gonzalez measure that gave thrifts until the end of 1994 to meet stiffer capital standards, and then made those standards even tougher than Gonzalez had. This formula—tougher on capital, more lenient on time allowed to get it—worked. The Gonzalez-Vento compromise passed by the surprisingly wide margin of 36–15. Again, it was Democrats who supported Bush—only four voted no. Meanwhile, eleven of twenty Republicans voted against the president's position and sided with the S&Ls.

Hoagland again went for the tougher standards. This time he was rewarded with some good ink, if of a very specialized kind. *Congressional Quarterly,* another insider magazine, did a brief story on him, with picture, headlined "A Tough Choice on New Thrift Rules." It was a tale of how a mere freshman had resisted the parochial pressures of a hometown S&L and cast his vote for the good of his country. Not bad.

Hoagland had been a legislator for years, which meant he'd introduced his share of amendments. So on the day he introduced the Yanney amendment, he didn't give it a second thought.

In Hoagland's experience, the press never paid much attention to markups. There was too much boring detail. How was he to know that this particular session would be so entertaining? How was he to know that it wouldn't be a very good time for a freshman to do his first favor for a wealthy constituent?

Hoagland's problems began, oddly enough, with a prayer.

Walter Fauntroy, the third-ranking Democrat on the Banking Committee, always seemed to look a little nonplussed. He was a black man with a round face, a spotty mustache, and eyes that never appeared to look anywhere but inward.

Perhaps Fauntroy was perplexed by his status. As the delegate from the District of Columbia, he represented over 600,000 souls. That was more than the populations of Wyoming, Alaska, Vermont, Delaware, or North Dakota.

Nevertheless, Fauntroy was not allowed to vote on the floor of the House. Oh, he could cast ballots in committees, even chair them. But when it came time to stand up and be counted on the floor, he was a "nonvoting delegate." Maybe that's what made him look so tentative.

Before Fauntroy became a nonvoting delegate, he was a pastor. That fact suggested another explanation for his inward gazing. Maybe he was in a kind of trance, communing with a higher power, to make up for the power he and his constituents lacked in this world.

Early in the markups, Fauntroy sought the aid of that higher power. Perhaps he had seen something untoward in the amendments stacked on his blotter, which would be presented during the day's session, and believed that a timely infusion of spiritual clout was the one thing needful. Fauntroy reserved a minute to address his colleagues. When his turn came, before the afternoon's actual marking-up had commenced, he did something he hadn't done "in nineteen years on this committee." He said a prayer.

"Help each of us," Fauntroy prayed, head bowed, eyes closed, "to rise above our own narrow self-interest. With every vote, give us purity of heart." You could almost hear the rolling of eyes among the worldly cynics of the press section.

But at least one pair of journalistic eyes brightened, with the light of inspiration. If Fauntroy's prayer did nothing else, tickled no divine ear, softened no legislative heart, it would grant this reporter *his* one thing needful on a long dry day in the regulatory desert of the Banking Committee: a juicy lead.

Immediately following Fauntroy's call for deliverance from "self-interest," a flurry of amendments were introduced to exempt specific banks and savings and loans from regulations contained in the bill. On another weary day in the Banking Committee, as in any other committee, this would not have been particularly big news. More like standard operating procedure.

But Fauntroy, like some wily PR genius, had given the affair a whole new spin. His cagey prayer had taken a dry ritual and soaked it through with irony, the kind that sells papers, or at least helps a story from the dismal banking beat break through the noise and win space on the business page.

The afternoon's first amendment was offered by chairman Gonzalez himself. It applied, he said, only to the Cross National Bank, in his district. The bank had made a loan to a bank holding company, which was secured by the stock of the holding company. Under the terms of the current bill, the security rights of the lender would be extinguished. The amendment was simply intended to assure that the security pledge remained valid. Gonzalez had no problem persuading his committee. The amendment passed easily: thirty-seven ayes, eleven nays. Hoagland voted aye, along with the praying Minister Fauntroy. Perhaps he believed God had a stake in Cross National.

Some members knew absolutely no shame when serving up the home-cooked legislation of special interests. Carroll Hubbard, the jowly Kentucky Democrat, who was not known for intellectual prowess, was having a hard time explaining how his amendment benefited "the homeowner," as he claimed. "To be completely candid," a reddening Hubbard said at last, "this [amendment] was a paragraph in a letter sent to every member of the committee by the Mortgage Bankers Association of America."

Though Hubbard plainly didn't even understand his own amendment well enough to explain it, the fact that he'd received it in the mail from the Mortgage Bankers was apparently all the "argument" a majority of the committee needed. It too passed easily, 34–15, despite compelling attacks on its merits; little things, like the fact that it ran completely against the grain of the legislation, benefited only a wealthy special interest, and put the deposit insurance fund at greater risk. The Mortgage Bankers, always generous with campaign cash, were well known to this committee.

Hoagland, the inside player, voted for that amendment too. He even spoke for it during debate. He may have believed what he said, that it was for homeowners, not mortgage brokers. Or he just might have been repaying Hubbard for agreeing to bring Banking's Oversight and Investigations Subcommittee to Omaha for a hearing on the Franklin Credit Union.

If Hubbard's record as a sleuth was any guide, the Franklin hearing probably wouldn't look under many rocks. During the eighties, amid a steady run of suspicious thrift failures, he seemed reluctant to turn his "watchdog" subcommittee on his friends in the S&L industry, from whom he'd gotten his share of campaign checks over the years.

Or maybe Hubbard was being repaid for what he'd done only moments before, when Hoagland had introduced his own "special interest" amendment. He did so at the behest of Mike Yanney, an

Omaha financier, who controlled two investment funds capitalized by separate groups of investors. One fund already owned S&Ls in California. The other fund had plans to purchase one or more S&Ls as well. But under the "cross-guarantee" provisions of the S&L bailout bill, Yanney's two separately capitalized funds would be liable for the losses in one anothers' S&Ls. Hoagland's amendment would eliminate that cross-liability, which he believed was unfair in this case. Why should investors in one fund be liable for the losses of another just because Mr. Yanney managed both?

Hoagland pointed out that his amendment was already "part of the Senate's bill," having been introduced there by Nebraska senators Exon and Kerrey. And it was cosponsored today by his Republican colleague from Nebraska, Doug Bereuter (bee-rider), who sat on the other side of the hearing room.

There were pangs of uneasiness among Hoagland's colleagues. "Exceptions for single institutions . . . bother me," said Mary Rose Oakar, a top-tier Democrat. Bruce Vento lodged a stronger objection. "I am very concerned about some of the amendments that were passed this morning for individual institutions, and I think this one really does not merit support."

But Carroll Hubbard, in what seemed an ongoing quid pro quo, went to Hoagland's defense. So what if this amendment only helped an individual constituent? "It would be a sad day if we couldn't help our constituents by being members of this particular committee," said Hubbard. After roughly five minutes of debate, the Yanney amendment passed by voice vote.

The Associated Press reporter covering the hearings made the most of Minister Fauntroy's prayer, and the feast that followed. His story appeared, among other places, in the following day's *Washington Times,* under the headline MEMBERS SAY GRACE BEFORE DIGGING IN. After Fauntroy's prayer, read the AP dispatch, "members handed out blessings to their constituents."

Some news stories live a long life. Thorough editors, or merely jealous ones, pass them along to the rewrite desk, where they are recast in their essentials, and elaborated on in their particulars. Some such process seemed to occur with the "prayer" story. The following day's *Wall Street Journal* contained a similar piece, in which Hoagland's name was mentioned as one who'd passed out a special favor. Alarm bells sounded in the office of the freshman from Omaha.

Gary said he "hit the roof" when he was told about the Yanney amendment—*after* it was introduced. He would have advised
against it. "It smelled like a rotten fish," he said.

Gary began to notice the story popping up elsewhere, especially in snide editorials, like "Praying over the S&Ls," in the
Washington Post. But Hoagland's name hadn't been mentioned
again—*yet.* Gary thought it best not to respond directly to the story
that *had* named Hoagland. To defend the amendment "on the
merits" would only draw attention to it. Since the Omaha media
hadn't done anything on the story yet, Hoagland's staff decided
simply to let it die.

But it didn't seem to want to do that.

A couple of weeks later, Gary got a call from a *Post* reporter
who was working on a story about special interest favors. Gary
said he explained the merits of the Yanney amendment, which he
now grudgingly acknowledged, and was able to talk the reporter
out of including Hoagland in the story.

But that still wasn't the end of it. Soon a *New York Times*
reporter called. She was apparently rewriting the *Post* story and
had done some digging. An account of Hoagland's amendment
appeared in the *Times* story as follows:

> Merrill Lynch and Paine Webber would benefit under an
> amendment offered by Representative Peter Hoagland,
> Democrat of Nebraska. Mr. Hoagland's amendment
> would exempt certain types of limited partnerships from
> liability if the savings institutions they own failed.

Merrill Lynch and Paine Webber! Was the feathery frosh from
Omaha now fronting for the heavy hitters on Wall Street? That's
what it looked like to anyone reading the nation's most influential
newspaper. But the *Times* had it all wrong. True, the two giant
brokerages were technically covered under the terms of Hoagland's amendment. It specified a date by which, if a limited partnership had filed its intentions to purchase an S&L with federal
regulators (as the brokerages had), it would be exempt from
"cross-liability." But you have to control *two* S&Ls to even worry
about cross-liability. Each of the brokerages had only applied to
buy one before the date specified in the amendment as a cut-off
point, so they couldn't possibly be covered under its terms.

Gary explained everything to the editors of the *Times,* who printed a correction a few days later. Still, this story was hard to kill. "It was like watching crabgrass grow on your front lawn," Gary said. "First you saw these little spots . . . then you looked outside and it was everywhere."

Late in the afternoon of the last day of full committee markups, a five-o'clock shadowy mood settled over the room. While the tiresome debates droned on, members eased back in their chairs, some reading papers, or swilling beer. Others, like Richard Neal, sat rigidly, arms folded, surrendering to a waxy boredom.

As the markups limped to an end, the blurred agonies of seventy-five hours began to show. Thoughts became scrambled. Tongues turned to rubber. Doug Barnard observed that not ignorance but "knowledge of the law is no excuse." Marge Roukema didn't want to "cast any aspirations" on colleagues. When Richard Baker was asked to yield the floor during a particularly foggy oration, he was candid. "I'm not quite finished obfuscating."

Finally, at around midnight, the committee voted on the entire bill. Members on both sides of the aisle agreed that it was "a good bill," "a tough bill." It stiffened capital standards, cut back on the risky activities thrifts could engage in, and put limits on state-chartered S&Ls, among other reforms. The legislation was approved overwhelmingly, 49–2.

Democrat Joseph Kennedy of Massachusetts, son of Robert F. Kennedy, was one of the two who voted no. He'd offered a plan similar to LaFalce's, for short-term financing, to cut down on the huge interest tab. It would have been supported by tax increases, on corporations and the wealthy. But Gonzalez ruled the plan out of order, since Ways and Means had jurisdiction over taxes. Because of that, and the defeat of Kennedy's amendment to track racial discrimination by lenders, he had opposed the bill.

Republican Jim Leach, who cast the other no vote, thought the bill "not tough enough." He said capital standards should be even higher, and that there were too many "special interest" favors in the bill.

But the overwhelming majority of the committee was very pleased with its work. Who would have suspected that before long some of these members would appear to be scrambling to remove their "fingerprints" from the bill?

* * *

Around 6:30 P.M., Hoagland left Rayburn 2128 and crossed Capitol Hill to the studios of C-Span. Someone on the station's staff had seen the story in *Congressional Quarterly* and invited the freshman to do a live viewer-call-in segment.

At 7:08, Hoagland sat in the boxy waiting room at the studio, accompanied by Gail and Jim. *Seven minutes to air.* Hoagland watched the interview segment preceding his own, staring at a monitor as he downed a tuna sandwich and mango soda for dinner. A message was superimposed on the picture: CONGRESSMAN PETER HOAGLAND—LIVE AT 7:15.

Things were going swimmingly for Hoagland. Here it was just May 2, he'd been in the House only four months, and he'd already gone through his first markup of a major bill, while many of his fellow freshmen were probably still hanging their diplomas. Not only that, he'd gotten two amendments passed, and he'd be bringing up his credit union measures later on the floor. His polls were up. He'd been featured in *Congressional Quarterly.* C-Span awaited. He was on a roll.

The sandwich barely gone, Hoagland was ushered into the hushed studio and seated opposite the program's moderator at a round table bathed in light. Behind each stood a manned camera. "You represent the district I was born in," the moderator said. The director counted down ten seconds to air.

Hoagland was asked to talk about being a member of the House. Looking directly at the moderator, hence not at the camera, he fretted the hometown chord. "About ninety percent of what's done in the House is nonpartisan," he said. "It's just a question of figuring out what's right." As he spoke, the red light on the camera opposite him was glowing, which meant he was *on.* The cameraman waved to get his attention, motioning that he should *look up at the camera.* Hoagland finally did, as the red light blinked off.

The next time Hoagland's light went on, he looked meekly into the lens and expressed his feelings about the S&L mess: "One of the greatest failures of government in this century." The bailout's cost, assuming it ended up at $100 billion, was "more than twice as much as the Marshall Plan," Hoagland said, "in real dollars."

Soon the moderator began taking viewers' phone calls. One man said that who was to blame for the S&L mess was not the issue. He was concerned about the bailout funding plan's cost. He didn't like the idea of issuing bonds and running up such a heavy interest tab. He echoed the refrain of Jesse Jackson that "those who had the party should pay for the party."

Members of Congress were convinced that the S&L issue hadn't yet sunk in among the folks back home. They were probably right. But C-Span's call-in audience was better informed than most.

"There are three parts to my answer," Hoagland said. First, some of the bailout money would be spent going after the S&L criminals, to recover what they'd robbed, and would save money in the long run. Second, "there's no fair way of spreading the cost, but the motto is 'never again.' "

That seemed to be a two-part answer, but who was counting.

Hoagland was defending the bailout legislation, even the onerous funding plan, as the best that could be done. Like most of his committee colleagues, he called it "a good bill," especially the House version. But one caller was really steamed about the bailout. "I blame *you guys*," he raged, "and you guys are asking *us* to pay for it—" Click. The moderator had cut him off.

"The congressman is a freshman," he said diplomatically, "and I don't think we can blame him for all that."

Suddenly, the crabgrass seemed to get out of control.

On May 17, the *Wall Street Journal* ran an editorial, under the title "Congressional Crack," that appeared to be heavily influenced by the "special favors" story in the *New York Times.*

> It may be the most horrifying sight in Washington, D.C.
>
> A gang is huddled together conspiring to steal from honest citizens to finance its costly addictions. The damage this activity does to the economy could easily run into the hundreds of billions of dollars. Someone better call Bill Bennett, the drug czar, and get him to send a posse of U.S. marshals after the city's worst addicts—who are holed up in the Rayburn House Office Building.
>
> We're talking, of course, about the Members of Congress now working on the savings and loan bailout bill. What they are doing is simply incredible. Faced with the task of trying to clean up this extraordinary mess,

many of the Congressmen are instead cutting deals and pushing expensive special breaks for favored constituents. You'd think just once they could resist this crummy behavior. But no, doing deals seems to have become a form of Congressional crack. . . .

Carroll Hubbard Jr. (D., Kentucky) made the day for mortgage bankers by getting an amendment extending federal insurance to the risky escrow accounts of mortgages sold by thrifts. . . . Peter Hoagland (D., Nebraska) has an amendment that would exempt four specific limited partnerships (including Merrill Lynch and Paine Webber) from liability if thrifts they take over flop. . . .

That the editorial had repeated the errors in the *Times* story was no comfort to Hoagland. The morning after it appeared, he looked dazed. "I tossed in my bed all night worrying about it," he said.

Meanwhile, the *World-Herald,* which had been silent on the issue, was sure to notice now. A letter to the editor appeared in its pages that referred to the *Journal*'s editorial, under the heading WHAT'S HOAGLAND DOING?

And poor Jim, hypersensitive to even the slightest hints of criticism in press coverage of his boss, was apoplectic. He kept repeating that it would cost "at least" $50,000 in campaign ad time to rebut the *Journal*'s charges.

11
ONLY HERE TO TEST MY HEARING AID

I n Omaha, just about everyone tells you the same thing: folks around here sure are *nice.*

The Nebraska department of economic development says the state's "number one asset is honest, friendly people." When the *World-Herald* asked readers what they liked most about living in Omaha, the most frequent response was "the people." When readers were asked what they liked *least* about Omaha, they most often answered that there *wasn't anything they disliked* about it.

The cozy skyline of downtown Omaha is composed of a snug, eclectic nest of office buildings on a grid of streets that are clean, safe, and almost never snarled with traffic. It's not the biggest, most exciting city you'll ever see, but most Omahans seem to think it is just the right size.

Omahans are proud of their solid Midwestern values. So much so, the place sometimes reminds one of mythical Lake Wobegon, where "all the children are above average." A recent *World-Herald* headline bragged: OMAHA STUDENTS ABOVE AVER-

AGE ON TEST SCORES. A related story ran the next day, after a school board member questioned the value of standardized tests, observing that "most school districts and all fifty states reported above-average test scores." That unboosterish item was buried deep.

Hoagland was not above stroking his constituents' collective self-esteem. "What Washington needs is more of Nebraska's values of clean government," he once told a local audience. He went on to praise the legislature in Lincoln, though in private he confessed that on some issues it was "strangled by the business lobby."

Omaha was once the kind of place whose people would be shocked at the sleaze quotient of coastal cities. Of course, as in all solid Midwestern towns, there was always a strain of indigenous crime here to amaze even the most jaded coastal fop. Only recently, a "ring" that dealt in stolen *cow gallstones* was broken up. The stones were ground up and sold in the Orient as an aphrodisiac.

During the eighties, Omaha began to lose its innocence. The city's tame streets were invaded by "Crips" and "Bloods" and all their sanguinary rites. Now, besides the homegrown cow-gallstone racketeers, there were gang-style killings in black north Omaha, and unsettling headlines: GANGS SAID TO SEEK WHITE GIRLS.

Omaha was doing its best to survive stormy times. The *World-Herald* was a rock to cling to. It recently found fully twenty-one movies out of twenty-three reviewed to be unfit for family viewing. If going to the movies was ill-advised, there were still things to do in Omaha. One could always visit the SAC base, just south of the city—housing the brains of our world-intimidating nuclear strike forces—and take in a "simulated red alert."

If that wasn't your idea of culture, there were concerts, ballets, and operas at the Orpheum Theater downtown, and a few tony restaurants down along the Missouri River waterfront, in the gentrified Old Market section. There you'd find a Chinese-French place called "Chez Chong," whose sign advertised an international reach: OMAHA–PARIS.

Omaha offered the enjoyments of a city, but it was small enough so that gossip could go across town in an afternoon. The place seemed like one enormous ear. That was partly how the

Franklin Credit Union affair had put such a nasty stain on the civic linen. Whispers about how high up complicity in Larry King's crimes reached were still heard over a year later. And most weren't talking about his embezzlements. More interesting to gossip mongers were details of a child prostitution ring that catered to . . . well . . . you wouldn't believe it! The characters of some of the city's most respected burghers were being assassinated. Investigations would be held and grand juries empaneled to look into all this. It was most unsettling for a city with a collective self-image that resembled former President Gerald Ford, whose birthplace was here: rock-steady, nothing flashy, there when you need them.

But Omaha has pumped more than a caretaker president into the nation's bloodstream. Johnny Carson worked at an Omaha TV station until, according to one account, he started setting fire to the neckties of interviewees. Fred Astaire took his first limber steps in Omaha, his birthplace. Marlon Brando, another native, had his first mood swings here. Shortly after Malcolm X was born here, he and his family were run out of town by the Ku Klux Klan. There were plans to build a Malcolm X Center at his birthplace.

After Hoagland landed in Omaha for a weekend of town hall meetings in early May, he roamed the airport parking lot for a few minutes and found his car, left there for him by his district staff, a faded, rust-colored, late-seventies-model Toyota. There were twin baby saddles hooked to the backseat, and layers of trash on the floor that seemed archaeologically significant. Hoagland is the kind of guy who has a name for his car. "Ol' Jenny's got over a hundred and forty thousand miles on her," he said. Tucked under the driver's seat was a computer-printed schedule, three pages long, of his weekend appointments, and the keys to Jenny.

Hoagland said his family's modest fortune was "long gone." House financial disclosure statements tend to conceal as much as they disclose. The one Hoagland filed in 1989 said that he had assets worth between $227,000 and $550,000. He collected somewhere between $13,200 and $42,000 in interest and dividend income from his portfolio of accounts and investments. Most came from the Hoagland Family Partnership, in which his stake was valued at $50,000 to $100,000. Whatever his financial status, Hoagland didn't appear as though he had a great deal of money.

Before Hoagland began a series of town hall meetings, he

had had a court date on a case from the law practice he was laboring to close out. He'd transferred most of his cases to other lawyers, but couldn't afford, he said, to get rid of them all.

The courthouse in Papillion (pap-pil-yun), just south of
Omaha, didn't look like a place to inspire one with faith in "justice
for all." But its courtroom was typical of newer models. Instead of
having high ceilings, marble columns, or mottoes inscribed in
Latin, it was decorated in an early Future Shock motif. There were
no windows in the low-ceilinged room. The only illumination
came from fluorescent lights, which gave an eerie lambency to the
tangerine color of the wall-to-wall carpeting and the upholstery of
the molded plastic chairs.

The judge presided not from a towering bench front and center, but from a platform in the corner, behind a spartan wooden
desk. Hoagland, dressed in his congressional blue suit, took a seat
in the last row of plastic chairs. His status didn't win him any
obvious favoritism in Sarpy County Court. He sat and waited
while the entire calendar of cases was called—mostly cocaine busts
—before his came up.

Hoagland was representing a truck driver who'd been injured
when, as he swerved to avoid an oncoming vehicle, he was struck
by one of the sides of beef he was carrying, causing him to roll his
combine. The lawsuit against the other driver was already won.
The plaintiff's doctors claimed a psychosis induced by the accident
had disabled him—he now saw trucks coming at him from closets
and dark rooms.

The only remaining issues to be decided concerned payment.
Curiously, Hoagland was now pitted *against his own client,* who had
already agreed with the insurance company on a lump-sum settlement. Hoagland was moving to block the settlement, in the belief
that his client would "squander" the lump sum—possibly on a
drug habit—and that he surely stood to get more money taking
smaller payments over time. Hoagland was convinced he was acting "against the client's wishes, but in his interests." If the man
truly couldn't work, he would need a settlement big enough to
take care of himself indefinitely. "He ought to be set for life,"
Hoagland said.

Hoagland clearly believed he knew what was best for his client. In a way, a willingness to act "against the client's wishes, but
in his interests" is a perfect trait for a congressman, who needs to

know when national priorities outweigh local demands. It remained to be seen how often Hoagland would apply this criterion in his public role.

Hoagland had every reason to be politically cautious back home. Nebraska was a sure winner for Republican presidential candidates. In 1988, Bush won the state with 67 percent of the vote. And though Omaha Democrats outnumbered Republicans, Bush won there easily as well, 58 percent to 42.

More to the point, before Hoagland, the district had elected Republican congressmen with disquieting regularity. Hoagland's rise might mark a change. But there was other evidence that if Omaha was changing, it was doing so in ways that benefited Republicans.

Though food processing was still a major local industry, Omaha was tilting toward the "service" sector—insurance, banking, telecommunications, and medicine. When people talked about a "stock market" in Omaha, they probably still meant a place where cattle were hammered into meat pies. But much of Omaha's stockyards had been bulldozed and replaced by highways and shopping malls. Livestock was now brought mostly to packers in the countryside. Population in the heavily Democratic middle-class sections of downtown was falling, the Republican suburbs were gaining, and Omaha's economy was changing collars, from blue to white. Not the best of news for a Democrat.

But, at a luncheon with about a dozen prominent—and mostly Republican—businesspeople at the Omaha Club downtown, Hoagland bravely stated that his "mandate" was to "do something about the deficit, even if that means raising taxes." Despite some disapproving groans, Hoagland didn't retreat.

When the topic of soaring health care costs came up, Hoagland really went out on a limb. He was intrigued by the Canadian system of nationalized health insurance. Canada had abruptly halted the growth of health care costs by cutting private insurance companies out of the picture. A similar strategy in this country would save untold billions. But it was extremely controversial—downright Communistic, some thought. When Hoagland began casually discussing it, his aides from the Omaha office went pale. People were always trying to paint him as a liberal. His wife said to be seen so is "the kiss of death in Nebraska politics." But there hadn't been any reporters around this morning—as Hoagland knew well—so his words probably wouldn't come back to haunt him anytime soon.

Hoagland's comments on the taboo subject of "socialized medicine" were partly just another manifestation of his "LIFO" style: he'd just seen a TV documentary on the Canadian national health care system. But he was rarely so candid at town hall meetings during these two weekends in the spring of 1989.

Hoagland was unfailingly patient with the halting attempts of ordinary mortals at town hall meetings to articulate their qualms about a distant and impossibly complex government. But when controversial issues came up, he liked to get out of the way, to "get the people debating among themselves," he said, so they would see "how hard it is to reach a consensus." When Hoagland was pressed for *his* views, the responses tended to be elliptical.

For instance, when constituents cornered him on the deficit— *why can't we balance the budget?*—Hoagland would answer, "The government is spending more than it's taking in." That was, of course, exactly the problem. But he left it there. Gone was the brave talk of "mandates" to raise taxes or cut someone's favorite program.

Moreover, on this trip home, Hoagland scarcely mentioned the S&L legislation at town meetings, despite the fact that he'd spent the last several weeks working intensively on it. He freely discussed it with bankers and lobbyists, who tended to be familiar with the nuts and bolts of the bill's far-ranging proposals. Some of those proposals would perhaps interest the politically involved types that attend town hall meetings, such as the elaborate funding scheme worked out by the Bush administration. But Hoagland didn't bring up the subject, though he had reservations about the plan himself. Because Hoagland seemed hesitant to discuss much of what was currently on his plate in Congress, these town hall meetings gave off the unmistakable odor of campaign whistle-stops, where the congressman was visible, but not too exposed.

Whenever Hoagland held town hall meetings, his office sent tens of thousands of postcard invitations, adorned with his name in bold letters, his picture, and the message that he wanted to meet with YOU! Even if the cards were trashed on sight, the onslaughts couldn't hurt his "name recognition." Unlike other forms of congressional mail, the volume of which was limited (somewhat) by law, town meeting notices were open-ended. Members could send them as often as they had meetings, at taxpayer expense. Hence, town meetings were a vital organ of democracy—even if no one came. Nevertheless, town hall meetings were a lot of work. Hoagland held them more often than his recent predecessors in office. Sometimes more than half a dozen in a single weekend of criss-crossing the district.

Hoagland's meetings were hardly the most popular show in town. Usually, only twenty or so came, mostly elderly pensioners, watching to see if he wavered about protecting their benefits. The gatherings often had the feel of social hour at a retirement home. At one, an elderly gentleman was approached by one of Hoagland's aides and asked to write his name and address on a sign-up sheet. The man shook his head and tapped a mechanism in his ear. "I'm only here to test my hearing aid," he said.

Instead of discussing S&Ls or other complicated issues, Hoagland seemed to be promoting a simple "theme" at his town hall meetings this weekend, in the hope of roping in some good media. At every stop, he talked about his recent vote for an amendment that would have cut tens of millions from the "Star Wars" missile defense program and devoted it to the "war on drugs." The amendment had lost narrowly.

One might wonder why Hoagland would tout a losing vote, and risk identifying himself with what sounded suspiciously like a liberal social program. But like many politicians in 1989, Hoagland seemed to be campaigning for this "war on drugs" precisely because he thought most people were in favor of it. At least, that's what pollsters were telling politicians.

The "war on drugs" was the sort of issue politicians can't help but love. Just as no one could be in favor of drunk driving, few could be in favor of drug abuse or drug gangs. Hoagland predicted, quite accurately, that drugs would "get more and more attention from public officials." It wouldn't be long before the president himself enlisted (loudly, if briefly) in the "war." Hoagland clearly thought there was "mileage" in the issue.

But his oft-polled constituents didn't seem excited about it. In a meeting at a high school auditorium near the SAC base, there was a good bit of fidgeting and eyebrow raising as Hoagland spoke earnestly about the need for spending to combat the drug menace. Finally, an elderly man piped up. The drug war, he said, was just "throwing money at a problem" without any real thought behind what was being done. Heads quietly nodded.

Perhaps the people in this neighborhood couldn't get excited about drug wars because they were preoccupied watching for real ones. At the time, one of SAC's Looking Glass planes was always airborne, to serve as a "flying command post" in case a sudden nuclear strike wiped out ground command stations. Earlier in the week, a tremor of alarm had spread when pieces from the engine of an airborne Looking Glass fell to the ground along nearby Cornhusker Avenue. This crowd, in the neighborhood of one of the biggest defense establishments in the universe, was hardly likely to be enthusiastic about cutting Star Wars to fund drug wars, no matter what pollsters were saying. The surrounding county was populated largely by current and former military folk, who toed the conservative line. Last November, Hoagland had lost here by eight points to Republican Jerry Schenken. It was not an area fond of "big government" programs, unless they were of the military variety, like the superexpensive B2 bombers.

Later in the year, as clear signs of the cold war's end were coming from Moscow, Hoagland wanted to vote against the B2 Stealth bomber project—which would cost the government $500–$800 million for each plane. According to an aide, Hoagland felt the program was the biggest waste of money he'd ever seen, and he thought the plane should be scrapped, but he simply couldn't vote that way right now. Maybe after he'd been there a few terms.

Down the road at the Papillion Town Hall, the audience couldn't get its blood up about the drug war either. "What good is it just to turn heroin addicts into methadone addicts?" one middle-aged woman said. Hoagland shrugged the question off, though it went to the heart of people's doubts about government programs. They might not mind spending money on them, if anything was really accomplished. Hoagland himself believed that the root cause of the drug epidemic—the desperate poverty of the under-class—had to be dealt with to solve the problem. Little in the "war on drugs" addressed that issue. It mostly seemed like a war on people who took drugs.

One of the few times S&Ls were discussed was when a couple of irate readers of the *Wall Street Journal* brought up the Yanney amendment. Hoagland had his defenses ready. "The *Wall Street Journal* completely misrepresented my amendment," he said, adding that the editors had promised to print "a retraction." Actually, they'd only promised to print a letter from Hoagland defending his amendment. And on the day it appeared, the *Journal*'s editors blasted him again.

The hometown media were much more cooperative. On this trip home, Hoagland talked a lot about wars on drugs, or his upcoming hearing on the Franklin Credit Union, and that's what got on TV and in the papers. One TV newswoman's description of his upcoming Franklin hearings sounded as if it were taken right out of Gail's or Gary's mouth: "Peter Hoagland is preparing for his most important challenge since he entered Congress, the upcoming Franklin Credit Union hearings."

There was a historical irony in Hoagland's apparent reluctance to discuss the intricate S&L funding issue with his constituents. Washington policymakers apparently found the matter unfit for public consumption, either too complex or too politically sensitive. Or they felt there was simply nothing to discuss, that a long-term bonding scheme was the only way to finance the bailout. The media seemed to agree, judging by their conspicuous lack of coverage. Hoagland claimed he didn't discuss the issue in town hall meetings because his constituents didn't bring it up. But since the media was studiously ignoring the matter, the home folks could hardly have been expected to have come to grips with it.

It was precisely this kind of knotty financial question—one considered outside the scope of common souls—that galvanized turn-of-the-century Populists. They were common farmers who built a movement that eventually flowered in Hoagland's hometown with the famous Omaha Platform. The movement also influenced such reforms as the single-house legislature in Nebraska and the direct election of U.S. senators, among others.

The Populist movement was a protest organized by farmers upset with the conventional financial wisdom of their day. In the late nineteenth century, farmers were whipsawed by a rapid deflation, which sent crop prices crashing, accompanied by tight money and usurious interest rates. Faced with steep drops in income, many were forced to put up their land as security against loans needed to purchase seed and equipment. As farmers inevitably lost their farms, bitterness turned to anger, and the Populist protest was born.

The Populists' main enemy was the gold standard. When

money was based on gold, its quantity tended to remain static, along with the gold supply. Not only did that tend to push interest rates higher, it depressed farm prices, which were already tending to fall because of improvements in technology that had boosted farm yields. The farmers devised a complicated scheme to address their concerns called the "sub-treasury plan." The plan called for the government to essentially create new money, expanding its supply, to make interest rates fall and crop prices rise. The Populists wanted the government to adopt a paper currency, and to put it into distribution by making direct low-interest loans to farmers and other "producers."

This audacious plan, which would have wrested control of the financial system away from banks, was naturally greeted with skepticism, to say the least, by the Eastern establishment. The *New York Times* called it "one of the wildest and most fantastic projects ever seriously proposed by sober man."

The mainstream press did not take the Populist program very seriously. After all, it was devised by normal people—dirt farmers at that. But the reformers spread the word, setting up lecture bureaus and newspapers. One of the movement's most important organs was the Reform Press Association. Its thousands of struggling weeklies around the nation kept the grass roots agitated about economic issues that the mainstream press ignored.

The Populists eventually built a mass movement around the sub-treasury plan and other home-cooked ideas. Though history generally records their passing with the defeat of William Jennings Bryan in the presidential election of 1896, they were actually neutralized before that, when the silver lobby took control of the Democratic Party agenda and turned it into a "shadow movement" for "the free coinage of silver."

But many of the ideas of these common folk, ridiculed at the time, eventually became policy, though not always in the way the Populists had intended. For instance, we now have a paper currency, and the government routinely "creates" money, through infusions of credit from the Federal Reserve system. But the infusions go to banks, which distribute the money largely as they see fit. The Populists wanted the new money to go directly to producers—factories and farmers—at low interest rates. Since the currency of a country belongs to all, the Populists figured it should be used for the benefit of all, not just bankers.

The Populists tried something that hasn't been attempted since—to wrest control of the banking system away from private financial interests. Today the "Fed," or Federal Reserve, controls the money supply. Though Congress created the Fed to be largely independent of political influence, banks exercise a good deal of leverage over it. And just as the Fed is said to be "above politics," complicated financial issues, such as those involved in the S&L matter, are almost entirely absent from public debate.

In *Secrets of the Temple,* William Greider writes: "Populism's brief and spontaneous drama was probably as close as the United States has ever come, before or since, to something resembling genuine democracy." Neo-populist groups today like the Financial Democracy Campaign, ACORN, and Nader's Public Citizen, were trying to get the word out on alternatives to the bailout's expensive funding plan. Meanwhile, mainstream media, following the cue of politicians, generally kept silent on the issue. Not surprisingly, Hoagland heard nothing about alternative funding plans from his town hall meeting audiences over the weekend.

None of Hoagland's town hall audiences showed any enthusiasm for his drug-war message until he delivered it at a library in north Omaha—make that mostly black, impoverished north Omaha. Hoagland had done very well in these parts last November. The crowd cheered when he announced the (failed) vote to direct Star Wars money to the drug effort. Not far away were the blighted streets lined with boarded-up buildings where most of the gang violence in the city was happening.

Hoagland's other gatherings had been like staid stockholders' conferences compared to this one, which abruptly turned into a revival meeting. But all the preaching came from the audience. First a grizzled, middle-aged white man in a plaid work jacket railed about increases in the budget for congressional operating expenses. He knew his figures. "Congress should set an example," he raged. "Instead of raising its budget seventeen percent, it should be cut ten percent."

"That's right," yelled one woman.

"You tell 'im," added another. No one shouted "Amen," but it was in the air.

A stocky black man rose next to talk economics. He didn't care what they said on television about there being no inflation, he *knew* there was. When gas was $30 a barrel, we paid $1.15 a gallon. Now that gas was $20 a barrel, we were still paying $1.15 a gallon. "Something's wrong," he said.

"That's right," several people shouted. Hoagland didn't seem to know quite how to react. He just stood there quietly, his mouth agape. Suddenly, a pretty young black woman shot out of her chair. "Our leaders treat us like we're a bunch of imbeciles," she roared. "They tell us there's no gang problem . . . we *live* with it." Though Hoagland could hardly have been accused of over-looking the seriousness of the drug problem, the audience response was immediate.

"That's *genocide,*" one woman said.

"That's exactly what it is," said another.

"Genocide . . . genocide," several others repeated, nearly chanting.

The young black woman was especially miffed with the slow response to gang violence in north Omaha. "If they go shootin' up white kids," she railed, "you can bet something's going to be done about it." TV cameras present lapped up the scathing scene. It was a sound bite on the evening news.

Meanwhile, when the woman was through, the vacantly staring Hoagland looked very much like a man who preferred confronting *his* social problems in textbooks. Finally, he managed a wan smile and said, "Thank you for your comments."

12

NUDE POLICE

Mike Yanney was the kind of man for whom the phrase "pillar of the community" was coined. When Omaha called, he answered. Name a commission, a board, a committee, a charity campaign, and he probably chaired it.

According to an item in the *Omaha World-Herald,* one day back in 1970, Yanney strolled out of the downtown Omaha National Bank, where he was a vice-president, over to City Hall to find a policeman. Instead, he bumped into the mayor, who asked him on the spot to become chairman of the new Riverfront Development Committee. Yanney accepted. Over the years, he helped lay plans that led to the refurbishing of abandoned warehouses and office buildings along downtown Omaha's riverfront. It was now a bustling strip of stylish shops and restaurants.

Yanney had a green thumb. The things he touched turned into money. In November 1977 he quit the bank to pursue "investments of my own," according to another item in the *World-Herald.* A news story the following May said he owned "several banks, insurance agencies and an agricultural company."

In August of 1980, the *World-Herald* reported that Yanney was one of "eight happy Omahans" who made up the local board of the Cox Cable company. After Cox was awarded the exclusive Omaha cable franchise by the city council, the happy eight saw an initial investment of a paltry $200 mushroom into a holding worth an estimated $9.7 million. Yanney's share was said to be worth $1.5 million.

Yanney was not a man who liked to grant interviews to the press. But he was outspoken nevertheless. He addressed graduation ceremonies, Chamber of Commerce breakfasts, and Rotary Club dinners, with pronouncements on the state of the state, and of the nation.

The self-made Yanney's politics were predictably conservative. Reports on Yanney's speeches in the Nebraska press quoted him as saying that Nebraska laid too heavy an income tax burden on "people who succeed," his euphemism for the wealthy. He called the Nebraska Aid to Dependent Children program "an atrocious failure" and said programs for the mentally ill were an "outrageous, uncontrolled expense." Yanney labeled such endeavors "massive doses of protectionism" that sapped people's incentive to work and prosper. His definition of "protectionism" was broad, including even the granting of tenure to state university professors. Not surprisingly, the Omaha Rotary Club named Yanney "Free Enterprise Person of the Year" in 1987.

Yanney said his father was born in "a sod house" and died when Yanney was eight. In amassing his considerable fortune, Yanney said, he had never had to "request help" from the government at any level. He was right. He didn't have to *request* help. But he managed to get it just the same. Even if one doesn't consider the award of a lucrative cable contract from the city government as "help," that was only the beginning of his government-sponsored boons.

Yanney's investment company, America First, organized a consortium known as a "limited partnership." The partnership bought Eureka Savings and Loan of San Francisco from FSLIC in 1988. Eureka was one of hundreds of failed S&Ls across the country that had been placed in receivership by the agency. FSLIC could have simply liquidated the assets and paid back the depositors of institutions like Eureka. But that would have strained its insurance fund—wiped it out, actually. So FSLIC decided to sell these institutions in a series of sweetheart deals the likes of which had never been seen before.

Yanney's partnership put up $100 million for Eureka. In return, FSLIC contributed $291 million in cash to make the institution solvent, and agreed to pay for all future losses from bad loans on Eureka's books. FSLIC also granted generous tax benefits to the partnership and guaranteed a profit on certain "troubled" assets in the thrift's portfolio.

Negotiating with FSLIC for failed S&Ls in 1988 has been described as taking candy from a baby. Congress disbanded the agency with the 1989 S&L bailout legislation partly because of overgenerous deals like the one given America First, which may have cost the government up to 40 percent more than simply liquidating those S&Ls and paying back the depositors. All told, Yanney's group got control of assets worth $1.74 billion for a mere $100 million investment, thanks to a beneficent government agency. Talk about "massive doses of protectionism." But it looked like one more dose might be needed.

Yanney formed another consortium of investors to buy more S&Ls. His first fund had raised $107 million from 10,900 investors. The second raised $300 million from 23,000 investors. But a slight hitch arose in early 1989. The Bush bailout bill contained a provision which said that two or more financial institutions which were "commonly controlled" would be liable for one another's losses. Yanney didn't think it was fair that investors in his second consortium would be liable for losses of his first consortium—or vice versa—just because he happened to be the common controller of both. He was in need of what lobbyists pedaling their services refer to as "legislative relief." So he contacted his attornies at the respected Omaha-based law firm of Kutak, Rock & Campbell.

The firm's headquarters in the elegant Omaha Building suggest its reach. A ten-story-high atrium serves as reception area, with a spiral staircase leading to the lawyers' offices. A "tone" is maintained by the Frankenthalers, Shahns, and Kawashimas adorning the walls. Adorning the staff are Roman Hruska and David Karnes, former U.S. senators from Nebraska, and John Cavanaugh, former congressman from Omaha. There are also ex-employees of the White House, the Securities and Exchange Commission, the Internal Revenue Service, and the Department of Justice.

KRC's legislative relief squad quickly went to work writing an amendment to the S&L bill for Yanney and securing support for it in the House and Senate. They found plenty. Among Yanney's champions in the Senate were both of Nebraska's senators, James Exon and Bob Kerrey, and Alan Cranston of California, home state of Eureka Savings. In the House were Doug Bereuter, Carroll Hubbard, and Peter Hoagland. Yanney could count most of the current (and former) Nebraska congressional delegation as members of his team.

Though Yanney had not supported Hoagland during the election, he'd quickly set accounts aright afterward, donating $5,000 to the new congressman before the end of 1988. Incumbency proved, once again, to be a magnet for cash.

Hoagland had sponsored a lot of amendments in his years as a legislator, but never one that attracted so much attention. He felt "blind-sided" by the *Wall Street Journal*. Initially, he'd seen "no downside" to the Yanney amendment. He'd been convinced that it served the public interest. But after the *Journal* lobbed its bomb, he turned the issue over again in his mind, "to make sure I hadn't done anything wrong," he said.

Hoagland got no grief about the amendment from the hometown media. He met with editors of the *World-Herald* to explain his position. He was getting good at drawing a diagram of Yanney's separate investment consortia, on napkins and scraps of paper. Hoagland argued that not only was his amendment fair, but the more private investors like Yanney could be encouraged to put up their dollars for the S&L bailout, the less would be soaked from taxpayers. Hoagland seemed to win the board over. They had nothing to say about the Yanney amendment on their editorial pages. "I could've gotten creamed," he said.

But Hoagland's opponent in the upcoming (five hundred days) campaign might not be so understanding. He or she could still feature a picture of the *Journal*'s blast in an attack ad, the kind that tends to inflate one's "negatives," and costs plenty to rebut, as Jim was sure to remind him.

For now, though, Hoagland was getting nothing but positive play back home. The Franklin hearing was a big winner. As investigations go, it was not among the most thorough. Most of the proceedings consisted of NCUA regulators—the people who had overlooked Larry King's spendthrift ways to begin with—recounting where he'd lavished the money he'd stolen.

While the hearings didn't produce much new information, Hoagland reaped a media bonanza, with lead coverage on all local TV stations and front-page stories in the *World-Herald*. The Franklin hearing capped a two-weekend district blitz. As the swing neared a close, Hoagland sounded pleased. "A measure of the success of a weekend is how much visibility you got," he said. "It's so important."

By the time the cherry-scented breezes of late April were upon Washington, it was becoming clear that the city was settling into a deep funk. The year that had begun with the humiliation of the congressional pay grab and the degradation of John Tower's lost weekends was hurtling toward new horrors. In early April, Jim Wright had been accused of, among other things, circumventing House outside income limits and accepting "financial favors" from his friend and business partner George Mallick, a man who had, it was said, "an interest in legislation." If so, Mallick might have been the only person associated with Congress to have cultivated such an interest. The ink on Wright's indictment was barely dry when it was revealed that his chief aide, John Mack, had served time in jail for beating a woman nearly to death—with a hammer. Television reports stopped asking whether Wright should resign and began speculating about when he would get it over with.

After Wright's inevitable fall, it was assumed that the amiable majority leader, Tom Foley, would be elected to replace him. That meant the majority leader's job, normally just a career-ending scandal away from the speakership, would be vacant.

One day Hoagland sidled up to Dick Gephardt, the gentleman from Missouri and recent presidential aspirant, to whisper something in his ear. Hoagland had been approached by Tony Coehlo, the majority whip, who wanted the freshman's vote in the race for majority leader. Coehlo was in the race "with both feet," Hoagland told Gephardt.

Coehlo was an infamous PAC panderer who many thought was exactly the wrong kind of standard-bearer for a party under siege. On the other hand, Gephardt, of the clear blue eyes and chiseled features, was referred to as an "Eagle Scout" for his All-American Boy image. Hoagland hoped the man might be considering running for leader, and would appreciate the intelligence. He was and he did.

According to Hoagland, Gephardt gathered a group of sympathetic colleagues in his office to sound them out about the race. Among those invited was the freshman from Omaha.

Gephardt had gone to Omaha to stump for Hoagland during the '88 election. Now he asked Hoagland to return the favor. The freshman was assigned a list of his peers to call and feel out about Gephardt's candidacy for majority leader.

Many such calls were heating up congressional phone lines as the scramble for power got serious. Their topics included more than a few nasty rumors about prospective candidates. One bit of malicious scuttlebutt was that Tom Foley, the majority leader, was gay. According to one version of the rumor, CBS had the story "cold" and would soon broadcast it.

On the day Foley was actually elected speaker, it became clear just how many of his distinguished colleagues had been whispering behind his back. An aide to the Republican National Committee distributed a press release entitled "Tom Foley, Out of the Liberal Closet." The memo compared Foley's voting record with that of Barney Frank, who was a homosexual. If one hadn't been on rumor-rife Capitol Hill, these cryptic references would have meant little. But the memo touched off a tempest in the press corps and among congressional Democrats, who'd been sharing the Foley rumor among themselves for days and knew exactly what the release was referring to. Barney Frank spoke for his party colleagues, accusing Republicans of dealing in "smear and innuendo." He threatened to point out gay Republican members if assaults on Democrats didn't cease. Cease is exactly what they did.

Lars-Erik Nelson, a columnist for the *New York Daily News,* tracked the source of the Foley rumor to the office of Newt Gingrich, the man who had launched the campaign that toppled Wright. Nelson quotes one of Gingrich's "youthful and eager female assistants" who had been giddily trashing Foley: "We hear it's little boys," she told Nelson, giggling. When asked if Gingrich was going to file morals charges against Foley, she blithely admitted, "Oh, no . . . we haven't done any looking into this at all."

Before Jim Wright resigned, Tony Coehlo beat him to it. Coehlo quit rather than face media scrutiny of a sweetheart bank loan given him by a California S&L official. A few days after Foley was unanimously elected to replace Wright, the rest of the leadership was chosen in a closed caucus: Dick Gephardt for majority

leader, Bill Gray of Pennsylvania for whip, and David Bonior of
Michigan for chief deputy whip.

While Hoagland was happy for Gephardt, he couldn't help
feeling sorry for Wright. To many politicians, the speaker's fall
seemed a case of yesterday's business as usual becoming today's
anathema. Any of them might become victims of fickle standards,
or a sudden bath of media scrutiny.

Despite the beanballs being pitched behind the scenes, many
doubted the new Democratic leadership would be aggressive
enough to contend with Republican sucker-punchers like Gingrich
and Atwater. Jim Wright had been their enforcer. Without him,
many thought Democrats would just roll over and expose their
soft parts again, as in the early Reagan years. Everyone respected
Tom Foley. But he was a man of the peace pipe in what looked like
a time for tomahawks. And Gephardt was known more for making
friends than picking fights.

But the three new leaders, in post-election speeches to the
press, vowed that the party would move aggressively to define the
American agenda. Bill Grey recalled a *Peanuts* cartoon that he
believed symbolized his party. Charlie Brown is slumped in his
beanbag chair watching TV. Along comes Lucy to make him
change the channel. "Why should I?" whines Charlie Brown. Lucy
shakes a fist. "See this?" she says. Charlie Brown, beaten again,
shuffles away. Staring helplessly at the fingers of his right hand, he
sighs and says, "Why can't you guys do that?"

Grey said Democrats were through being chumps and were
gonna put up their dukes.

For all the trouble congressfolk were getting into, it was hard
to believe they worked short weeks—Tuesday through Thursday
was the routine for almost everyone. Members liked to go back
home on weekends to water their roots.

The bumper harvest of scandal, combined with a singularly
unproductive session, had made Congress the target of every pun-
dit with a weekly quota of bromides to fill. But there was at least
one publication that didn't lash out. Just as members are accustomed to gentle treatment from the hometown paper, Congress
has a hometown paper of its own, a little tabloid named *Roll Call*
that covers Capitol Hill from the bottom up—everything from
special elections to the rat that ate the wiring in the Rayburn copy
machine, plus generous dollops of gossip.

Like any good hometown paper, *Roll Call* is a booster of local enterprise. In this case, that means Congress. So it was hardly surprising when the editors decided to swim against the media tide by choosing "What's Good About Congress" as the theme for their annual "Guide to Congress" issue. The choice was especially risky, since *Roll Call* editors have been accused of being little more than airhead cheerleaders for their favorite legislature. They deny it, of course. But there was a telling omission from the editorial on August 3 announcing the theme issue. "We are mindless Pollyannas," announced *Roll Call*'s editors, presumably omitting the word "not." They concluded by saying, "We know that there are lots of things wrong with Congress, too. But the balance has swung too far . . ."

When the S&L bill finally got to the House floor on June 15, the honeyed words were flowing between Peter Hoagland and his committee chairman, Henry Gonzalez, who were among two dozen or so members participating in debates. After Gonzalez yielded the floor to his freshman colleague, he was rewarded with a fusillade of flattery.

"I appreciate our illustrious chairman of the full Banking Committee yielding time to me and appreciate his gracious handling of those complex issues in committee, and now on the floor," Hoagland enthused, and he was just warming up. "It is a great pleasure to serve with the gentleman from Texas. He has done the nation and our Congress proud with his handling of this bill."

Gonzalez responded in kind, lauding the "very brilliant, honest, hardworking performance" of the gentleman from Nebraska, and citing his "stalwart" support of necessary reforms.

This was shaping up to be a triumphal day for Hoagland. He'd been granted a "rule" by the Rules Committee to offer his credit union measures later on the floor. That would give him a crack at managing part of a debate. And if all went well, he'd have four amendments in the bill by the time it passed that night, a remarkable harvest for a freshman.

But the big issue on the agenda this day, all were agreed, was again capital standards. Some members were conducting a campaign to preserve "goodwill" for thrifts as if it were a moral crusade.

Goodwill was the product of regulatory alchemy, an attempt to turn red ink into cash. Actually, it allowed S&Ls with red ink to risk other people's money. New standards would make owners risk their own money first.

But there was much sympathy for the goodwill crusaders, especially among House Republicans. Their probusiness feelings were wounded by the idea of breaking the government's "solemn contracts" with many S&Ls, which were to be allowed to count goodwill on their books for as long as forty years hence. "A deal," they argued with emotion, "is a deal."

The bill now called for getting rid of goodwill after only five years. Some argued that raising so much cash so quickly to offset goodwill losses would be the ruin of thrifts—requiring further bailouts in the future. And why would they face ruin? Precisely because "they tried to help their government."

The S&Ls' goodwill lament naturally made many a Democrat's eyes mist over as well. But most were thought to be lining up behind the president. Despite appearances of bipartisan comity, however, politics were being well played. Stacks of amendments to restore goodwill had been submitted to the Democratic-controlled Rules Committee by members of both parties. But "rules" for floor consideration were granted only to Republican-sponsored capital measures. If S&L reform was killed by an excess of goodwill, so to speak, Democrats wanted Republican fingerprints all over the weapon.

Hoagland sat among the small cluster of members around the majority bill manager's table throughout most of the long hours of debates, soaking up the oratory. He was here primarily to lend an ear. But he'd also agreed to "whip" certain members on the goodwill issue for the Democratic leadership. To whip was to corner a fellow member and bring him around to the party's way of seeing things. And the party hierarchy was seeing goodwill as a loser, and supporting the president as a winner. For one thing, it seemed like the only sane policy. But perhaps another compelling argument against goodwill was, as Hoagland had observed, that doing away with it was unquestionably "where the media is."

When the press dealt with the complex S&L morass at all, its focus was almost exclusively on the issue of capital. Pundits weighed in as one to denounce the corrupting fiction of goodwill. The press loved a fight, and this one had an interesting angle: not only did it pit the president against Congress, his main opponents were congressional *Republicans.* The press had chosen sides in this fight. Goodwill supporters were portrayed as "the bad guys," said Minority Leader Bob Michel.

Still, in the days leading up to floor consideration of the bill, many grew convinced that the goodwill forces could elicit enough sympathy to win. The average congressman seemed to identify strongly with S&L owners. Perhaps it had something to do with the remarkable fact that both owners and members wore expensive blue suits, solicited big cash deposits, and opened branch offices. Or maybe those S&L campaign contributions really had made a difference.

The first sign the crusade was stalling came when Republican James Quillen of Tennessee withdrew his amendment to retain the status quo. A button rode Quillen's lapel carrying the slogan "A Deal Is a Deal." But his extreme approach was no deal, and he knew it. Goodwill forces put their faith in Henry Hyde, Republican from Illinois.

Hyde was among the best debaters in the 101st Congress, a man who played righteous avenger and devil's advocate with equal brio. Though a stoutish sixty-four-year-old, he still managed to project an air of elegance. When Hyde waded into a debate, his white mane flashing, one glimpsed a quality rare among the faceless ranks of legislators: presence.

Mr. Hyde was deeply conservative, and quite capable of living up to his sinister namesake, especially in his rabid support for the Contra war in Central America. And his unyielding "prolife" crusade helped shape a policy so intolerant it wouldn't spend federal money on an abortion for a rape or incest victim.

But today, that Hyde gave way to the calm, reasonable Dr. Jekyll in his nature. His amendment wouldn't change the stiffer capital requirements in the committee version. It merely said that regulators must give S&Ls a hearing, a chance to prove their goodwill deals with FSLIC were binding, before shutting them down for inadequate capital. That was "the same consideration that five blocks away from here rapists and drug dealers and murderers get, a hearing before you are punished," Hyde said.

Listening to Hyde, one began to see S&L owners as a persecuted class, herded to the back of the bus and fed leftovers at the kitchen door. One might have forgotten that reformers were merely asking owners to stop booking pretend millions and start risking the real stuff.

Hyde's "due process" approach had been defeated in the Judiciary Committee. Opponents said it would "gut the bill" because "high-flying" owners could continue their reckless ways while waiting for hearings in an inevitably backlogged system. By the time regulators got hold of them, their S&Ls could be milked dry. For regulation to work, speed was everything.

"I just want to say to Mr. Hyde . . . that I have a good deal of sympathy," said Steven Neal, Democrat of North Carolina and Banking Committee member. "This was, frankly, the most agonizing issue that we had to deal with in committee." Hoagland too had his difficult moments. "It is with considerable reluctance that I oppose the Hyde amendment," he said in his halting floor remarks. "It has not been an easy decision. . . ."

Bob Michel provided a rationale for reluctant defectors from the worthy cause of goodwill. While Hyde's amendment "may be responsible," he said, "is it really right?" After warning that an economic crisis could befall the nation if the S&L issue was mishandled, Michel concluded, "We have to be not only responsible, but we have to be right today." That the leader of the party of business could deem it "responsible" for our financial institutions to continue pretending that *no* money was *lots* of money was just one remarkable aspect of this day.

Troubling as it was for the House, it managed to defeat the Hyde amendment decisively, 326–94, to the great surprise of all concerned. Then a measure to prohibit S&Ls from investing in junk bonds, which had failed in committee, passed by a similarly lopsided 303–114. Hoagland voted with the majority.

It seemed that the recent flurry of editorials condemning "business as usual" on S&Ls had the House spooked. Many who'd been sympathetic to thrifts in the past seemed reluctant to cast any vote that could be interpreted as a vote for S&Ls. The House appeared to have become a chamber of paranoia. "It's weird in there," Curt Prins said, according to an account in *Congressional Quarterly.*

After the Hyde amendment went down, the talk in the press gallery was that the story was "over." But a vote later in the afternoon, on an amendment offered by John LaFalce, also told an interesting story. LaFalce still wanted to change the bill's method of funding the bailout. His proposal—novel by the standards of 1980s Washington—was simple: Why not face this thing like adults, pay now, and save hundreds of billions in borrowing costs? Since just about every member of Congress ritually promised to end deficit spending, one might have expected LaFalce's argument to have some bedrock appeal.

LaFalce's idea was finally going to get thrashed out in the arena of democracy. But if you didn't happen to be in the arena, you might never have known it. Here was a legislator saying he could cut the overall cost of the S&L bailout *by two-thirds*—from $300 billion to $100 billion—yet the press ignored him.

The reason LaFalce was ignored was that, by and large, there was no fight over this issue. The president and congressional leaders agreed that long-term borrowing was the way to go. How could there possibly be a story in LaFalce's lonely crusade?

One way politicians control the news agenda is when both parties stop talking about something. Then the press often won't talk about it either. Despite its vaunted aggressiveness, the press sometimes seems to have a yellow streak. It doesn't like to get "out in front" on issues. It likes to follow the leader. One reason the S&L problem had grown so immense was that in earlier stages, when it could have been solved much more economically, politicians in both parties agreed to bury the issue and the press played along. Commenting on the press's failure in the S&L mess, Hobart Rowan of the *Washington Post* said: "I fear that in the past, we in the media have been more attentive to protecting the establishment than protecting consumers and taxpayers."

Now that S&L fraud and failure on a huge scale were out of the bag, however, the political establishment seemed to want protection on another aspect of the story, funding the bailout. Again, since it was a "bipartisan" project, the press was likely to play along.

During the debate on LaFalce's proposal, it became clear that not its economics so much as its politics were "flawed." Gone was the "agonizing" over taking pretend money away from S&L owners. Patronizing took its place.

Thomas Downey, a Ways and Means Democrat, cautioned his colleagues against LaFalce's childish fantasy. "Please, please, don't be silly," he said. His own committee had already rejected

LaFalce's approach. "Recognize that the Ways and Means Committee deals with the world as we know it," Downey said. "In the world that you should live in, the LaFalce amendment would make perfect sense . . . a world without Gramm-Rudman . . . where the president would be prepared to face the reality of raising revenues or cutting spending."

Congressional Democrats could have shown their fists and challenged the president's plan. But they were scared to take the lead on taxes. As far as Democrats were concerned, the only fit question for debate was whether long-term borrowing—through the sale of bonds—was to be done "on-budget" or "off-budget."

Republican Bill Frenzel called LaFalce's proposal "the real truth in budgeting amendment," as opposed to the on-budget bonding plan. But then he suggested that to vote for LaFalce was a childish impulse that, while best resisted, might be indulged just this once by those who "feel overpowered by urges to be wholly honest and make good their pledges."

The barrel-chested Ways and Means chairman, Dan Rostenkowski, called LaFalce's measure "a bold amendment, which comes at the wrong time." The right time would perhaps be when political courage flourished in Washington. But surely then a "bold" amendment would hardly be needed.

The House was looking at its own image in the mirror. Where it might have glimpsed craven opportunists afraid to challenge the president, it chose to see statesmen dealing in hard political realities.

But not everyone saw that. "I absolutely refuse to accept the fact that this House cannot and will not act," raged Congresswoman Lynn Martin, Republican of Illinois. "Is it any wonder that people have lost faith in us if we do not face this honestly?"

Despite Martin's plea, LaFalce's foredoomed amendment lost. But it garnered a respectable 171 votes, against 256 nays. There's no telling how many of those votes were symbolic salutes to "truth in budgeting" as Frenzel foresaw. Hoagland voted for the LaFalce amendment, but he did so with just 0:15 remaining on the clock. "I hadn't really thought it through before," was Hoagland's explanation for his late vote at the time. But legislators sometimes voted late to show support for a measure only after it was clear it would *lose,* so they could gain credit for trying. Hoagland subsequently denied that his late vote on the LaFalce amendment was such a "symbolic" vote. However, his reasons had changed. He now claimed he had "supported the LaFalce amendment in committee," not, as he had earlier said, that his first chance to think it through occurred during the floor vote. The LaFalce amendment never came up for a recorded vote in the Banking Committee.

At around 9:00 P.M., Jim called the House Democratic Cloakroom and got Hoagland on the phone. Jim was worried that an "end run" by credit union lobbyists might yet kill Hoagland's amendments. To keep their support, Hoagland had already agreed not to bring up the looted Franklin Credit Union in his floor remarks.

Hoagland would present his amendments last, just before the vote on final passage of the entire bill. As the time drew near, members began crowding the floor, and they were in a rowdy mood, talking loudly and laughing, impatient to get away for the weekend.

Word was fast spreading around the chamber about another end run in the works, a "motion to recommit" the bill, to eliminate all "special interest" provisions. One such motion is normally permitted just before the final vote on a bill, to give opponents a last chance to change or defeat it. But they almost never pass, maybe once every Congress. If this one succeeded, the "Yanney" amendment would be one of the casualties.

The motion was being offered by Iowa Republican Jim Leach, Hoagland's old friend. The fair-haired Leach was as independent as they come in Congress. He was a heretic in the eighties, voicing shrill criticism of Reagan's foreign policy. And throughout the S&L markups, he was a consistent scourge of the thrift industry and champion of stiffer regulations. Leach, who did graduate work at the London School of Economics, was well informed and articulate. But some members resented his stridency. They said he could afford to take principled stands, since he took no PAC money, and could rely in a pinch on family wealth to fund his campaigns.

To avoid trouble, Hoagland walked across the center aisle to the Republican side to "visit with" his old friend. Hoagland made the case that his "special interest" amendment actually served a legitimate public policy purpose, by bringing more private capital into the S&L bailout effort.

Leach was sympathetic. But he wasn't about to show favoritism in the midst of an effort to banish favoritism from the bill. Unfortunately, his old chum's amendment would have to go if the others went, for the sake of consistency.

Around 9:45 P.M., the last major item of contention was being decided. The Banking Committee had passed an amendment, sponsored by Gonzalez, to require Federal Home Loan Banks to set aside $150 million annually for low-income mortgages. It was a relatively trifling amount in this megabillion-dollar undertaking. Still, it had sparked intense opposition, mostly from Republicans. Steve Bartlett, a Texas Republican, presented an amendment to strip the measure from the bill, calling it a "hidden tax" on the S&L industry.

Housing programs hadn't fared well during the Reagan years. Liberals were now anxious lest the S&Ls get away with a massive bailout while again nothing was done to promote housing—the mission of S&Ls in the first place. And they resented the liveliness of the opposition they were running into, on this relatively minor housing initiative, after they'd gone along with most of Bush's far-reaching, infinitely more expensive bailout plan.

Hoagland, who had voted with the winning side, now strode to the podium for his maiden voyage in debate managing. The chamber was in commodities exchange mode. Bartlett panned the amendment as a rush job, poorly thought out, and inferior to existing housing programs. In reply, Frank vented the spleen of liberals, in his amusingly brusque style. As for how well-drafted existing housing programs might be, Frank recalled that Bartlett hadn't supported those either. "There is no formula that would get the gentleman from Texas to vote for this measure," he decided, "unless it was one which was slipped into his drink."

The chamber filled quickly for this last big fight before final passage. The vote itself was the closest of the day, stoking the competitive fires of the assembled partisans. Every uptick or downturn in the tally got a lusty reception.

With only a minute left, the vote was tied at 200. When the nays nudged ahead by a few, throaty cheers exploded from the Democratic side of the aisle. Then the yeas pulled slightly ahead. The other side roared.

A brief hush fell when the vote knotted again at 206. Then

Democrats erupted again: nays 207, yeas 206. The final tally: nays 208, yeas 206.

"The amendment is not agreed to," announced the speaker pro-tem.

Backs were slapped and hands were shaken all around the rambunctious Democratic side. Frank walked up to Gonzalez and gave him a hug.

Very soon after, when Hoagland strode to the podium for his maiden voyage in debate managing, the chamber was in commodities exchange mode. Everywhere you looked, groups of lawmakers were loudly yammering, oblivious to the proceedings. The House was decidedly not in order.

"Mr. Chairman," Hoagland said, his trembly voice barely a rumor in the hellcat din, "I would like to offer an amendment today which is technical and conforming in nature, but very important in substance."

Loud cries of "VOTE, VOOOOTE" came from the back of the chamber as Hoagland read on from his prepared statement. There wasn't much patience left for "substance," especially of the technical and conforming variety. It was late. Important business was done. Let's go.

"VOOOOOOOOTE."

Hoagland offered more boilerplate praise for his committee chairman's "excellent" work. "I ask for order," Gonzalez demanded, mock-forcefully. "The gentleman is saying very nice things about me."

But order was not in order. When Hoagland finally got through his shaky, inaudible spiel, fellow Nebraskan and cosponsor Doug Bereuter spoke up for the amendments, followed by Carroll Hubbard (again), and Mary Rose Oakar of Ohio. No one cared. The measures were rubber-stamped on a voice vote.

So that was that. No credit union end run. No problems. The biggest bill of the year was now just about home free, and Hoagland could count four amendments with his name on them. Not bad for a shy late-bloomer from Nebraska.

Then Hoagland learned the meaning of "easy come, easy go."

Just before the vote on final passage, Leach stepped up to the podium, amid the loud hubbub of his impatient colleagues. While all around him was *opéra bouffe,* he delivered lines from a tragedy.

"Personally, I believe capital standards are inadequate," Leach announced in scolding tones. "I also believe that estimates of the depth of the hole in the insurance fund are insufficient and that we will have to revisit this bill in eighteen to thirty-six months."

Though Leach had many problems with the bill, on the advice of Republican leaders, he was offering a motion to recommit that would only strike "special interest exceptions." He'd itemized them in a devastating hit list. In a stroke, he hoped to undo the work of platoons of lobbyists.

"Mr. Speaker, we are looking at the greatest debacle, the greatest lapse of legislative judgment in the history of this republic," Leach railed, turning his guns on his colleagues. ". . . now is the time for reform, not politics as usual."

Annoyed grumbling was heard in the chamber, especially on the Democratic side. No one liked a grandstander, especially a sanctimonious one.

Gonzalez challenged Leach. "Mr. Speaker," he said wearily, "I am opposed to this motion. . . . [W]hat it does is say that any provision that affects a narrow group is bad, no matter what, no matter why. I might not like or support all of these provisions he refers to, but the motion gives me no way to distinguish between them." That, said Gonzalez, was "grossly unfair."

On the voice vote, the nays appeared to have it. But Leach demanded a recorded vote, and got one the likes of which the House seldom saw.

Republicans threw up a block of votes for their guy very quickly, as they often did, hoping to scare Democrats into swimming with the tide. Usually, it didn't work. But after a few minutes, the tally was a surprising one hundred yeas and only sixty nays, and the latter were all Democratic votes.

If the split had continued along strict party lines, the Democrats, being the majority party, would have won. But what would they have won? A lot of headlines about themselves as the party that voted for special-interest giveaways? Talk about a Pyrrhic victory. All at once, Democrats began to change their votes.

On the tally board, red lights blinked off and were replaced by green ones. The nays sank to thirty . . . twenty-two . . . twenty . . .

Hoagland stood in the aisle next to Bereuter. They were already discussing ways to remove the "special interest stench" from the Yanney amendment and get it back in the bill in the House-Senate conference committee. Right now, it was getting a glorious stomping.

Dave Nagle, from Nebraska's neighboring state of Iowa, hurried down the aisle to Hoagland shouting, "Change to yes! Change to yes!" according to Hoagland. The freshman hadn't voted yet. But he and Bereuter finally did vote yes, helping to kill their own amendment. After all Hoagland's hard work, his sleepless nights fretting over the *Wall Street Journal* editorial, all he could do was smile philosophically.

The nays were down to ten, then eight. In the end, only seven votes stuck against Leach's motion. Gonzalez had cast one. His special interest amendment for Cross National Bank had been at stake too. A thumping 412 voted with Leach. The House had spoken. A few minutes later, Hoagland voted with the majority as the newly sanitized savings and loan bailout bill sailed through 320–97.

The S&L bill moved through Congress like a bad joke. It kicked around in the Senate for only seven days, including debates, mark-ups, and floor consideration, before it was passed 91–8. It lasted a few months in the House–which is four times bigger than the Senate–and that was still a remarkably quick turnaround compared to its normal pace.

Washington is not exactly known for handling thorny issues with such dispatch. How to explain it? After years of avoiding and even covering up the matter, had the president and Congress finally risen above politics to pass a tough policy without dilatory partisanship? That was the view of many in Washington. But there were those who read the situation differently.

The complicated S&L affair was never a made-for-TV scandal. So far, the medium had paid very little attention to the bailout. But the day after the House passed the bill, this tale of recklessly squandered billions was deemed lurid enough even to crack the lineup on *Donahue,* taking its place among "Nude Police," "Incest," "Ugly Babies," "Kept Women," and "Buns and Bellies," all recent topics on the show.

Gripping the microphone, Phil charged at his audience. "The question is," he shouted, "has Congress . . . ramrodded through a bailout that they assume you are not going to understand, and therefore not beef about, that is going to cost you money, when the real responsibility should lie in the laps of the people who have these high-rolling good times . . . ?"

Consumer groups were complaining that after years of delay, politicians were suddenly rushing a bailout bill through Congress so that public opposition to aspects of the plan would lack time to coalesce. Near the end of the process in the House, after the Wright affair had died down and whispers of debate on some aspects of the S&L bill had filtered through to the public, its effects were seen in some nervous votes on the House floor. But later in the year, flag-burning and federal funding of "obscene" art would get a much more extensive airing in the media.

One index of the public's lack of information was the trickle of mail received in Congress on the issue. Hoagland said his S&L mail was almost exclusively from executives of financial institutions, a group well represented at House markups. "We have received fewer than five letters from the general public on the bill," Hoagland told the *World-Herald*. (Hoagland did his part to inform the home folk about the bailout in a newsletter he sent to constituents in November, months after the bill had been signed into law.)

When the media did cover the S&L issue, its information was often wrong or incomplete. Estimates of the bill's cost often didn't include interest payments, which would be more than two-thirds of the eventual bill, or the amounts pledged by FSLIC in the 1988 deals. And the media—taking their cue from politicians—behaved as if no alternative to the long-term bonding plan were conceivable. Almost nothing about the issue was reported on television.

When the bonding plan *was* discussed, it seemed as if the media didn't understand it. On the day the LaFalce amendment was defeated, the House adopted the "on-budget" plan to sell long-term Treasury bonds to finance the bailout. That evening, on the *McNeil-Lehrer Newshour,* the "intelligent" alternative to shallow network news, Jim Lehrer reported that the House had "rejected a proposal to finance [the bailout] through the sale of bonds."

On *Donahue,* Phil summed up his take on the bailout. "I think the word on the Hill is that you won't understand this anyway, it's very complicated, and let's get out of here."

13
UNION DOWN

O n the roof of the House of Representatives, near the southern face of the Capitol dome, the flag of the United States was hoisted up a pole, permitted to flap once or twice, then yanked back down. Another flag was raised and jerked down just as quickly. Then another. And another. The ritual continued for around two hours, on each of three poles. In all, some three hundred flags were aired out by employees of the architect of the Capitol. These men were performing a seldom-publicized service, mass-producing flags "flown over the United States Capitol," as advertised in the newsletters of just about every member of Congress.

In truth, the flags aren't so much flown as *exposed* over the Capitol. Constituents buy them at slightly above cost from congressional offices, complete with certificates inscribed with the member's name and a dedication written by the buyer. Since the fifties, when the architect's flag pull got into gear, more than 1.3 million have been "flown" over the Capitol. The all-time record for hoistings in a single day was set on July 4, 1976—the bicentennial—when an expanded flag crew set up eighteen poles on the roof to handle 10,471 requests. They started at midnight and didn't quit until seven the next morning.

Each flag comes smartly boxed in red, white, and blue, with a long set of instructions on the proper handling of Ol' Glory. The flag should be displayed only from sunrise to sunset, though when "a patriotic effect" is desired, nighttime hoistings are okay if the flag is properly illuminated. The flag "should be hoisted briskly and lowered ceremoniously," and should not be displayed in inclement weather (unless it's a waterproof model).

The flag must not be flown in a position inferior to any other flag. It should never touch anything beneath it, nor be used as a covering for a ceiling. And the flag should never, never be displayed with its "union"—white stars on a field of blue—facing down, "except as a signal of dire distress in instances of extreme danger to life or property."

On June 21, 1989, the Supreme Court added to the already long list of rules for flag handling. In deciding the case of *Texas* v. *Johnson,* the court said that when a political statement is intended, it's okay to *burn* a flag.

The afternoon before the S&L vote, Jim Crounse was seated at his desk in Hoagland's office. His usual genial grin was gone, replaced by a look of pouty frustration. "It's Nicole again," Jim said when asked what was wrong.

The *World-Herald*'s junior Washington scribe had once more violated Jim's idea of proper journalistic practice. It happened in the wake of the second mugging of Hoagland by the *Wall Street Journal.*

On June 9, the *Journal* had printed a letter to the editor from Hoagland, in which he explained how his amendment was "a necessary refinement" to the S&L bill's overly broad provisions. It "strengthens, not weakens," the bill, he wrote.

Across the page from Hoagland's screed, the hardly chastened editors denounced the "amendment chutzpah" concerning the S&L bill, which had reached "incredible" levels in the House. Among the guilty, they cited "Two Nebraska congressmen, Republican Doug Bereuter and Democrat Peter Hoagland," cosponsors of the Yanney amendment. Not only was Hoagland dragged into the police lineup again, but he'd pulled his fellow Nebraskan along with him. Hoagland had been a mite unstrung by the paper's first swipe. Now he was angry. "Maybe we can sue them for libel," his staff heard him say.

The day of the *Journal*'s second strike, Nicole Simmons called Hoagland's office and made a routine appointment for an interview with him. Jim said that when Hoagland called back, Simmons "sprang" a question about the second editorial. Since she hadn't specified this topic when she called to request the interview, Jim thought the question was unfair, and later told her so.

There are stories in Washington of public officials who before accepting invitations to dinner parties instruct their secretaries to inquire what the topics of conversation will be. But it was surprising to find open, straightforward Nebraskans so jumpy about unscripted questions, especially when the subject matter wasn't exactly something they had to study up on.

Even Jim admitted that Simmons's story on the Yanney amendment the next day was balanced and fair. But he didn't like its headline, PAPER CHIDES HOAGLAND, BEREUTER. No doubt he was mentally computing broadcast rebuttal fees already.

For an anxiety specialist like Jim, June had been a pretty busy month. On the 28th, Gerald Solomon, a conservative Republican from upstate New York, had offered an amendment on the House floor to a foreign aide bill. It would have made some State Department employees subject to random drug tests.

Solomon was an ex-marine whose perennial squint and frown made his face look like a clenched fist. He was best known for a series of amendments, pressed with tireless zeal, that barred people who'd avoided registering for the draft from getting student financial aid, job training funds, or work on defense contracts. Solomon now announced a new crusade. He promised to try to attach his drug test amendment to "all authorizing bills for our federal agencies and departments."

Mandatory drug tests tend to make hash of Fourth Amendment protections against unreasonable searches without probable cause. Before the vote, Hoagland told Jim that he could not, in good conscience, support random drug tests in this case. But Jim's political radar was blipping like mad. Drugs were a hot issue. He sensed a Republican trap. As Hoagland recalled it, his aide advised: "Couldn't you just vote 'present'?"

When Hoagland got to the floor to vote, he was shown a memo from the State Department, which was opposed to Solomon's amendment too. In other words, the Bush administration was opposed. "The amendment is unnecessary and would duplicate existing law and regulation," State's memo said. What possible harm could Republicans do Hoagland for supporting the president? He voted against the amendment, as did many Republicans, and it was defeated 212–204. Recalling the vote later, Hoagland was disappointed in Jim's take on the issue. "Jim is excessively political," he said, shaking his head.

But the next day, Jim's prescience was proved. Newsrooms in Omaha got a faxed press release from the National Republican Congressional Committee, the GOP equivalent of the DCCC. Across the top of the release was the question "Is Congressman Hoagland Really Serious About the War on Drugs?" The rest was vintage guerilla politics:

> "Congressman Peter Hoagland may talk tough about fighting the war on drugs, but when he came face to face with the enemy, he went AWOL," according to Ed Rollins, Co-Chairman of the National Republican Congressional Committee.
>
> On the afternoon of June 28, an amendment was offered on the floor of the House . . . which would require random drug testing in the State Department and the Agency for International Development. The amendment fell four votes shy of passing, Congressman Hoagland was one of those votes.
>
> Rollins said, "In essence Peter Hoagland is saying it's OK to do drugs if you work in the State Department. . . ."

Needless to say, no NRCC press releases appeared in the districts of any of the thirty-four Republicans who voted against the Solomon amendment. Nor was the president accused of condoning drug use in the State Department.

Hoagland wasn't attacked on a whim. He was an official NRCC "target," one thing that added to the anxiety level in his office. Since his race had been so close in '88, his seat was viewed as a very possible Republican pickup next time around, and he could expect more such salvos from the NRCC.

But as it worked out, no damage was done this time. The Omaha media, after consulting with Hoagland's staff, decided not to do any stories based on the releases. Nevertheless, Hoagland didn't want the NRCC to simply get away with such sleazy tactics. He failed to interest some Washington reporters in the story, but *something* needed to be done.

More nervous times visited Hoagland's office in the wake of the Supreme Court's flag-burning decision. In *Texas* v. *Johnson,* the court ruled that Gregory Lee Johnson had engaged in politically "expressive conduct" protected by the First Amendment when he burned a flag outside the Republican National Convention. Finding the "overtly political" nature of Johnson's act "both intentional and overwhelmingly apparent," the court threw out his conviction for violating a Texas law against "desecration of a venerated object." Similar laws in forty-eight states were nullified.

It wasn't long before Congress, that old flag clearinghouse, whipped itself into a patriotic pother. The day after the court ruled, a long line of House members cued up to deliver their one-minute reviews of the decision. The same words and phrases were bleated over and over: "sad day for America," "shocked," "this time it has gone too far," "the symbol for everything this country holds dear," "would shock our Founding Fathers," "an affront to every American," "makes me sick," "more than one million Americans have died defending the flag," "outrageous," "a slap in the face to every American," "disgusting," "save the colors."

Bob Stump, a fiercely conservative Republican from Arizona, was in no mood to just wring his hands and whine. "I am not a very big guy," he said, "but . . . I say to those who would choose to desecrate the flag, they had better not try it in *my* presence."

Douglas Applegate, Democrat from Ohio, was "mad as hell" (censors of the *Congressional Record* changed that to "mad as heck"). This new thinking on the court puzzled him awfully. "What in God's name is going on?" Pointing to the huge flag draped behind the speaker's rostrum, Applegate thundered, "The flag right here in this chamber that we pledge to, we can take it down, throw it on the floor, step on it, defecate on it, do anything we want, burn it, as long as we have a message, and the court is going to say it is all right! . . . Are there any limitations? Are they going to allow fornication in Times Square at high noon?"

There was a mood to "do something" about the decision quickly. Changing the Constitution, to spell out protections for the flag, didn't seem too radical a remedy, even if that meant editing the Bill of Rights. Almost as many constitutional amendments were dropped in the hopper on this day as there were outraged speakers in the House.

But in this chamber laden with lawyers, there wasn't a word uttered in defense of the judges of the Supreme Court, those most exalted of the legal breed. Many members seemed sure these justices represented pointy-headed . . . something or other. Not *liberalism,* certainly, since two of the justices who voted in the majority were conservative appointees of Ronald Reagan. But something!

Marilyn Lloyd of Tennessee said the Court's reasoning showed "no understanding of what America is about." Applegate didn't want to stop at amending the Constitution. He drew a bead on the Court itself, proposing an amendment to limit the terms of justices.

President Bush's first response to the flag case was tempered. "I understand the legal basis for the decision and I respect the Supreme Court, and as president of the United States, I will see that the law of the land is fully supported," Bush said. He added his emotional response—"Flag burning is wrong—dead wrong." But he didn't seem ready to join the jihad stirring in Congress.

That changed quickly. After Bush huddled with his political adviser Lee Atwater, a master of the hair-pulling, scratch-your-eyes-out, divisive politics of "values," he seemed to decide the issue was too good to pass up. It was another tool to separate the liberals from the "Americans."

Republicans had scored off Michael Dukakis for his "legalistic" refusal to disobey a court order and make children in Massachusetts recite the pledge of allegiance in school. Now they had another "issue" to make Democrats squirm. Bush proposed a constitutional amendment of his own to protect the flag. He and his advisers were probably guessing that many Democrats would be reluctant to rewrite the Bill of Rights, and hoping their reluctance would look "unpatriotic" right about now.

Some thought Bush was using the flag, a symbol of union, to polarize the nation. Wasn't this one more sordid example of the slimy tactics of campaigning being imported into the realm of governing? Wasn't Bush draping the flag with its union down, not to mention dragging it through the mud of politics?

Network news shows were airing pictures from places like Findlay, Ohio, which, by an act of Congress, had been designated "Flag City, U.S.A." Amid a forest of flapping flags, Findlay's citizens posed for the cameras. They were *angry* at the Supreme Court and wanted something *done!*

Newsweek published an instant poll that said 70 percent of Americans supported a constitutional amendment to "protect" the flag. Some might have thought that supporting the Supreme Court and the Bill of Rights was a fairly conservative position. But if any Democrats thought that way, they weren't saying so just now, as pressure seemed to be mounting to pass a constitutional amendment, whether one was necessary or not.

One of the few voices raised against the flag frenzy among lawmakers belonged to Senator Gordon Humphrey of New Hampshire, who was retiring at the end of the term. Before the Senate voted 97–3 to register its "profound disappointment" in the court's ruling, Humphrey said, ". . . this just seems to me an exercise in silliness and even a little bit of hypocrisy, if I may say so."

It was only Tuesday, Congress's first day of the work week, but by 4:00 P.M. Hoagland already looked exhausted, wiped out in fact. He sat slouched in his chair, his eyelids heavy, his face paler than usual.

"What a miserable day this was," Hoagland said, rubbing his temples. He'd been up at 4:00 A.M. to catch his flight back from Omaha, where he'd just completed a fully booked four-day weekend of appearances, meetings, and paperwork. The flight was late, so he didn't get to Washington until noon, and missed a journal vote. Such votes were meaningless. They decided whether the House would "approve" the previous day's journal. It was always approved. Why wouldn't it be? Nevertheless, journal votes counted in the averages, and Hoagland had gotten up early so he wouldn't miss it.

When Hoagland got to the floor shortly after noon, he was already spent. He wanted to slip off to the House gym. Not to do curls in the weight room. He liked the gym's sleeping cubicles. He would sometimes retire to one during a lull in a long day, close the door, and catch a nap.

But before Hoagland could leave the floor, one of Tom Foley's staffers tapped him on the shoulder. "The speaker wants to see you," he said. "I didn't know if I was in trouble or what," Hoagland recalled.

Hoagland walked down to the rostrum, where Foley stood presiding over the quiet House proceedings. With no preamble, the speaker handed the gavel to the freshman. "I've got to go," Hoagland recalled him saying. "I'd like you to preside for a while." Then Foley was off.

Speaker Pro Tem Hoagland was sort of at a loss. He wasn't expecting to be sitting aloft in the big, high-backed chair, over-looking the whole chamber. Even if the place was nearly empty, he would still have to make *rulings* from time to time. What then?

A member made a routine "unanimous consent" request. Hoagland blanked out. Though he'd heard the standard ruling a thousand times, it wouldn't come to him. Luckily, a woman sitting nearby who worked for the clerk of the House noticed his plight. "Pssst," she whispered. "Say, 'Without objection, so ordered.'"

And so ordered, Hoagland did as he was bidden, and the House managed to grind on.

The weary Hoagland sighed when asked about the Supreme Court's flag decision, which he appeared to support. "You shouldn't go to jail for burning a piece of cloth," he said, shaking his head. But he was in no hurry to go on the air with that view.

House Democrats were looking for ways to respond to the apparent public mood without rushing to amend the Bill of Rights. Jack Brooks, chairman of the Judiciary Committee, drafted a "resolution" which expressed the "profound concern" of the House about the court's decision. Democratic leaders hoped a vote on the resolution would at least stall the growing clamor for an amendment, which now had the president's support too.

Gail Handleman, one of Hoagland's media aides, peeked into his office. She'd gotten a call from a reporter at an Omaha TV station. He wanted to know if Hoagland supported Bush's amend-ment proposal.

Hoagland and Gail seemed a trifle paranoid about the ques-tion. They believed the reporter was cleverly avoiding asking about Brooks's resolution, preferring to press Hoagland on the more controversial Bush amendment proposal. Intriguing as that sounded, it hardly seemed likely. Bush had been on all the networks beating the drum for his amendment. Meanwhile, who outside of Washington had heard of Brooks's "profound concern"?

Hoagland gave Gail a reply for the newsman. "Tell him I haven't read Bush's amendment proposal, so I can't comment on it, but I've read Brooks's resolution and I support that." It was standard evasive strategy. Shelved for now was the bold opinion stated moments before about "a piece of cloth."

Hoagland didn't like hiding out on this issue. But every time he brought up his desire to be honest about it, "Jim and Gary waved polls at me," he said.

After Gail left, Hoagland's aides saw his door open and took their opportunity. One by one, they filed in to get a rare word with him.

Hoagland absently signed this and approved that. But in between, his musings revealed a bunker mentality. He wondered aloud how the newest *Wall Street Journal* swipe might be used by an opponent. "Hoagland says he's fighting a drug war," Hoagland said, in mock announcer style, "but he's addicted to congressional crack." This was two days before the vote on the Solomon drug-test amendment that drew enemy fire. At least Hoagland had known which direction the shells would be coming from.

The next day in Hoagland's office, the only things missing were shouts of "incoming!" and people diving under desks covering their heads. "We were attacked," Jim said, eyes wide with excitement. Gail was taking and making a flurry of phone calls. "We were attacked," she enthused into the receiver.

Officials of the Douglas County Republican Party had criticized Hoagland for his "intolerable silence" on the court's flag ruling. Unlike many of his colleagues, Hoagland had been curiously mum on the issue.

Jim and Gail quickly made contact with all the reporters on their beat. This rapid response had "deflected," they believed, the negative story. "I think the media has taken our message," Gail said.

The message was that Douglas County Republicans were "out of touch" with the "bipartisan deal" in Washington. Gail was referring to an agreement by House leaders to vote on Brooks's "profound concern" resolution, which had passed 411–5. Hoagland was not one of the five opposed.

Of course, there was nothing in that agreement that kept anyone from speaking out about the flag one way or the other. Nor would it stop a constitutional amendment from eventually coming to the floor. Nevertheless, no one ever said "messages" peddled to the media had to be true. They just had to be "taken."

"If someone wants to burn the flag, that's their business," said Michele Swoboda. Then she remembered where she was, and blushed. On Capitol Hill these days, them was fightin' words.

"Will you still speak to me?" she asked Hoagland.

As you might have guessed, the free-speaking Michele was no member of Congress. She was a reporter for a local television station doing contract work for Nebraska public TV. She'd come, with a camera and light crew, to interview Hoagland, who was leaning back in his chair, mentally reviewing responses to her likely questions, too distracted to hear her.

Michele needn't have worried. But she couldn't have known that this congressman harbored heresies of his own about the flag, and wasn't feeling too good about keeping them hidden. A few minutes before, Hoagland had walked into the office wearing a tiny American flag pin on his lapel. When asked if the pin gave him protection, he blushed, then sheepishly yanked it off and put it in a drawer.

Hoagland had spoken to several members about the flag amendment. Most were against it, but would feel compelled to vote for it should it come to the floor. He estimated that in a secret ballot, at least three hundred members would vote against it. But out in the open, he thought, it would pass nearly unanimously.

All his evasiveness with the media on this issue was getting Hoagland down. "I lost about *that much* of my self-respect yesterday," he said at one point, holding his thumb and index finger an inch apart. He would presently get a chance to shed a bit more.

Most of the interview concerned Hoagland's views on the Omaha drug problem. But near the end, Michele asked the inevitable flag question. Speaking slowly, professorially, Hoagland called the court's decision "unfortunate." Then he grew bolder, saying that "you can't help but admire what the judges were trying to do to protect free speech."

After the interview, Michele wanted to borrow Hoagland's office to shoot "re-asks"—footage of her asking the questions he'd just answered. "I really hate to do this," she said. But Hoagland was agreeable. "Fine!"

Before Hoagland left, he dropped a deck of photographs in Michele's lap. "Here are some pictures of the kids you can look at," he said, beaming. Hoagland spent most of his free time with his children. Outside of work, he talked of little else. Michele's screwed-up smile seemed to say, "Are you serious?" Not a close friend of the family, she appeared to find his suggestion incongruous. But while her crew rearranged the equipment, she sat flipping through the pictures.

Two elderly lady lobbyists from the School Nurse Association were waiting in the front office to meet with Hoagland. They wanted to talk about the child-care bill moving through Congress. Since his quarters were occupied, he escorted them upstairs to his annex.

On the way down the hall, the ladies noticed that every congressperson's door had a pair of flags guarding it—a U.S. flag on one side and a home-state flag on the other. "How come you don't have flags up in front of your door?" one of the ladies asked Hoagland. He didn't hesitate. "Those are put out by conservative members," he said. "They cost about two hundred and eighty dollars, and I didn't think we needed them that bad."

"Oooooooh!" said the ladies, a trace of awe in their tone.

14

MESSAGE FROM AN ANGEL

In Washington, it's often hard to know where symbolism ends and policy begins. Steve Szmrecsanyi (Smur-shonni) had reason to wonder where the boundary was. Szmrecsanyi was the legislative aide to the director of Boys Town, that famous sanctuary for troubled boys (and girls, since 1979) in Omaha. Boys Town was established by Father E. J. Flanagan, the man who said, "I never found a boy who really wanted to be bad."

Szmrecsanyi managed to reserve a narrow slice of time on Hoagland's schedule—from 3:00 to 3:10 P.M.—on an afternoon in late June. He hoped to win support for youth programs of the type sponsored by Boys Town, the sort that steers kids away from drug abuse and other dead ends. And he was also planning to invite the congressman to visit Boys Town's Flanagan High School, on Omaha's "near north side," the poorest, most crime-plagued neighborhood in town, where local drug gangs reigned. Hoagland's aides had said such a visit would fit snugly with his interest in the "war on drugs."

But when Szmrecsanyi sat down in the congressman's office, Hoagland couldn't seem to concentrate. He interrupted his visitor to talk with aides, then for a picture-taking session with his interns and the House photographer.

Szmrecsanyi, a patient, soft-spoken man, eventually got the chance to invite Hoagland to visit Flanagan High School in the near future. The congressman now sat up in his chair and focused on his guest. "I'd like to link up my visit with a theme," he said deliberately, "so we could get the TV cameras in." Szmrecsanyi nodded politely while Hoagland laid out a scenario. "Maybe we could announce some phase of my war on drugs."

No one flinched as Hoagland talked of *his* war on drugs. So far it wasn't a shooting war.

Hoagland and his staff were planning a town hall meeting on "drugs and gangs" for September, which would air on local television. As Gail prepared press releases for the event, she had trouble finding a single drug bill with Hoagland's name on it. Some examples were needed for ammunition on the only front that seemed truly active in Hoagland's war, the public relations front. John finally dug up two defense appropriations Hoagland had voted for that had some relationship to combating drug use.

After the visit, Szmrecsanyi went back to Boys Town to discuss Hoagland's plan with Father Peter, the current director. Both men agreed they should stick to standard Boys Town policy and not turn Hoagland's visit into a "photo op." They didn't want their children exploited.

Szmrecsanyi called Hoagland's office and "laid down the guidelines very gently and respectfully," he said. Hoagland was still more than welcome to visit Flanagan, a school meant to deal with teens who were otherwise unteachable, in an area of Omaha "full of drug users and drug pushers," according to Szmrecsanyi. A drug warrior might learn a lot there. But the media and their cameras and lights would not be welcome.

Gail Handleman of Hoagland's office told Mr. Szmresanyi that the congressman would still be happy to visit Flanagan. But the date suggested for the visit by the congressman's office was one on which Father Peter was booked up, and Hoagland's visit never took place. Gail said that since the academic year was soon to be over at Flanagan, another date could not be found to accommodate Hoagland's visit.

                              *   *   *

The House and Senate didn't sit down together to iron out their
differences on the S&L bill until July 11, when their delegations
met in Rayburn 2129. The scene looked like the aftermath of a
coup. On the ascending tiers of the congressional dais, behind
nameplates marked "Mr. Annunzio," "Mr. Wylie," "Mr. Leach,"
etc., strange faces were arrayed. Most of them belonged to the
usually anonymous "banking beat" reporters. Meanwhile, the
often anonymous elected officials were crammed in at ground
level, where press and public normally sat. It was the only place
most of them could fit. Henry Gonzalez's idea of a conference
committee had called for a little redecorating.

    Partly because Gonzalez wanted to be fair and democratic,
and partly from other motives, he had decided that participation in
this conference, concerned with the most important bill in many a
year, should be wide. He wasn't kidding. Gonzalez appointed all
fifty-one Banking Committee members to the House's delegation.
Ways and Means added twenty more, and twenty-three came from
three other committees. In the end, the ninety-four-member delegation included over a fifth of all House members. The Senate,
meanwhile, sent a lean squad of eight.

    Gonzalez believed he had good reasons for packing the place.
Conference committees are often arbitrary creatures. Provisions
can be stripped out of a bill, or new ones added, that neither
chamber had approved of. The antidemocratic nature of these
gatherings was one thing that led George Norris to fight for a
unicameral legislature in Nebraska.

    Gonzalez divided House conferees into "subconferences,"
whose members would only vote on certain issues. To these
groups he assigned people who had supported the committee's
position on the issue in question during markups. This was viewed
as a way to ensure that *his* pet provisions, for consumers and low-
income homebuyers, were not removed. Only people who'd
voted for them in markups would be in a position to decide their
fate now.

    The actual differences to be worked out between the House
and Senate versions of the bill appeared to be relatively slight. But
with so much raw democracy in one room, there was bound to be
chaos. The huge House group couldn't even fit all at once at the
rectangle of tables set up on ground level in 2129. "Subconfer-

ence" delegations joined in only as their subjects came up. But
with all the rotating in and out, progress was slow. After the
smoke cleared on day one, only a single section of the long bill
had been worked through.

Discussion of the "special interest" provisions ginned out of
the House bill by Leach's dramatic floor maneuver got a little
tense. Senate conferees agreed to strike such provisions from their
version, taking a bow in the intensifying spotlight on the issue. But
how to decide just what a "special interest" provision was? The
conferees opted to let House and Senate staff members bang out a
list of offensive articles still hiding in the bill. Many were in the
Senate version, which contained duplicates of favors washed out of
the House bill.

Curt Prins, Annunzio's chief aide, was amused by the procedure. "How would you like to be the staffer who decides who is
on the list of special interests?" he said to someone on the re-
porter-infested dais. Prins then demonstrated how he would handle the swarms of jittery lobbyists waiting outside the staff room to
hear the fate of their prized amendments. "I would have walked
out of that room with my wallet open," Prins joked. "Give me a
hundred thousand dollars or you're on the list."

When "the list" was finally ready for inspection, it touched
off a minor crisis. The chairmen of both delegations had said many
times that no copies were to be given to the press until the conferees had reviewed it. But even before the list was passed out to
members, word swept the room that a photostat had been found,
with a message scrawled across the top: "For Kathleen Day—
Washington Post." Several other reporters were said to have copies.

Members were angry, and not only at the apparent porous-
ness of their staff. Carroll Hubbard complained aloud that the list
members got did not identify sponsors alongside the provisions.
"We don't have a list with sponsors," Hubbard said testily into his
microphone. "The press has that." Apparently some staffer meant
to keep the pressure of publicity on the committee.

Hoagland's name didn't appear on any of the lists as far as he
knew. Though his Yanney amendment had been scrubbed in the
House, it was in the Senate bill, introduced by Exon and Kerrey.
On one list of questionable Senate provisions, Nancy Granese, a
lobbyist with KRC who was working with Hoagland, saw the
words "special deal" written next to the Yanney amendment.

* * *

Hoagland met in his office with Nancy Granese and David Karnes. Granese, a tall, conservatively dressed woman in her late thirties, was the head of Kutak, Rock & Campbell's lobbying division. Karnes had been the mustachioed junior senator from Nebraska until his defeat the previous November by Bob Kerrey. Now he was another lobbyist with KRC.

Hoagland leaned back in his chair and sighed. "It could have been just a routine corrective amendment," he said of the Yanney provision. Now it carried a certain stench, which put it in considerable jeopardy. But no one was content to just let it drop.

Yanney had a lot at stake. If the bill passed without the amendment, he could probably get a waiver from FDIC to specify that his two funds weren't liable for each other's losses. But what if he had to wait sixty days? Should he then go to the expense of contacting thousands of investors to tell them their actual liability was now higher, if only temporarily? That could hurt his reputation. So might *not* telling them. And what if he couldn't get a waiver? If the amendment could somehow survive, a lot of problems would disappear.

Granese read aloud from a list of the names of conference committee members, stopping when she thought one might be persuadable to their side. "We need either Wylie or Leach," Hoagland said. Wylie was the respected ranking Republican. Leach was the man whose motion had put the scarlet letter on Hoagland's chest.

Hoagland wanted to find a Republican to speak for his amendment, not just vote for it. Granese suggested that someone at Yanney-controlled Eureka Savings and Loan could contact Norman Shumway, a Republican from California. They would also talk to every senator on the conference committee.

When the meeting broke up, Granese was left in Hoagland's office with Nancy Nagle, whom the congressman had assigned to assist her. "Shut the door," Granese barked as she began punching up numbers on the phone.

Hoagland's staff was ambivalent, at best, about the Yanney amendment. Nancy thought it was "sorta weird" to be working so closely with David Karnes, the man she'd helped to defeat as a volunteer on Bob Kerrey's Senate campaign. As for Gary, though he saw the public policy rationale of Yanney's amendment, he didn't like the idea of Hoagland keeping his door quite so open to lobbyists who made "hundreds of thousands of dollars protecting the interests of rich people."

Gary and Jim also weren't thrilled about Hoagland's possibly attracting more bad press, especially after his amendment was tarred so publicly by the Leach motion. Both had asked him to quit going to bat for Yanney. Hoagland said they were "furious" when he decided to keep fighting.

Hoagland wasn't too worried about more bad publicity. He'd already taken a hit in the *Wall Street Journal.* How much worse could it get? Besides, the *World-Herald's* editors had been very understanding.

Hoagland now saw the Yanney amendment as a matter of pride as much as anything. He believed that the only way he could be cleansed of the taint of "special interest" deals was to keep battling for this particular special interest, and to convince the conference committee his amendment made sense as policy. He also aimed to "show people here"—lobbyists and other members —that he could come through when the going got tough.

"You hold before you the most valuable gift we can give you," read the message on the title page of *The Success Quiz: A book written by angels.* Bound in a dark-blue soft cover, the book arrived in the daily sack of mail dumped on Hoagland's office. Congress-folk always get their share of wacko correspondence. But this looked like a breakthrough in the genre.

The book was a patchwork of incomprehensible "meditations," apparently about the imminence of the apocalypse. As such, it belonged to the tradition of eschatological missives received by public officials and journalists on every level. But most of these communiqués take the form of a few single-spaced typewritten pages of lunar babble. This tract's "physical author Mark," however, had gone to great expense to vanity-publish an actual book, which he intended to distribute to ALL THE OTHER HUMAN BEINGS IN THE WORLD.

Rummaging through the congressional mailbag turned up letters from cranks expelled from every school of thought. A man who wanted the United States to adopt "a new flag" to represent "our Lord and Savior, Jesus Christ" enclosed crayon-colored mockups of a replacement for Old Glory. A woman objected to "cohabitation in missile silos." Another strung together two sin-

gle-spaced pages of quotations from the King James Bible. "People who are wise shall live by King James Bible law," she wrote.
"Only the wicked, who cannot understand, will continue to up-
hold United States law, which is Satan's law."

Then there were the barely legible "mad as hell" notes that
came from time to time. This one was scrawled on the back of a
telephone message memo form:

> I am writing to all of the Demacrats in Congress. I am a
> housewife and mother I don't have a high School Educa-
> tion But any Dummy Can see how corrupt you people
> are . . . I seen how you's slander the Judge that Presi-
> dent Regan wanted in. I seen how you Put Vic. Dan
> Quayle through the mud and to top it off you's are really
> doing a good job on Ollie North Tell me something how
> do all of you's sleep or do you's have a *conscious*. . . . If
> you all like being around Communisms so much Why
> dont you go to China or Soviet Union or Cuba Because
> this is what US is fiting for. If you people dont wake up
> and get some Morle Values We have to get good *Leaders*
> instead of *Greddy* people that only think abouth them
> self's We Elected President Bush not the Congress to
> make his *dicisions*. . . . Hope you people wake up and
> see whats going on. You better put God back in our
> school's.

Hoagland's staff didn't pay much attention to the crank mail.
But the rest was carefully husbanded. Letters were logged by subject matter and answered. But that was only the beginning of their
usefulness.

Names and addresses of letter writers were stored on a computer file according to the subject they'd written about. Hoagland
also bought lots of mailing lists, of small businesses, doctors, den-
tists, retirees, peace activists. Then both sets of lists were used to
generate "targeted" mail on issues that people had written in
about, or that their particular subgroup was likely to care about.

With this technique, called "narrowcasting," constituents
could be told what they wanted to hear—and only what they
wanted to hear. It was even better than broadcasting because messages were personalized: "Dear *your name here.*"

The bottom line on Hoagland's letters read: "Sincerely, Peter," under which his "signature" appeared. Of course, Peter actu-

ally signed few letters. His staff sometimes compared their forger-
ies of his signature, to decide who had "the best Peter." Eventually, Hoagland requisitioned stationery with "built-in" signatures
for mass mailings. There was even ink available that smeared to
the moist touch of a constituent.

Hoagland actually saw few of the letters sent him. His staff
prepared a weekly one- or two-page correspondence summary,
listing the names of writers and a blurb about what was on their
minds: "outraged about events in El Salvador"; "ban alcohol advertising on TV"; "upset Peter supports override on rape & incest"; "does not want tax $ to pay for abortions"; "opposes pay
raise for Congress & judges and their pensions."

Jim had become something of an expert on targeted mail at
the DCCC. He also made sure Hoagland's newsletters were on
the cutting edge. The trend was to downplay words and concentrate on layout, graphics, and pictures—like *USA Today.* Hoagland's newsletters were so text-light they looked like freeze-dried
TV spots.

Newsletters are fine for getting your name and face out there,
as they say. But targeted mail is the saturation weapon of choice.
Besides the "warmth" factor, there is another thing members like
about it: there is no upper limit on the number of mass mailings
that can be done with targeted mail, but there is with newsletters.

Newsletters aren't addressed to anyone in particular, but to
"postal patron." They go to every box in the district. Because of
their usefulness as propaganda, and their uselessness for any other
known purpose, the House capped postal-patron mailings at six
per year in 1989. But there is a loophole big enough to drive an
oil tanker through: targeted mailings to specific addressees are
unlimited. Naturally, congressfolk have cranked up their PCs and
churned out mail-merged personalized letters in postal-patron volumes.

Hoagland's office unleashed blizzards of this targeted mail. In
just one weekend in October, four printers ran almost nonstop in
his seventh-floor annex, spewing over 165,000 letters. (Postage
alone for such a mailing cost over $40,000.) The staff gave the
overworked printers nicknames: Moe, Larry, Curly, and Shemp.
John Minter reported that after twelve hours of continuous printing, "Larry blew up" and had to be replaced.

15

OUT OF THE CLOSET

H oagland's spotlight cravings sometimes amused even him.
Bob Armstrong, chairman of the Omaha Housing Authority,
was a popular local official. He'd gotten "national attention" for
programs to improve the prospects of dwellers in Omaha's public
housing. "We must make sure that the children of public housing
don't become public housing adults," he said, according to an
account in *The New York Times*.

Armstrong offered students modest bonuses—a $100 savings
bond for a year's perfect school attendance—and warned parents
that failure to keep their kids in school could lead to eviction. His
carrot-and-stick approach was well received in high Republican
circles. Housing and Urban Development Secretary Jack Kemp,
former Buffalo Bills quarterback and current gravel-throated per-
sonification of "tough-love," was soon to pay Armstrong a visit to
review his program.

Hoagland wanted to crash that party in the worst way. There
were bound to be shutters clicking in Omaha when a cabinet secre-

tary came to town. But the Republican Kemp wasn't likely to cooperate in promoting a Democratic congressman. When Armstrong stopped by Hoagland's Washington office, the congressman outlined an audacious plan to infiltrate the Kemp meeting. "I'll jump out of the closet when he's there," Hoagland said with a playful smile.

When it came to the Supreme Court's flag ruling, Hoagland was still safely in the closet, along with his peers. But on July 18, a senator spoke out strongly in defense of the Supreme Court. In so doing, he may have shown his nervous breed a novel way to get publicity—by doing something courageous.

It so happened that this bold, outspoken soul was Hoagland's fellow Nebraskan, freshman Senator Bob Kerrey. While a few others had spoken up against the mob's wounded outcry, Kerrey's remarks seemed to carry more weight. He was, after all, a war hero, with a plastic stump where his right foot had been to prove it. He'd also been awarded the Medal of Honor. No other politician in this town, not even the president, had one of those. It just wasn't possible to question Kerrey's patriotism.

Shortly after the Fourth of July recess, Kerrey rose to speak in the midst of a Senate "debate"—a very one-sided "hang the flag burners" affair—on the amendment. At first he'd been "outraged" by the Court's decision. He'd voted for the Senate's message of "profound disappointment" in the ruling. "It seemed ridiculous to me that flag burning could be a protected act," he said.

But during the Fourth of July recess, Kerrey read the text of the decision. To his surprise, he found the argument of the majority "reasonable, understandable, and consistent with those values which I believe make America so wonderful." He said the Court "broke no new ground" in holding that "the First Amendment applies to conduct as well as pure speech."

Kerrey said a constitutional amendment to protect the flag would "create problems rather than solve them." He didn't support an anti-flag-burning statute either, being "skeptical about the need." "There is simply no line of Americans outside this building or in this nation queuing up to burn our flag."

Recalling Chief Justice William Rehnquist's "disappointing dissent" in the Supreme Court's ruling, Kerrey trotted out his credentials to take on the jingo juggernaut. Rehnquist said our soldiers fought for our flag in Vietnam. "I do not remember feeling this way," Kerrey said. "I remember that my first impulse to fight was . . . a feeling that it was my duty. . . . I do not remember giving the safety of our flag anywhere near the thought that I gave the safety of my men."

Kerrey, his doelike eyes aglow with emotion, recalled one more thing that would be much quoted in days ahead. "I remember most vividly on the night that I was wounded, with the smell of my own burning flesh in my head, that I knew I was going home, and how happy I was in that certainty. America, the home of the free and the brave, is my home, and I give thanks to God that it is. America . . . does not need our government to protect us from those who burn a flag."

Kerrey immediately became a leading voice in what was finally a two-sided discussion on the flag. His emotional comments landed on editorial pages across the country. Some politicians, who wished they could speak out themselves, resented the "immunity" from political harm Kerrey's plastic leg gave him. There was probably much truth in that. But his principled stand hadn't come risk-free. Nebraskans, if one can believe polls, were solidly in favor of Bush's flag amendment.

Though both Hoagland and Kerrey were Nebraska boys, their political styles were about as opposite as two styles can be. Hoagland was very much a Washington mold politician. He went to the schools that influential people go to, and developed the patient, compromising temperament of a "policy intellectual" so respected in the corridors of power.

Kerrey, on the other hand, had gone to the University of Nebraska, where he studied pharmacy, and didn't seriously consider politics until he was much older. From the moment he entered the chase, he was a young pol in a hurry. In his first run for office, at the age of thirty-eight, he challenged the sitting Republican governor of his Republican state, Charles Thone. When Kerrey won, by a little better than seven thousand votes, he reportedly said, "I was confident of victory, but I don't know why."

After sitting in the Senate for only three months, Kerrey proposed a controversial amendment to the S&L legislation. It would have changed the makeup of the agency established to shut down insolvent thrifts and sell their megabillions worth of assets. Kerrey saw in this agency "a potential scandal of immense proportions."

The Bush bill said the agency's board should include the treasury secretary, the attorney general, and the chairman of the Federal Reserve. Kerrey believed these officials were simply too busy to oversee "the largest liquidation of assets in the history of the United States."

Kerrey's amendment, strongly opposed by Bush, was beaten on a tabling motion, 66–32. That wasn't surprising. That he'd even offered it was. He wasn't a member of the Banking Committee. And though the Senate is traditionally more open to floor amendments from any quarter, controversial measures on major bills aren't commonly offered by one so newly arrived.

But Kerrey didn't seem to worry much about the standard rites of passage. Though he sat on the Agriculture and Appropriations committees, he talked of making major initiatives in health care and education. He also came out in favor of national health insurance.

Like Hoagland, Kerrey was originally a Republican. He switched in 1978. But the two men's orientations to public service are as different as their personalities. Kerrey grew up in a middle-class home where lively discussions of political issues were a staple at the family table. According to accounts in the Nebraska press, his high school classmates remember him as "very competitive." Part of the reason he entered public life seems to be that he'd simply run out of challenges. At thirty-eight, he was already a millionaire restaurateur and businessman.

Hoagland didn't talk of public service as a challenge so much as a sacrifice. His sense of it was shaped by his parents, who were active in the local art museum, the Junior League, the Red Cross. "They are selfless people," Hoagland has said of his parents. "They believe in giving something back."

Politics to Hoagland wasn't an invigorating contest so much as a monastic discipline. "I'm drawn to public life like some people are drawn to the priesthood or teaching," Hoagland once told a reporter. "It's a way of making your years on this earth count for something more than just yourself."

Hoagland and Kerrey also differed in their assessments of Washington. Hoagland generally liked what he saw. "My impression is that the House is a meritocracy," he had said. "Members are smart, personable, and well-motivated." Kerrey was less sanguine. "Everyone's slow to solve things that seem the easiest to solve," he said, according to an account in the *World-Herald.*

The differing styles of the two freshmen from Nebraska were evident in their reactions to the Franklin Credit Union affair. When Kerrey confronted National Credit Union Administration officials at a Senate hearing, he was unsparing. "I see massive fraud and regulatory ineptitude," he said of the Franklin case. "Massive fraud on the part of the credit union, and regulatory ineptitude on the part of you." Kerrey couldn't fathom why NCUA's suspicions weren't aroused about Larry King, "an eighteen-thousand-dollar-a-year employee with a one-million-dollar American Express bill, with a five-thousand-dollar-a-month apartment in Washington and another place in Los Angeles, with limousines and planes at his beck and call. The people in Nebraska say, 'If you can't regulate that kind of activity, what can you do?' "

Kerrey liked to lead public debate, Hoagland was more comfortable following it. But when Hoagland chose to cooperate with NCUA officials rather than chastise them, he got some legislation out of the arrangement. Some questioned whether Kerrey would ever be a legislator who got things done. Jacob Weisberg, writing in the December 1989 *New Republic,* said Kerrey's career in the Senate might be marked "more by leadership on selected issues of conscience (the flag) than by legislative achievements." Weisberg also criticized Kerrey for embracing "discarded Democratic dogma," like national health insurance and federal aid to education.

Kerrey's quixotic temperament troubled some. One Hoagland staffer thought he simply enjoyed being contrarian, like some electoral Evel Knievel, getting his thrills cheating political death. "The essence of patriotism is standing against the mob," Kerrey said before his flag speech. He did seem to relish taking such stands. A month later, he spoke against the move to restore military pension benefits taken from Oliver North after his felony conviction. North was about as popular as the flag back in Nebraska. Even Jesse Helms, keeper of the conservative flame, was impressed. "He does not pussyfoot on issues," Helms was quoted as saying of Kerrey.

And there were the "Cosmic Bob" stories. Weisberg referred to Kerrey's "visionary streak," which, he wrote, "raises some legitimate concerns." This vein of criticism usually focused on Kerrey's "baffling" decision not to run for a second term as governor, and his "spacey" musings about such esoterica as "sacred places" or "the limitless." Weisberg wondered if Kerrey wasn't too much of a dreamer to last in the gray world of policymaking. "He might simply walk away again if it all becomes too 'unreal,' " he wrote.

When Hoagland said he wanted to stay in office for the long haul, earning seniority and clout that would benefit Nebraskans, you believed him. His whole life long, he'd patiently positioned himself to be where he was now. Meanwhile, Kerrey admitted that his mind wandered. "I look out this window and see how nice it is out there today," the *World-Herald* quoted him as saying a few months into his Senate term, "and I wish I was doing something else."

But part of the sniping Kerrey got from the Washington "big-think" crowd seemed tinged with resentment, no doubt because of the speed of his sprouting into "presidential timber." Kerrey's constituents probably wouldn't be disappointed to learn that he might not want to spend the rest of his life in Washington. They also might appreciate his not taking ten years becoming an "expert" before addressing a problem.

The two freshmen from Nebraska weren't close personal friends. But Kerrey had nothing but praise for Hoagland, the man many believed had ridden his coattails to Washington. "He's an excellent politician," Kerrey said, adding that he meant that as praise. "He's interested in serving people who work for a living . . . he's thinking about teachers . . . families . . . the farmers out there, he knows who it is he represents."

Shortly after Kerrey spoke out on the flag, House Majority Leader Dick Gephardt asked Hoagland to accompany him across the Capitol to palaver with Nebraska's junior senator. Gephardt was shepherding anti-flag-burning legislation—as opposed to the more drastic constitutional amendment—to the floor of the House.

Gephardt wanted to persuade Kerrey to speak out in favor of the anti-flag-burning bill. It was going to pass anyway. But Gephardt wanted the votes of flag-amendment supporters, to head off a later move in that direction. He thought Kerrey's unique position of moral leadership on the question would provide "cover" to wavering politicians whose hearts weren't really in the amendment drive.

Kerrey politely refused, according to Hoagland. He didn't support the bill, and didn't think anything needed to be done—

period. Kerrey thought his role was to continue sniping at the president, as he'd done in his floor remarks. "President Bush . . . did not offer words that calmed us and gave us assurance that the nation was not endangered," he said. "Instead of leading us, President Bush joined us."

In late July, the House Ways and Means Committee held a lavish, PAC-underwritten formal dinner party to celebrate its two hundredth anniversary. "Celebrating two hundred years of taxation," a press gallery wag remarked.

The tax-writing committee wasn't the only place where things were hopping. Congress was finally running flat out. Members were actually clocking in on the Hill five days a week! Everyone wanted to finish "pending business" in time to take the "traditional summer recess"—in other words, the entire month of August off.

Hoagland was still intensely lobbying for the Yanney amendment. He'd persuaded a pair of Democrats to speak for it, but no Republicans yet. And he was cautiously arming missiles, to return some of the fire he'd taken lately.

As usual in midsummer, Washington was steamier than a Turkish bath. Even in air-conditioned Longworth there was a certain soupiness. Hoagland sat at his desk in shirtsleeves, while behind him the smokestacks of the power plant fed the shimmering afternoon haze.

Hoagland, his brow thoughtfully creased, pored over a letter outlining a potential weapon for politicians wronged by sloppy or treacherous journalism. A lawyer had written it, after hearing Hoagland complain at a luncheon about the shabby treatment he'd received at the hands of the *Wall Street Journal.*

Hoagland believed the *Journal* had acted irresponsibly, if not downright maliciously, in misrepresenting his amendment and then refusing to print a retraction. The lawyer proposed introducing legislation, perhaps to be called "The Public Figure's Clear Your Name Act of 1989," to give people thus wronged modest relief. The law would set up a board to determine the truth or falsity of something purveyed in the press. If an item was found false, the organ in question would be required to retract it in print. Hoagland said the idea was "similar in spirit to the old Equal Time rule of the Federal Communications Commission."

Hoagland sent a copy of the letter to a lawyer friend to get his opinion. Whatever the proposal's eventual chances of enactment, the fact that Hoagland was pondering it was a telling peek at his mind-set in these dog days.

Hoagland also had a score to settle with the National Republican Campaign Committee. Its "attack memo" on his vote against random urine tests in the State Department didn't sit well. It was a cheap, sleazy gambit. The president himself was against the bill. So were thirty-four House Republicans. But no one tried to smear them.

Hoagland didn't think these foul campaign tactics had any place in governing the country. He and a few other Democrats who'd been NRCC targets planned to go straight to the top with their grievance. They drafted a strongly worded letter to the president and circulated it to other Democrats for their signatures.

Hoagland wanted to hold a press conference when all the signatures were in, to expose the Republicans' rank hypocrisy. After all, it was Bush who'd gushed about his "offered hand" of bipartisanship to the Democratic Congress. When Hoagland and his fellow victims reached out their hands to grasp George's, they were "slashed . . . ferociously," said the letter.

While the counterattack was being mounted, more incoming missiles hit. Back in Omaha, attempts were being made to implicate Hoagland in some sort of cover-up in the Franklin Credit Union scandal. A former Franklin teller, Edward Hobbs, said he handed Hoagland a memo in 1984 about "embezzlement, homosexual activity and favoritism" at the credit union. Hoagland, a state senator at the time, recalled seeing Hobbs in his law office, but nothing about any memo. Hobbs "presented us with a rather bizarre story," Hoagland said, "I didn't give it a whole lot of credibility." Hoagland did call the state banking commissioner and sent Hobbs to see him.

Now Nebraska State Senator Ernie Chambers, the fire-tongued voice of black Omaha, wondered why Hoagland had withheld this information from his own investigating committee. "You loudly injected yourself into the [Franklin] matter with great noise, bombast and fanfare," Chambers wrote in a letter to Hoagland and the news media. "Yet, curiously, you never breathed a word about your direct knowledge of the memo."

Hoagland hadn't thought it necessary to tell the committee of Hobbs's "trivial" visit. In any case, he believed he'd "done everything I should have done" in 1984 by contacting the banking commissioner.

Jim dismissed Chambers's charges as "a three-day story."

16

A RISING STAR

B ack at the House-Senate conference on the S&L bill in Rayburn 2128, normalcy had returned. House conferees were
once again seated in their ascending tiers. The Senators were
camped at the witness table below them. When the day began,
Gonzalez assured the senators that the new seating arrangement
was not meant to exalt House members. "But we've always exalted you," said a grinning Don Riegle, chairman of the Senate
detachment.

Not many laughed. The long, punishing days of fine-print
haggling had left conferees on both sides rheumy-eyed and listless.
Gonzalez's plan to let a hundred flowers bloom hadn't panned out.
The senators weren't crazy about working in "subconferences"
with House members traipsing in and out as their topics came up.
Days before, the Senate had come to the House with a package
deal that covered most of the issues dividing them.

The prickly Gonzalez was angry at first. The Senate, after all,
had written its bill in closed meetings, unlike the wide-open "free-

for-all" in the House Banking Committee. Now the senators had
cobbled together a compromise package in private too. Gonzalez
believed legislating "in the dark" bred shady deals. He spoke of
the senators as if they belonged to a species of bats. "Here, for the
first time, they are in the glaring spotlight," he said, according to
an account in *Congressional Quarterly*, ". . . and they're unaccus-
tomed to it."

Perhaps Gonzalez had reason to be wary of these particular
senators. Two of them, Democrats Alan Cranston of California
and Don Riegle of Michigan, would become notorious as part of
the "Keating Five," a group of senators who pressured regulators
in San Francisco to lay off Charles Keating's Lincoln Savings and
Loan, despite evidence of flagrant criminal behavior. That affair
was not yet widely publicized, but it was common knowledge in
this room. Meanwhile, another member of the Senate delegation,
Republican Jake Garn of Utah, was a principal author of S&L deregulation in the early eighties.

But Gonzalez mellowed after studying the Senate's offer
overnight. It was a sweet deal for the House. The senators bought
the tougher capital standards in the House bill, made them even
stiffer, in fact. And they swallowed most of the low-income-hous-
ing and consumer provisions that Gonzalez cared so much about.

Gonzalez agreed to abandon the unruly subconference approach and draft a counteroffer. Two sticky issues were left to be
resolved. The House had put the bond sale that would fund the
bailout "on-budget." The Senate, like the president, wanted it
"off-budget." Meanwhile, the Senate contingent had new plans for
FSLIC chief M. Danny Wall, whose dubious testimony about the
S&L crisis leading up to the '88 elections had earned him the
nickname M. Danny Isuzu among some federal bureaucrats. The
senators wanted Wall to run the new thrift oversight agency. But
they didn't want him sweating out public confirmation hearings in
the Senate, as the House was demanding.

The House finally dropped its demand that Wall be confirmed
by the Senate. The next day, the senators accepted the House's on-
budget plan when Cranston switched his vote. Gonzalez said no
"deal" had been struck, but he believed the House's switch on
Wall had been necessary to move Cranston.

It was clear that the senators' top priority was to keep the
spotlight of a public confirmation hearing off of Danny Wall,

where "the subject of Keating would certainly be brought up," according to a *New York Times* article on the conference.

When Danny Wall was named Federal Home Loan Bank Board chairman to replace Ed Gray, he went the Keating Five senators one better. Instead of merely pressuring San Francisco regulators to lay off Lincoln, he actually took them off the case and transferred it to FHLBB's Washington bureau. No further action was taken against Lincoln until it went bust and was a $2 billion liability for the taxpayer.

Danny Wall had another thing going for him. He had once been on Garn's staff, and was married to one of the senator's current employees. No wonder the man accused of covering up the biggest financial disaster in history seemed to have the safest job in Washington.

Near the fag end of the conference, Hoagland was ready to storm the barricades one last time to get the Yanney amendment into the S&L bill, and save his good name in the doing. "Chairman Riegle, Chairman Gonzalez, and conferees," he said creamily, "I would like to take a minute or two to speak to you about an amendment on cross liability."

It was a weary, walleyed crew of conferees that listened to Hoagland's presentation. Compared to them, he was looking quite fresh, in his seldom-seen beige suit and brown striped tie. With a little luck, he might sneak this amendment through without anyone noticing how problematic it was.

Hoagland really had no business offering his amendment again. It had been stripped from the bill along with the other "special interest" provisions listed in Leach's motion to recommit. Besides the procedural problem, Hoagland was taking no small risk reintroducing the measure. The press might easily paint him again as a shameless tool of the rich. But he believed the amendment was "good public policy," and he aimed to prove it.

Looking across at the fading senators, Hoagland made his case. "In my opinion," he said, the amendment "is not a special interest provision." Although it applied only to "a limited number of institutions," that, said Hoagland, was "not necessarily bad."

Hoagland pointed out that the thousands of investors in Yanney's two funds had no common link other than Yanney himself, whose company owned a mere 1 percent equity interest in each fund (and a slightly larger management interest). "It is simply unfair," he said, to ask the investors in one fund to be liable for the investments of the other, as the Bush bill would do. Besides, the funds were pumping over $400 million in private capital into the S&L salvage effort, which was clearly in the public interest.

When Hoagland was finished, Shumer and Frank, both in shirtsleeves and looking like players at an all-night card game, spoke up for the amendment. So far, so good. It looked as if the thing might just sail through.

But not so fast.

Jim Leach, Hoagland's old friend, but the enemy of "special interests," had reserved a "point of order." During Hoagland's remarks, Nancy had propped up a chart to help clarify the amendment. "I have no charts," Leach now proclaimed, "but I do have righteous indignation."

Leach's voice could get downright shrill when raised—as it was now. "First of all," he began, this amendment was thrashed on the House floor, along with all the others of its kind. After that, it was only in the Senate bill, which meant "they have the right to bring it to us, we do not have the right to bring it to them."

Leach also noted that the amendment was now different, which was true. In order to avoid the "special interest" stigma, Hoagland had recast it to apply to *all* limited partnerships that had filed—or might yet file—to buy an S&L prior to the date the law took effect. Leach thought the new approach was, frankly, "nuts!" "Anybody you know, good guy, bad guy, crook . . . can go and make an application," Leach wailed, "and . . . it is automatically approved."

Soon Schumer, Frank, and Gonzalez were haggling with one another and with Leach. Meanwhile, Hoagland, turning his head from side to side to watch them, looked like an umpire at Wimbledon.

Leach might have been a scold, but he was a constructive one. He wasn't out to thrash Hoagland's amendment again, merely to make his friend accept a substitute that applied less broadly. That was fine with Hoagland. But now he had other problems. Leach's keening had waked up the Senate.

Senator Paul Sarbanes, speaking slowly, like one newly risen from a nap, interrupted the hassling House members. "I am not clear on the procedure that is now being followed," he said.

Thanks to Leach, Sarbanes now understood that "there is no provision in the House bill on this subject." That didn't sit well with him. Did it mean that any member now could "free-float" amendments? If so, Sarbanes saw "a hole opening up . . . the possibilities on that are enormous." The meaning of Sarbanes's veiled threat was clear enough. The House and Senate had struck a deal. If the House was now going to start asking for new amendments, a "hole" would open up in the deal, and things just might leak out.

Now just about everyone agreed that the House had gotten the better of the Senate in the bargaining to this point. And Gonzalez was not about to let the deal on the biggest bill of the year come apart over Hoagland's little amendment. "The senator from Maryland is quite correct," Gonzalez said wearily. He was ready to rule on Leach's objections. In this context, that could only spell death for Hoagland. But before the gavel fell, Frank intervened.

It was okay for the House to offer this amendment, Frank argued. It was merely a "compromise" on an amendment that was already in the Senate bill, just like all the compromises offered by the Senate about things in the House bill. While everyone was digesting Frank's new argument, Leach abruptly, and adroitly, withdrew his "point of order," so Gonzalez couldn't kill the amendment by ruling on it. In the meantime, he and Hoagland had hammered out a new version. Hoagland spoke up for it. The conference should "just adopt it and get on with it" he said, punctuating his remarks with a nervous smile.

But now Riegle wavered. He thought the amendment might still be too general, might apply to things and persons unknown. The weary Gonzalez had heard enough. Looking like a man battling to stay conscious, with eyes like slits in a grapefruit, he asked Hoagland, "for the sake of making progress," to please withdraw his amendment.

Hoagland saw his prize slipping away. He couldn't very well refuse his chairman. Even if he did, the amendment would never pass over Gonzalez's objection. But before Hoagland could say anything, Barney Frank again galloped to his defense, asking Gonzalez to "slightly amend" his request and let Hoagland withdraw now but bring his measure back later with improvements.

When Frank was finished, Senator Garn pleaded in Hoagland's behalf. "Don't cut him off," he implored. "Work something out to keep that four hundred million bucks" in private capital. Apparently, lobbying the Senate was paying dividends.

These appeals appeared to soften Gonzalez. It now seemed to him that the amendment fell into the jurisdiction of the conference after all, since it *was* in the Senate bill, as Frank said. And Riegle now seemed agreeable to just sleeping on it, and letting Hoagland come back in the morning with a redrawn proposal.

But nothing is easy when a bunch of tired lawyers get together. Sarbanes grabbed the mike on his side again. Hoagland's proposal "may have a lot of merit," he said, but it was the *procedure* that irked him. Maybe the amendment *had* been in the Senate bill at one time, but "we scrubbed it out." Now the House wanted to bring it back from the dead. Well, there were a lot of other dead issues littering the conference-room floor. This amendment might be "the open door" to bring them back too.

Gonzalez knew exactly what that meant. It was the old "hole in the deal" problem. He asked Hoagland a second time to withdraw his amendment.

Hoagland wore the doomed look of an animal trapped on the highway with the headlights bearing down. If no one else leaped to his aid, he would surely have to withdraw. All that hard work up in smoke. The slings and arrows of the *Wall Street Journal* suffered for naught.

But an unusual thing happened. The late Senator John Heinz of Pennsylvania, the young millionaire ketchup potentate, broke ranks with Sarbanes. "I am not sure that Senator Sarbanes speaks for the Senate side," he said. Delegations of conferees normally hang together like bloods. But Heinz was known to lack the common touch, so his remarks probably didn't surprise his fellow senators. Still, Sarbanes didn't say any more about "holes." And now Riegle suggested that maybe, just this once, they would allow the House to present the amendment to the Senate, which would then study it and offer it back to the House.

This "simple" solution was finally agreed to. The House delegation approved the amendment on a voice vote. Then it was sent across the room to the Senate, where it was to be taken up the following morning and, it was warmly hoped, passed with dispatch.

Phew!

* * *

But next morning, the septuagenarian Banking Committee chairman didn't appear to have slept well. Or perhaps he had slept too well, because he was in a fighting mood. When Riegle brought up Hoagland's amendment, expressing the hope that it could be dealt with "in a minute or two," Gonzalez balked.

After all the haggling of the day before, Gonzalez went right back to square one. He said Hoagland's amendment "poses a real dilemma." He was talking—again—about how Leach's motion had killed it. Everyone else in the room had assumed that problem was settled. But Gonzalez didn't think it was fair to make exceptions for Hoagland.

But maybe Gonzalez wasn't really out for fairness here. Maybe he was really hunting other game, namely, the special interest scold from Iowa. As Gonzalez spoke on, it became clear that he was powerfully miffed with Leach. What, he wondered, would happen to "the other hapless authors" of special interest amendments who weren't able to reach Mr. Leach for his "imprimatur"?

Gonzalez hadn't liked Leach's special-interest-killer amendment to begin with. On the floor, he'd argued against it, because it meant that "any provision that affects a narrow group is bad, no matter what, no matter why. . . . the motion gives me no way to distinguish between them." Now that he'd been proved right and distinctions were obviously desirable, *Leach* was the one making them.

Leach had set himself up as the Saint of the Savings and Loan Bailout, damning "special interests," then handing out blessings to poor supplicants like Hoagland—at least, that's how Gonzalez seemed to view things. He wanted Leach to be consistent with his own motion to recommit. Either special interest amendments "are all children of God," he sneered, or none are.

Leach was one of the more articulate members of Congress. But he was practically sputtering now. "I have done my very best, sir," he railed, "not to attempt to claim any sort of presumpting [sic] of authority."

Hoagland felt as if his amendment were a mouse caught between two clawing cats. He looked to the Senate side for aid. "Perhaps it would be helpful," he said evenly, a voice of calm in a sea of strife, "to remind all of us that yesterday the House ap-

proved this amendment and tendered it to the Senate." And now
the Senate was sending it back to the House. Remember.

But that wasn't going to work. Riegle said he would not "pre-
sume" to interfere with an "unresolved parliamentary issue" on
the House side. In other words, *you boys fight it out.*

A member of Congress knows he's in trouble when his colleagues start talking about how much "respect" they have for him.
It's the perfume on the dagger. Frank Annunzio, Hoagland's subcommittee chairman, spritzed some of it now. He was still smart-
ing from his loss on capital standards. Hoagland had been one of
the votes against him. "Now I have a lot of respect for you,"
Annunzio said to Hoagland, "but . . . I think you should withdraw" the amendment.

Gonzalez appealed to Chalmers Wylie, the conservative Republican with the wild pompadour. On the night the bill passed,
after the vote on Leach's motion, Wylie had followed with another
motion that also passed. It instructed House conferees not to accept any special interest amendments *from the Senate.* Didn't that
mean the House side could not now accept Hoagland's amendment from the Senate side—even if it wanted to?

"Technically, you are correct," said the fastidious Wylie. But
he agreed with Leach that the changes in Hoagland's amendment
had cured it. Gonzalez still wasn't satisfied. He told the conference
to proceed to other matters, while House members straightened
out the Hoagland mess among themselves.

The amendment wasn't dead yet, but it was in a deep coma.
Hoagland took no chances. Having exhausted reason and argument, he decided to resort to more direct means: begging. Hoagland sat down and wrote a note to his aged and cantankerous
chairman. According to him, this is what it said:

> Chairman Gonzalez
> I really need this amendment.
> I won my race by only 3,000 votes.

Whether it was the note, or the nod from Wylie, or the fact
that, in the interim, the Senate moved another "cured" special
interest measure to the House, Gonzalez now blessed Hoagland's
amendment. "If the conferees on your side wish to offer the
Hoagland reply," Gonzalez said shortly after reading the note,
"we'll entertain it." The amendment now passed easily and be-

came part of the bill. Meanwhile, Mike Yanney's lobbying bill from Kutak, Rock & Campbell was mounting. It would top $99,000 by year's end, according to a report filed with the Clerk of the House.

Robert Garsson, a reporter for *American Banker,* was impressed with Hoagland's handling of the Yanney matter. Garsson wrote a story about the freshman, which appeared in the August 8 issue of his magazine, under the headline HOAGLAND'S STYLE WINS POINTS IN HOUSE.

The article, which did not mention Hoagland's last-minute prostration before Gonzalez, called him a "Rising Star" of the freshman class, and quoted some of his committee colleagues singing his praises. "He's soft-spoken, but a strong contributor," said Paul Kanjorski. "He's straight as an arrow and does his homework," said Henry Gonzalez.

The article noted that Hoagland had "few preconceived notions" about issues important to the banking community—the magazine's prime audience—like loan write-downs to Third World countries, or the coming fight over bank deregulation. That was understandable for a freshman and the way our system works it probably wouldn't hurt his chances to get contributions from the banking industry. His having opinions on such matters, even ones that favored banks, might make them less prone to try to influence him with their cash.

But the article had a wider audience than the pinstripe set. The *World-Herald* featured a slightly abridged version of it prominently on its editorial page, under the heading HOAGLAND CALLED "RISING STAR"—"HE DOES HIS HOMEWORK."

17

I'M NOT FAMOUS

All the elements were in place for a boffo "media event." A podium that wore the congressional seal was centered in front of a floor-to-ceiling window curtained in stately blue. An American flag drooped from a pole off to the right. Beside the podium, Congressman Peter Hoagland, also, of course, in blue, was flanked by three Democratic colleagues. Fully eighty-one House Democrats had signed the strongly worded letter to the president of the United States that would be delivered to him, and the media, today:

Dear Mr. President:

We are a group of Democrats who have taken seriously your call for a bipartisan, rational consideration of issues on their merits. We agree that the most difficult and potentially divisive questions that face our nation can be solved only through this approach.

Today, attacks by certain members of your party

have compromised our willingness to continue voting for
positions urged upon us by your administration. . . .

 . . . Fifty years from now, the cleverness of Mr.
[Ed] Rollins . . . will be of no consequence. . . .
What will matter is what you have done and what we
have done to augment the vitality of our nation. . . .

 To pursue your agenda you need our votes. . . .
we need your . . . assurance that when we vote with
you on difficult issues . . . we will not find that bipartisan spirit so shamelessly betrayed. . . .

Almost a third of the Democratic caucus signed on to this
single-spaced, two-page reply. But the media didn't seem to
care—at least, not the right media. Sure, there were ten print
reporters sprinkled around the room. But none from any of the
big papers (one was from *Rollcall*). As for television crews, there
was but one, a hayseed outfit from "someplace in the Northwest,"
said Gail.

But the congressmen—Ben Jones, Richard Stallings, Bill
Richardson, and Hoagland—went gamely through the motions.
Hoagland spoke in his usual monotone. "I don't feel I should
have to pay a political price" for supporting the president, he
said.

Jones, also a freshman, had been an actor ("Cooder" on the
TV series *The Dukes of Hazzard*). He knew how to put some steam
into his pitch. "This is sleaze, this is garbage, this is obscene, and
this . . . is a lie," he railed, waving an NRCC press release sent to
his district, which charged that he supported "sexually explicit and
antireligious works of art." He had voted to fund that old smut
peddler the National Endowment for the Arts.

As the congressmen protested their shabby treatment at the
hands of Republican sleaze merchants and policy thugs, a passing
band of olive-uniformed Boy Scouts paused in the doorway to
gawk. If they sensed that unscoutsmanlike conduct was being discussed, they showed no sign. It was Jamboree Week, and scouts
from all over this land were swarming like locusts over Washington's tourist attractions. This one did not hold their interest for
long.

After opening statements were gotten off congressional
chests, questions were directed at Jones, Stallings, and Richardson.

But there were none for Hoagland, one of the instigators of this counterstrike, who slouched meekly to one side, his blue suit seeming to melt into the stately curtains.

"What a flop," Hoagland groused as he emerged from the press conference, squinting in the midday sun. "That was a major screwup." Hoagland regretted that his staff hadn't booked the studio in the House Press Gallery for the event. But perhaps it wasn't too late. He decided to round up the other participants and simply move the event to where the media were. All but Jones went along for take two. He seemed to have gotten his fill of "exposure" for one afternoon. But the lure of the Press Gallery was not something Hoagland could easily resist. "There's always a row of cameras waiting to film anyone who comes in," he said, as the entourage hurried across Independence Avenue to the Capitol. "CNN is always there, they'll carry it."

But congressmen are not like presidents, who, by simply holding a press conference, can fill a room with eager lapdogs ready to scarf up their every pose. As with most things in life, these lawmakers were learning by doing. When they got to the House studio, they were informed, politely, blushingly, that they couldn't simply *hold* a press conference there, but had to be *invited* to appear by the reporters. Talk about the tyranny of the Fourth Estate!

Hoagland, a little embarrassed, settled for a tour of the radio and TV section of the House Press Gallery, from the woman who ran the place. Her plush office, with its expansive view of the Mall and the Washington Monument, made his look like a broom closet. "I always worry when members see my office," she said. She worried they would want it for themselves.

The boxy little studio, where members are invited to meet the cameras, consists of little more than a podium and rows of stainless-steel chairs for reporters. There are no windows, only banks of bright lights. And the place is swathed with carpeting and padding and otherwise soundproofed.

Behind the podium is a bookshelf/backdrop decorated with designer "books." They are actual books sawed-off, with only the spines, plus an inch or two, remaining. Among the titles, before which our leaders address the nation, are *Bartlett's Familiar Quotations* and *The Hydro Electric Handbook*.

* * *

Later in the day, Hoagland slumped in his office chair, looking bone-weary, as he so often did. He was reassessing his job again. "I've gotta start thinking about getting on another committee," he blurted out of nowhere. "Maybe Foreign Affairs." At Stanford he had been an International Affairs major.

Hoagland suddenly felt there was no future on Banking. Too many members had too much seniority. But something else seemed to be troubling him. Discussing his disappointment with the committee, he said, again out of the blue, "I didn't come to Congress to help Mike Yanney with his problems."

It wasn't just the committee that was getting Hoagland down. He didn't particularly like being a freshman. "Too much running around," he said. He was looking forward to being a sophomore, though it was hard to see how things would change very much.

A few days after the press conference "flop," Hoagland was again disappointed by the media. He had an interview scheduled in his office with a *New York Times* reporter. Hoagland waited nearly an hour, but the reporter didn't show up. He'd forgotten about Hoagland and had been interviewing Senator Cranston instead.

The White House held its annual Congressional Barbecue on the evening of August 1. The timing didn't sit well with some. That was also the night of the annual congressional baseball game, a contest taken very seriously by those involved, some of whom were in training weeks beforehand. Naturally, the mode was *hardball.* Professional umpires were hired. The commissioner of baseball threw the first pitch. Republicans routed Democrats 8–2, for their second straight win. They rubbed it in by displaying the trophy on the minority leader's table the whole next day.

Meanwhile, there was still a respectable massing of congressfolk at the White House for George Bush's Tex-Mex barbecue, which featured the rambunctious sounds of the Oak Ridge Boys.

Hoagland was a good tennis player—he'd lettered in the sport in high school—but wasn't among the obsessive jocks of Congress. He and Barbara opted for the barbecue instead of the ball game. Picnic tables covered with gingham were set up on the huge south lawn of the White House. Nearby were grandstands stuffed with journalists, snapping pictures and taking notes. Having an army of reporters ogling you through dinner "felt sort of weird," said Hoagland.

When Hoagland got his few seconds on the receiving line with the Chief, he didn't bring up his recent letter. After all, this was a social occasion. But Hoagland asked the president if he wouldn't consider phoning the mother of a young Omaha man, Dan Hotz, recently murdered in Washington. Mrs. Hotz had called the White House in the hopes of speaking to the president about "the social problems that afflict Washington and all U.S. cities," according to the *World-Herald.* She left a message for the president, which he naturally never saw. But now, at the request of her congressman, Bush called Mrs. Hotz that very evening after the barbecue and they chatted for around ten minutes. "He was very nice," said Mrs. Hotz, according to the *World-Herald.* Naturally, this was big news in Omaha, and Hoagland was in the spotlight again. "The call was a result of efforts by Rep. Peter Hoagland . . ." read the second paragraph in a page-one *World-Herald* story.

The next day, Hoagland got one of Bush's famous handwritten notes in the mail thanking him for "calling this to my attention." Bush sent about two hundred such notes a week. But somehow he never saw fit to reply to the letter from eighty-one House members about sleazy Republican campaign tactics.

A few days after the White House barbecue, Barbara Hoagland made one of her rare visits to her husband's office. Memories of arriving at the president's house and being gawked at by the crowd on the avenue were still fresh. "You see all these tourists lined up outside waving at you and taking pictures and it's rude not to wave back," she said. "But you feel like saying, 'Hey, I'm not famous.' "

On August 3, the S&L bailout bill was only a couple of steps away from final passage. Members were anxious to get it over with so they could adjourn for the August recess. The House was debating the conference report, the compromise version of the bill hammered out by the House-Senate conference committee. It was expected to pass, but there were still speed bumps in the road ahead.

The president threatened to veto the bill if it passed with the on-budget financing plan agreed to in the conference. Meanwhile, a group of forty-one mostly Republican senators had written a letter to the House, announcing they would vote against the bill. That was more bad news for supporters of the on-budget plan. In the Senate, sixty votes were needed to pass any measure that exceeded Gramm-Rudman spending limits, which this bill did, because of the on-budget financing. Ironically, if the funding plan were put back off-budget, more money would be spent, but because the money wouldn't be counted in the budget, Gramm-Rudman's fiscal "discipline" wouldn't be violated. At least, that's what the president and congressional Republicans were calling "discipline."

Compared to the overall $300-billion-plus cost of the bill, the difference between the off-budget and on-budget plans was relatively slight—$5 billion over thirty years. LaFalce's pay-as-you-go approach, on the other hand, could have saved hundreds of billions, and would not have violated Gramm-Rudman limits, since new spending would have been matched with new revenue, not paid for with costly long-term bonds. But few wanted to fight that battle.

House Democrats thought the president's insistence on his off-budget scheme was unreasonable, and based on cheap political calculations, especially since he'd gotten everything else he'd wanted in the bill, and then some. "The president of the United States has the constitutional right to act like a spoiled brat," Barney Frank carped during floor debates on the conference report, "but we're under no obligation to indulge him." (The word "brat" in Frank's remarks was changed to "child" by censors of the *Congressional Record*).

The conference report passed the House, 221–199, mostly on Democratic votes. Many Republicans who'd voted for the bill before the conference now voted against it to protest the on-budget plan, at the president's request.

Hoagland voted for the bill, as he had right along in committee. He believed it was a good, tough law that absolutely had to pass. But depending on what the Senate did, it was far from clear that he had voted his last on the issue. The subject was plainly on his mind.

Shortly after the House adjourned to await Senate action on the conference report, Hoagland stood in his outer office, musing on the philosophy of voting. "The safest thing to do is to vote against a bill that passes, or vote for a bill that fails," he said matter-of-factly.

In this case, Hoagland explained, voting against the bill, should it pass, was "very safe." For one thing, the bill was creating, in the RTC, an asset clearinghouse the size and scope of which the world had never seen. So many assets changing hands under government supervision seemed certain to breed scandal. Those members voting for the bill risked being associated with that. Besides, the bailout was among the most expensive measures ever considered in Congress. When *that* sank in, people would be hunting scalps. A no vote on the basis of cost alone was safer.

So voting no on the bill, if it passed, was hard to beat from an individual standpoint. The bill would begin addressing the problems, and you'd be off the hook for any unpleasant by-products or political pain.

On the other hand, if the bill failed, and you voted for it, that was almost as good. You could claim "it was a grave problem, and I tried my best," Hoagland said. But since it had failed, you wouldn't be on the hook for any problems it might have created.

If the Senate passed the conference report, Hoagland would be on record as having voted for a controversial bill that became law, a vote that might be unearthed later by a political opponent and used against him. But if the Senate defeated the bill because of the on-budget financing plan, which seemed likely, it would come back to the House after another conference, and Hoagland would have to think this vote through one more time.

At 5:30 P.M., Jim and Gary sat Hoagland down to plan his upcoming special town hall meeting on the drug problem. They'd been trying to discuss it with him for days, but conference committee sessions and other appointments got in the way. Now they had Hoagland cornered, weary though he was, slouched deep in his chair, peering from red-streaked eyes. Earlier, out of his aides' earshot, he'd complained, "I just want to sleep."

The idea behind the special town hall meeting was to gather experts together to "educate Omaha citizens on the drug problem," Hoagland said. But Topic A this afternoon was, as usual, "coverage." The meeting was to be held on a Sunday evening. "It should be a fairly dead weekend," Jim said. That meant Hoagland's event would be featured on the local news Sunday. Gary pointed out that it would probably get airtime the following day too, since Sunday stories were often repeated on Monday. So they were looking at two days' worth of "free media" for one event.

Besides, the whole two-hour-long affair was to be broadcast live on local television.

The plan was to empanel a group of experts from local and federal agencies that dealt with the issue. Each would make a brief statement. Then the audience would generate concerns and questions, the experts would generate expertise, and Hoagland would moderate. But Jim and Gary wanted to add a slight twist. They had visions of Hoagland roving out among the audience, microphone in hand, Phil Donahue–style, taking questions and pitching them back to the experts on the panel.

Hoagland was hardly one for histrionics. Frowning, he squirmed in his chair. Ever sensitive to his boss's moods, Jim tried to reassure him. "It's basically what you do in a town hall meeting anyway," he pleaded, "but it gets you out from behind the podium."

Hoagland wasn't buying it. He wanted Jim and Gary to consult with one or two members who had experience with drug meetings, before their planning went too far. "I'd hate to see us reinvent the wheel," he said. Jim and Gary stiffened. They didn't appreciate Hoagland's attitude. They felt he should trust their judgment. "Jim and I have been planning these events for years," Gary said later.

But Gary leaned over to the telephone and punched up the number of Charles Rangel, the representative from Harlem, a place that had its share of problems with drugs. Rangel, a stout, dapper black man with a raspy voice, often appeared on television to discuss the issue. Hoagland put him on the speakerphone.

Rangel said the topic was too complex to deal with in one meeting. "Unfortunately, most people focus on law enforcement," he said. Then Rangel remembered who he was talking to. "But Omaha . . ." he said incredulously, his gravel voice strained to a shrill rasp. "What kind of problems you got out there—crack?"

Hoagland smiled. "We've got the Crips and the Bloods," he said. Rangel, apparently suffering from the New Yorker's View of the World syndrome, sounded genuinely puzzled. "It must be in the urban part of your district," he said at last, "right?"

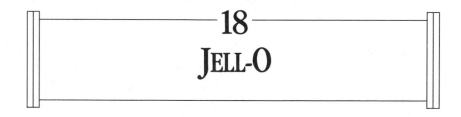

18

JELL-O

Hoagland stopped in the middle of the block-long hallway in Longworth. A row of windows ran from one end to the other, overlooking a gaping courtyard that seemed to ripple in the August heat. One of the windows was stuck open. Hoagland, grunting, struggled to close it. "The air conditioning is escaping like mad," he said.

Such things bothered Hoagland. He didn't like extravagance, and he hated waste. He always saved half-eaten sandwiches for later. He still drove his weather-beaten Toyota. And of course, there was his all-purpose basic blue suit.

So Hoagland was certainly alive to the magnificent wastage still going on in the nation's savings and loans. He understood how important the bill now emerging from Congress was in putting a stop to it. A lot of money was oozing from the fisc through insolvent S&Ls. Amounts were reckoned at anywhere from $20–$30 million a day to over $1 billion a month, depending on how much someone wanted to scare you. This bill was needed to close down those S&Ls and stop the hemorrhaging. Hoagland had often said, "The bill's gotta pass." But he was having doubts just now about whether or not his vote would help close that particular window.

As expected, the Senate defeated the conference report. Though fifty-four senators voted for it, that was still six short of the sixty votes needed for the exemption from Gramm-Rudman made necessary by the bill's on-budget funding plan.

So it was back to the conference committee late Thursday night, where a new compromise was worked out on funding. With OMB Director Richard Darman and Treasury Secretary Nicholas Brady looking on, the House and Senate split the difference. Of the $50 billion authorized by the bill, $20 billion would be on-budget, $30 billion off-budget. Darman and Brady assured the conferees that the president would go along with that.

But many House Democrats were unhappy. Of course Bush would accept that compromise. The $20 billion in so-called on-budget spending wouldn't hurt him politically at all. It would be spent in the *current* fiscal year. Since the Gramm-Rudman deficit-reduction "snapshot" for the current year—the comparison of actual spending with deficit-reduction targets—had already been done, there would be no painful cuts needed in other programs to compensate for the added spending. Meanwhile, the budget deficits for upcoming fiscal years, the ones that counted politically for Bush, would not show the impact of S&L spending. For those years it was still off-budget.

Bush had argued that the House's plan—to put the whole $50 billion on-budget and exempt it from Gramm-Rudman targets —was a "dodge" that undermined the deficit-reduction law's "fiscal discipline." But many Democrats saw the new compromise itself as just another trick. Backdating spending so that it wouldn't exceed the upcoming fiscal year's targets was one of the oldest gambits in the budget game. And the $30 billion in spending placed off-budget would not only "dodge" Gramm-Rudman, but would increase interest payments over the life of the bill by anywhere from $1.5–$20 billion, depending on whose figures you believed. What kind of "fiscal discipline" was that?

Many Democrats were convinced that those extra billions would be spent not out of concern for Gramm-Rudman "discipline," but to buy political cover for Bush. "Their lips say

'Gramm-Rudman,' " one Democrat reportedly quipped, "but their hearts say 'cop-out.' "

Opponents of this new compromise had a painful choice to make. If they voted against the bill, they risked seeing it defeated. But if ever-mounting losses in insolvent S&Ls weren't stanched, those losses might soon even exceed the money that would be saved with an on-budget approach.

To prevent any such thing from happening, the leadership had promised to keep Congress in session until it produced a bill. So a vote against the conference agreement was a vote for delaying the "sacrosanct" August recess. That was serious business.

By Friday evening, Capitol Hill was a ghost town. Hallways were deserted, parking lots nearly so. Congress was still in session, but it looked as if most people had already gone home.

The Senate was particularly depopulated. It was said that seventy senators—maybe more—had already left town for the August recess. But the Senate had yet to vote on the new S&L conference report. Meanwhile, the House couldn't do anything until the Senate acted. At 6:30, Hoagland got a phone call from Nebraska's senior senator, Jim Exon, who happened still to be in Washington. "There's some kinda stallin' goin' on," Exon said of the syrupy pace.

Hoagland thought he had the situation sussed. He explained his theory to Exon. All day long, powerful Democratic committee chairmen had been lobbying to sink the bill, including Dan Rostenkowski of Ways and Means and Leon Panetta of Budget. They were angry about Bush's stubbornness regarding the off-budget plan, as were many Democrats, and even some Republicans.

The leadership was still in favor of the bill. So was the Banking Committee chairman, Henry Gonzalez, one of the architects of the new compromise. But Democrats were expected to defect in hordes, and the president had been told that Republican votes would be relied on to pass the bill.

Hoagland thought Senate leaders, in cooperation with the president, were executing a devious strategy, drawing out the evening as long as possible, in the hope that House Democrats, unwilling to cancel plane reservations, would simply leave to begin their vacations. That didn't sound so silly when one saw the wasting effect the delay had had on the Senate's population. If House members also melted away in sufficient numbers, it might be possible for the bill to carry with a majority of Republican votes.

"If the vote had been this morning, it would have gone down two to one," Hoagland purred into the receiver. "Now they're just fighting a war of attrition, trying to wear us down."

Hoagland had plane reservations for Sunday, so he could withstand a recess delay of another day or so. But he still wasn't sure how to vote. His heart told him to join the rebellion spreading among House Democrats. It was "infuriating," he fumed, that the president was "going to charge the taxpayers five billion dollars just to make himself look good."

Democrats like Hoagland had been voting with Bush right down the line on the tough issues, like capital standards. Meanwhile, Republicans had run from him. But now, on an issue that was important to Democrats, George Bush, Mr. Bipartisan, Mr. "Offered Hand," was suddenly getting all hairy-chested, threatening vetoes, and putting their recess in jeopardy, just to protect his precious image. "It's calculated," Hoagland complained to Exon of Bush's apparent ploy. "Cynical."

Worse yet, after all the help Democrats had given Bush, what *could* they expect in return for their votes tonight? "The Republicans are going to send press releases into my district a year from now," Hoagland predicted, "saying I supported a thousand dollars in taxes for every man, woman, and child because I supported this bill."

Gathered around the speakerphone with Hoagland were Jim, Gary, and Pedr Bartling, a summer intern from Omaha. It was Pedr's last day on the job, and he was waiting to go to an Orioles baseball game in Baltimore with Jim, along with a few others on staff who'd already left. But Jim, tuning in to Exon, was finding it hard to tear himself away. "I want you to know I'm going to publicly oppose this," Exon told Hoagland.

Exon read from the speech he would later give on the Senate floor, earning chuckles from Hoagland's retinue at the juicy bits. Referring to George "Read My Lips" Bush, Exon said in his Nebraska back-country drawl, "I am weary of reading lips that drip, if not with outright deceit, certainly with insincerity as far as fiscal responsibility is concerned."

Brave as those words sounded, this was not a night to make a nation proud of its Senate. As Congress considered final passage of

one of the most significant, most expensive pieces of legislation
ever to emerge from its mazy folkways, it now seemed clear that
barely two dozen senators remained in Washington. That was
enough to get up a decent game of touch football, but far short of
a quorum.

An agreement was reached among the distinguished senators
who stuck till the end. The bill's fate in the Senate would be sealed
on a voice vote, to avoid embarrassing the missing with a record of
their absence at this crucial juncture. House Democrats were already miffed with the Senate for not passing the on-budget plan.
Now senators wouldn't even stand up and be counted on the final
vote, leaving their colleagues in the House to go on the record
and take all the heat.

House members tended to think of themselves as workhorses
and senators as showhorses, policy-hobbyists, wealthy windbags,
who left the serious work to the true legislators on the other side
of Capitol Hill. Times like these certainly didn't improve the reputation of the "other body." In a speech later that evening on the
House floor, Barney Frank compared the strength of the Senate's
character to Jell-O.

But House members were no more eager than senators to
have their fingerprints on this legislation. And despite the indignant bleatings of certain Democrats, some suspected that they
were simply using the on/off-budget issue as a convenient excuse
to "jump off" a bill they wanted nothing to do with.

There were, after all, some very good reasons to go along
with the latest compromise. To vote the bill down now would only
send it back to conference, where, as the August hourglass emp-
tied, the House would be under mounting pressure to save what
was left of its recess. In such a weak bargaining position, not only
might the funding fight be lost, but housing and consumer provisions, so prized by House Democrats and despised by Republicans, might go as well.

Hoagland was considering voting against the final version of
the S&L bill. He said it was because he opposed the administration's off-budget plan. But his statements about the plan were in-
consistent. Only a few days before, he'd told a reporter that "the
on-budget/off-budget issue is a tempest in a teapot." After the
defeat of the LaFalce amendment, which would have paid for the
bailout with little or no borrowing and saved perhaps hundreds of

billions in interest costs, the on-budget/off-budget issue did indeed seem like "a tempest in a teapot." Instead of the perhaps hundreds of billions of interest savings promised by the LaFalce plan, the on-budget approach would save only 1.5–20 billion at most. Supporters of the new compromise contended that it wasn't worth jeopardizing passage of the bailout bill to recoup those significant but much smaller extra costs, since the defeat of the bill would also add to the eventual price of the bailout, perhaps substantially.

The issue was difficult for Hoagland. He'd consistently voted against congressional budget resolutions because they seemed to him based on fiscal chicanery, something that didn't go down well in Nebraska, where the state government is required by law to maintain a balanced budget. The bill's "off-budget" accounting certainly looked like more of Washington's budgetary smoke and mirrors. On those grounds alone, Hoagland probably could have sold his vote back home politically. But there were institutional pressures at work. Many of his colleagues, including his committee chairman, believed the new compromise was the best that could be done, and that to defeat the bill for the sake of on-budget accounting alone risked running up the huge price of the bailout by even more money than such accounting might save. Hoagland himself felt that the bill simply had to pass. And he had a large personal investment in the legislation, which carried four of his own amendments.

During the hours before the new S&L conference report came to the House floor, Hoagland was still undecided as to how he would vote. He sought advice from every quarter.

Hoagland unwrapped a half-eaten tuna hoagie and spread it out in front of him. Then he dialed up his brother, Laurie, the St. Louis investment manager and "family genius." Peter told Laurie that while he was angry about the off-budget plan, he didn't want to miss the Big Picture, as one tended to do in Washington. And in the Big Picture, "the bill's gotta pass."

Laurie was sympathetic, but didn't think his brother should surrender principles. Dishonest budgeting was dishonest budgeting.

But there were some principles that an outsider couldn't see. Hoagland felt their tug. His committee colleague Barney Frank, recalling that Hoagland had four amendments in the bill, had urged him to resist the temptation to vote no, in the interest of maintaining good relations with their cantankerous chairman, if nothing else.

But Hoagland was getting conflicting advice from Banking Committee Democrats. Schumer was furious about the new conference deal and was definitely voting no. Meanwhile Vento, who'd been assigned to whip Hoagland on the bill, was practical. As far as the on-budget plan was concerned, "We just don't have the votes," he said. "You can't cause a train wreck over it." When Hoagland chuckled at that, Vento added, "I'm serious."

But Hoagland wasn't convinced that voting the bill down would cause a "train wreck." He thought it would simply mean going back to conference to "get it right." Laurie agreed, though he knew nothing of consumer and housing provisions that might be risked. "You'd be making a statement of principle that the budget deal stinks to you," he said. Before ringing off, Laurie relayed a personal message to his little brother. "I love when you call about these things," he said, "so don't hesitate."

Hoagland now seemed to have his mind made up. To cast a vote against budget chicanery was, he said, "what Nebraskans would want me to do." He lifted the tuna hoagie to his lips and tore off a decisive bite.

In any case, it looked as if the bill was going to pass. By Hoagland's own reckoning, that made a no vote quite safe. He got a current "whip count" from the office of Bruce Morrison, another Banking Committee Democrat: 130 Republicans were said to be voting for the bill. If that was true, only around ninety Democratic votes would be needed to make a majority, less if the House's numbers were depleted by early departures, which seemed likely. When the conference report passed the House only to die in the Senate, just thirty-nine Republicans had voted for it, with 182 Democrats. So it looked like the Republicans would save this bill for their president after all. But the word was they were "furious" at Bush. Well, who wasn't?

When House Republicans looked back over the past few days, they may have seen a stubborn president, protecting his own image at their expense. If Bush had only accepted the initial conference report—passed with mostly Democratic votes—Republicans would have been home free. When the whopping cost of the bailout hit home with Joe Six-pack and the bill was brought before the court of public opinion, it would have been covered with Democratic fingerprints. Republicans could have bludgeoned Democrats senseless with an issue like that.

Alas, that was not to be. Republicans were being forced to put themselves on the line to protect Bush, to keep the funding off-budget, so it wouldn't swell deficits on his watch. Now this hugest bailout in the history of the race was going to be *their* bailout.

The Orioles had long since taken the field in Baltimore. But Jim was still here, tickets peeking from his shirt pocket. Meanwhile, George Bush, the man whose stubbornness was detaining Jim, and an increasingly sulky Pedr, was at the ball game.

Jim had advised Hoagland to vote for the bill to protect his chummy relations with Gonzalez. But Hoagland wanted to vote no. He planned to submit a statement, for the record, explaining why. Jim now wanted him to descend to the well and make a speech besides, a *Mr. Smith*–style critique of Washington's budgetary flimflamming. Assuming a pose of wide-eyed, wounded piety, Jim demonstrated. "Back in Nebraska, where I come from, we do things differently," he said. In Nebraska, where the constitution requires a balanced budget, the government doesn't spend more than it takes in. "Why? Because it makes sense," Jim said, in tones of gentle remonstrance.

Jim wanted Hoagland to use his status as an untainted "newcomer" to deliver a sincere appeal to cynical Washington, direct from the virtuous heart of the country. Hoagland seemed to have nothing against this "shame on you" approach, but he wasn't sure he could reserve floor time. He assumed only the "big hitters" would get that. But he'd try. Meanwhile, Jim went to his keyboard and started banging out a draft. Gary did the same. Later, they'd combine the best of each. None of them ever dreamed their little speech would offend anyone. Why should it?

The Senate had a minor scare when the conference report finally reached the floor. According to an account in *Congressional Quarterly,* Senator Kent Conrad seemed ready to upset the well-laid plans for an anonymous voice vote. He made it known he wanted the roll to be called. Not only would that have been embarrassing, it might have changed the outcome. A dozen Democrats and five Republicans—on this night almost the whole Senate—said they would vote no if the roll was called.

Conrad reluctantly went along with the voice vote. But then another malcontent, Charles Grassley, demanded a vote by "division," which meant those in favor of the bill would indicate that by standing. Their names wouldn't appear in the record. All they had to do was stand and be counted. But requiring even this negligible degree of public commitment made passing the bill harder. At first, with only eleven senators on the floor, the vote went *against* the bill, 7–4. Then someone hastily objected that a quorum was not present, nullifying the vote. After ten more Senators were rounded up, the bill passed on the second standing vote, 17–4. Some of its earlier opponents were apparently swept up in the new "groundswell" of support. To the Senate's great relief, no one objected that a quorum wasn't present for the second vote. They might have stayed through August looking for one.

As Hoagland sat back and watched the Senate on C-Span, he was struck by the number of staffers orbiting the few senators present. "Look at all those staff!" he marveled.

"Yeah," said Gary, "they've all got fifteen people working for them."

Hoagland was half watching, half going over his brief speech, both versions, blending, crossing out, scribbling in, eliminating the scolding tone, which just wasn't him. "No wonder they can make those long speeches," he said, looking up. "Fifteen pages here, twenty pages there."

Around 9:30, the whip phone—the direct line to the Democratic whip's office—rang. The House would reconvene at 10:08, a prerecorded voice said. Apparently the whip's office did not believe in rounding off.

Hoagland was in no hurry to get to the floor. He knew Gonzalez would be waiting to lobby him. How could he refuse the old man, after going down on his knees to him in the conference?

While Jim typed up the final draft, Hoagland called the staff at Ways and Means—whose chairman was managing opposition to the bill—to book floor time. At around 10:00, they strolled over to the Capitol, while Gary stayed behind to fax a copy of the speech to Dave Beeder, the *World-Herald*'s beat reporter. Beeder was probably home this Friday night getting set to watch the House on C-Span, Hoagland surmised.

Hoagland, tubed speech in hand, crossed the avenue with Jim, swimming in the heavy jungle heat. Spotlights caromed off the Capitol dome and streaked the muzzy air. Hoagland still wasn't quite sure about all this. "Do you think I'm gonna alienate Gonzalez?" he asked Jim.

"Sometimes," Jim said with a sigh, "you just gotta do what you think is right."

Hoagland shook his head, recalling what his friend Rep. John Spratt had told him earlier in the day. "It can't hurt—sometimes—to show a little independence," he said. "On the other hand . . ." Hoagland smiled. "In this business," he said, "for every 'on the one hand' there's always an 'on the other hand.' "

There were a lot of empty seats in the House chamber when it reconvened at 10:21. But the rate of attrition wasn't quite so high as in the Senate. Fifty members had gone home, leaving 385, instead of the usual 435. So the majority needed to pass the bill was down from 218 to 193. That would make it easier for Republicans, with a minimum of Democratic help, to get it done.

Shortly after Foley called the House to order, a messenger holding a foot-high pile of papers appeared at the back of the center aisle. "Mr. Speaker," his escort announced, "a message from the Senate." The messenger proceeded down the aisle and deposited the pile at the speaker's rostrum.

Members on both sides were clustered in small, talkative groups as Gonzalez read a letter from the president to open the debate. Hoagland stood among a particularly boisterous bunch of Democrats in the well. As Gonzalez was speaking, they erupted in loud laughter. "Mr. Speaker," Gonzalez objected sharply, "I ask for order. This isn't a laughing matter. I'm reading a letter from the president of the United States."

Hoagland seemed to avoid Gonzalez when he came to the floor. He showed his speech to other Democrats in opposition, soliciting a few comments and scrawled changes.

The president's letter endorsed the new conference agreement. Gonzalez did too, reluctantly, because "we must have a bill." He'd favored the on-budget plan too, but now thought the time for fighting had passed.

Chalmers Wylie was also on board. "It is always easier to vote no," he said. "I have done that a lot of times myself. But I truly believe that a responsible vote tonight is an aye vote." Frank Annunzio called the on-budget plan a "lost cause," and urged a vote for the bill too.

So the highest-ranking members of the Banking Committee all came down in favor of the conference agreement. Rostenkowski, leader of the opposition, made no opening speech but yielded first to Moody of Wisconsin. Was the House going to pass this measure simply "because we want to get out of here?" asked an incredulous Moody. "What kind of crazy priorities are we setting for ourselves? . . . What kind of discipline are we instilling here?"

After Moody had, appropriately enough, set the mood for the dissenters, Rostenkowski made a point of mentioning that his next speaker was "a member of the Committee on Banking, Finance, and Urban Affairs." He would be the first from that panel to speak in opposition, the gentleman from Nebraska, Mr. Hoagland.

Members from "marginal," highly competitive districts, like Hoagland, are normally given a lot of slack on controversial votes, especially when they are freshmen. If duty to party or country calls, the leadership usually looks the other way when such members cast what might be perceived as a safe vote. That's not to say Hoagland didn't believe in what he was doing. But if he'd quietly voted no, it's likely that no one would have found fault with him. But to *speak* against the bill, to rise and openly oppose his chairman, well, that was another matter. Gonzalez was livid, according to a source close to him.

"Mr. Speaker," said Hoagland, in a low, quavering voice, "I'm the first to acknowledge that I am new to this body. I have only been here for a little over seven months." Perhaps that inexperience was showing. Hoagland would not be the only Banking Committee member to openly oppose Gonzalez tonight. In a few minutes Schumer, one of the man's staunchest allies, would rise to say: "I respect the chairman." Of course, the dagger would swiftly follow. "Obscene, obscene," Schumer would cry of the deceitful, wasteful, off-budget plan.

But Schumer hadn't gone to Gonzalez on his knees begging for an amendment, which, no matter how it might serve the commonweal, was also a favor to a wealthy Omaha investor. Hoagland had done that. And now his Yanney amendment was one of very few such favors to survive the conference. And the freshman had three other amendments in this legislation as well, on which he'd received much help from Gonzalez's committee staff. "What did Hoagland want that he didn't get in this bill?" a source close to Gonzalez later asked, not a little indignantly.

"I still have a great deal to learn," Hoagland acknowledged in his floor remarks, ". . . but people from Nebraska, my home state, would simply shake their heads over this financing scheme. They would think it was concocted on Mars."

After slamming the Martians, Hoagland went through his litany of problems with the bill, all well understood by most members. They had, after all, supported the on-budget plan in overwhelming numbers. When Hoagland said that off-budget financing would add "billions of dollars in financing costs," Republican Steve Bartlett, a Banking Committee colleague, stepped up to the mike on the minority side and barked, "Will the gentleman yield?"

Bartlett clearly had something to say. But Hoagland, perhaps because he was nervous, or because he wasn't yet used to hearing himself addressed in the third person, didn't notice. As Bartlett waved and repeated, "Will the gentleman yield?" Hoagland went right on talking as if Bartlett weren't there. Finally, Mike Synar, the Democrat from Oklahoma, turned in his front-row seat and motioned to Bartlett to sit down. It was as if Synar were saying, "He's just a freshman, he doesn't know from 'yield.' "

Since the decibel level in the chamber was rather high as Hoagland spoke, probably not many noticed when he flubbed part of his prepared summation. "I was elected to be part of the problem," he said soberly, "not part of the solution." (Censors of the *Congressional Record* generously reversed the order of "problem" and "solution.") "So let's roll up our sleeves once again," Hoagland concluded. ". . . Let's go back to conference, do this financing provision right, and complete a bill that is excellent in every respect."

Loud groans greeted Hoagland's call to go "back to conference." But he wasn't alone in advocating it, even at the draconian cost of a delayed recess. Pete Stark, a Democrat from California, denounced those who would vote for the off-budget plan just so they could catch their planes. That amounted to "a three-billion-dollar ticket home," he said. Then Stark ripped up his own $190 ticket to Oakland so he could stay and win an on-budget plan worth "three billion bucks" for his constituents.

Before the debate was over, LaFalce raised his voice one last time. "Most everybody in this body has discussed on-budget or off-budget," he said. "That is all the media has reported. I don't

want to say that's a phony issue, but it isn't all that relevant."
LaFalce's plan—to pay in cash, not to borrow—could have saved
hundreds of billions, not $1.5 to $20 billion. Though it would
have required a large expenditure of political courage. LaFalce was
voting against the bill not because the bonding plan was left off-
budget, but because the real issues had never been seriously debated by the public.

The balloting on S&L conference agreement II was fairly close,
but it passed, 201–175. Republicans provided 119 votes in favor,
Democrats only eighty-two. Voting against were 135 Democrats
(including Hoagland) and forty Republicans. Five voted "present." Fifty didn't vote (not counting the speaker, who by tradition
seldom votes and didn't on this bill).

Coverage of the event was typically light. The following day,
CNN broadcast a thirty-second item on the passage of the S&L
bailout and its megabillion-dollar cost. The report was immediately followed by a relatively "in-depth" three-minute piece on
congressional sex scandals.

Shortly after the bill passed, Barney Frank rose to address the
House. "Mr. Speaker," he said, "having consulted with the very
distinguished and objective parliamentarians, and with the
speaker, on reflection, it does seem to me that my comparison of
the U.S. Senate to Jell-O was not totally in keeping with the tradi-
tions of this institution . . . and I therefore apologize."

Republican Dennis Eckart had a better idea. "Mr. Speaker,"
he said, "perhaps the gentleman should offer his apology to General Foods," makers of Jell-O.

Epilogue
A PINK HOUSE

O n a Sunday afternoon in mid-November, Peter Hoagland lounged in the House Democratic Cloakroom. Congress was in the midst of its standard crush of pre-adjournment business, similar to exam week at a university, when a whole year seems to get crammed into a few painful days and all-nighters.

The House was on standby, waiting for a stack of bills to be delivered from the Senate and voted on. Several members were relaxing in the cloakroom watching a football game. Hoagland considered watching football "a waste of time." He flipped through a stack of members' photographs kept at the desk of the cloakroom manager, memorizing the faces and names of the thirty or so Democrats he hadn't mastered yet. "A good way to goad someone into learning your name is to learn theirs," he said.

Getting to know your colleagues was a basic requirement of the job, but it wasn't always a happy experience. The better Henry Gonzalez got to know Hoagland, the less he seemed to like him. According to a source close to Gonzalez, the chairman was seriously miffed with Hoagland, not so much for voting against his S&L compromise but for having had the gall to speak against it on the floor. After all, Hoagland had asked for a lot on the S&L bill—even going so far as to beg Gonzalez for his nod on the Yanney amendment—and the freshman had been given every blessed thing he'd wanted. Then, when the compromise Gonzalez had worked out was under siege from various quarters, Hoagland had joined the attackers.

Getting on the wrong side of one's committee chairman would certainly have consequences, maybe serious ones. Hoagland had already gotten a taste of what it could mean. During Banking Committee hearings in October on Lincoln Savings and Loan and Charles Keating, Hoagland had asked Gonzalez for time to make a brief statement on the need for campaign finance reform. The hearings were getting a lot of media attention; C-Span was covering them almost continuously. Members generally milked such visibility for all it was worth. But Gonzalez said Hoagland's speech wasn't "germane," according to Gary Caruso, and refused his request for time.

Keating had generously donated to the campaign funds of the infamous Keating Five, and of scores of other legislators besides. He admitted having done so to buy influence. And though campaign finance reform wasn't in the jurisdiction of the Banking Committee, to make a speech on such a topic was simply business as usual. But not for Hoagland, at least not for now.

Among the bills House members ramrodded through at the end of the session was a fat pay raise for themselves. Some thought that particular measure had been approved a little too quickly, and that members just wanted to get it passed before the public had time to react. The last time Congress was contemplating a raise, it had balked before a wave of public outrage fueled by saturation media coverage. This time, House leaders seemed to select the time they announced the pay-raise vote for minimum visibility.

On the day that Lech Walesa, former leader of Poland's Solidarity trade union, addressed a joint session of Congress, as all Washington hailed the progress of democracy in Eastern Europe, the state of democracy at home was made plain. House leaders casually announced that a vote would take place—the very next day—on an "Ethics Reform" bill, which, by the way, included a

33 percent pay raise for members, to bring their salaries from $89,500 to around $120,000.

The revised pay boost wasn't quite as large as the 51 percent bonanza that had been stampeded to death in January. But it also included a 33 percent increase in Congress's already quite generous pension benefits. In exchange, members agreed to relinquish honoraria from special interest groups, which many used to supplement their incomes, with few scruples about conflicts of interest.

According to Ralph Nader, what congressional leaders were saying amounted to this: "We'll stop doing *some* unethical things if we get a thirty-thousand-dollar pay increase." Nader thought members of Congress had "no shame." He listed their unmet challenges, including "the biggest ethics scandal of them all," campaign finance reform. "I think [Congress] should reform campaign finance now, reform their ethics now, and talk about any pay increase later," Nader said.

No doubt most Americans would have agreed with Nader again. That's exactly why House leaders wanted to get a vote on the raise as soon as possible, before protesters started pelting members with tea bags and surrounding them in angry mobs as in February. It was very hard to vote for anything in the teeth of that kind of opposition.

On the evening of Walesa's speech, Hoagland was in the Democratic cloakroom. Several members were watching a network news broadcast. After a long story on Walesa's visit, the anchor began a piece on the pay raise. The room hushed. Everyone braced for the worst.

But only the barest mention was given the pay proposal. No tapes were aired of February's angry mobs. The surprisingly neutral segment lasted all of twenty seconds. Hoagland recalled that when it was over, the room exploded in cheers and applause. The sense of relief was palpable.

The House leadership had also devised a plan to limit any future political damage to members who voted for the pay raise. Republican and Democratic leaders agreed that no candidates would use the issue against an opponent during the 1990 congressional campaign. Any candidate who tried would be denied funds from the party's war chest.

One of the arguments members used for the raise was that it

would go into effect only after the 1990 elections, so voters would get a crack at them before they got the money. But this gag rule was an attempt to make sure that the subject wouldn't even come up in the campaign. Since the issue could only hurt members currently serving, the leaders of both parties were, in effect, taking a weapon out of the hands of challengers in each, and providing incumbents with yet another insurance policy.

Though the TV networks weren't saying much about the raise, talk-radio jocks around the country again tried to get the word out. Hoagland's office in Omaha got a lot of calls, all but one of which was negative. "Who was that, my father?" Hoagland quipped.

Hoagland believed the raise was needed. He wanted to be brave and vote for it. But that seemed out of the question on such a visible, volatile issue. Party leaders were whipping their caucuses to support the bill. But since Hoagland was a freshman in a targeted seat, he was given a "free" vote. In other words, there would be no hard feelings if he voted no, which he did. The raise passed the House handily nevertheless.

Members viewed this issue as among the toughest they faced. Only they could raise their pay, and there seemed to be no such thing as a good time to do it. For instance, right about now, most Americans, perhaps with good reason, simply couldn't accept that $89,500 wasn't plenty of money for a member of Congress.

Members invariably argued that Washington was an expensive place to live, especially if you had to keep a home there and one back in the district you represented. When the Hoaglands moved to Washington, their standard of living hardly improved. They hadn't even considered owning two houses. Their home in Omaha, a comfortable red-brick, three-bedroom on a cozy street of tall trees, was up for sale. It would probably bring only around $100,000. Meanwhile, the house they'd bought in Washington cost over $400,000. And it was no prize.

While the family was house-hunting, Hoagland's youngest daughter, Kate, lobbied him. She simply loved the color pink, preferring pink hair ribbons, pink tennis shoes, pink skirts, pink wallpaper, and pink doll clothes. She now "wanted to talk seriously about buying a pink house," said Hoagland. His answer was diplomatic, in the Seussian mode: "Kate . . . your mom and I love pink, but not for houses. I don't think I've seen a pink house more than once a year. But it would be a beautiful thing to have."

The Hoaglands' criteria for housing, factoring distance from public transport, access to schools, and play safety of neighborhoods, narrowed their options to a small, pricey section of Chevy Chase, Maryland, just over the District of Columbia's northwest border. Most homes there cost half a million or more, enough to buy a mansion in Nebraska.

As things worked out, Kate's instincts proved uncanny. Their broker found an affordable house in the neighborhood they wanted, a three-bedroom place on a very pretty street, selling for a little over $400,000—a good deal for the location. And there was an added "attraction": the house was stucco and brick—*painted pink!*

Though Kate may have been pleased, the grown-up Hoaglands saw the house as a compromise, to state the matter politely. Compared to their place in Omaha, it was a dog!—make that the runt of the litter. Besides its obvious, well, pinkness, the driveway was too narrow, the front door was off-kilter, the basement was periodically flooded, and the "rec room" added to the first floor was so long and narrow you could almost hear bowling pins crashing together. But this house was the only one affordable where the kids could go to the highly regarded Somerset Elementary School nearby. Even the janitors there seemed to score in the 90th percentile on aptitude tests.

Hoagland began to joke with his colleagues, "Did you hear about the eighty-thousand-dollar house I found in Chevy Chase?" After they showed due amazement, he delivered the punch line. "Yeah, we paid four hundred thousand for it." Of course, there were cheaper houses for sale over the line in the District—in the $200,000-to-$300,000 range. But living there meant sending the kids to D.C. public schools, whose reputation isn't among the best, or to expensive private schools. To the typical member of Congress, living in the District with a family is simply not an option.

The day after the raise passed the House, the measure moved across to the Senate, where the vote promised to be closer. Hoagland went to the Senate chamber with some House colleagues to watch the debates and see how the other half lived. Hoagland found the Senate more livable than the umbrous House chamber, which he likened to a cigar box.

Some House members were lobbying senators to support the raise. They asked Hoagland if he would talk to Bob Kerrey, who was said to be on the fence, and get him to vote for it. Hoagland agreed. But he felt funny about asking Kerrey to vote for a bill that he himself had been scared to support. He talked to Kerrey all right—"about anything but" the raise.

In the end, the Senate "millionaires' club" defeated the pay boost, which, under the arcane procedure of this bill, meant that the House would get the extra money and stop taking honoraria, but the Senate wouldn't.

Members of Congress hoped that voters would forget all about the raise—if they had heard of it in the first place—by election day. That seemed likely to happen. The campaigns were almost a year away, both parties had promised to keep mum, and the public didn't pay much attention to "off-year" races anyway.

Of course, election day was rarely far from the minds of some members. Hoagland had been looking ahead to his 1990 campaign since before he was sworn in as a congressman.

Hoagland's reelection prospects were looking surprisingly strong. To his great relief, Jerry Schenken, the man who had come within three thousand votes of winning last time around, had decided not to run this time against an incumbent. Events like the Franklin hearing and the drug town hall meeting in September had gotten Hoagland intensive exposure in the Omaha media. He was also helped when House Speaker Tom Foley visited his district to attend a fundraiser for him in September. "We had Peter Hoagland picked out from the moment he arrived as one of the stars of the 101st Congress," Foley told the well-heeled crowd of Hoagland boosters, "and I think we were right about that."

In between these major events, Hoagland's regular town hall meetings kept a steady blizzard of postcards blanketing the district with his name and picture. And his staff doggedly flacked the press, which paid off in consistent TV, radio, and newspaper coverage the year round—almost all of it favorable. As the 1990 election approached, Gary had difficulty thinking of even one critical local story about Hoagland. He finally cited only the piece by Nicole Simmons on the Yanney amendment, done in response to the *Wall Street Journal* editorial.

Tom Kenworthy, congressional correspondent for the *Washington Post,* did another front-page story on Hoagland in March of

1990, headlined "Incumbency's Winning Ways." The piece stressed how Hoagland had skillfully used his office to strengthen his political base. The *World-Herald* reprinted most of it on page one, captioning a picture of Hoagland with an outtake from the story, a quote from a DCCC staffer, who said of the freshman, "He's done everything right."

Hoagland's political adroitness, and the advantages of incumbency, showed in his numbers. His Washington polling firm, Garin-Hart, prepared a very optimistic report based on a benchmark poll of Omaha voters. Their analysis showed "the breadth of voter esteem for this freshman congressman," according to the report.

When Hoagland was matched head to head with his only announced Republican opponent, Ally Milder, who had lost the GOP primary two years before, he was leading by 63 percent to 21 percent. Hoagland's support "far exceeds the majority threshold so pivotal for an incumbent," the report said. Apparently Hoagland had welded a favorable image of himself onto the public mind of Omaha. But other things about him were less clear and distinct to his constituents. "Volunteered impressions indicate that the Congressman has a fairly well-rounded image," said the report, *"although voters are understandably not yet as familiar with his issue stands as is typical for an incumbent* [italics added]."

Though Hoagland's polls were encouraging, Garin-Hart's analysts warned him not to "take this campaign lightly." There was little chance of that. Despite his impressive numbers, he still managed to worry. For one thing, he thought some votes might come back to haunt him, particularly the one in favor of spending federal funds to finance abortions for rape and incest victims. He'd once pledged not to vote to spend federal money for abortions, but this exception seemed like the right thing to do. It was also, it must be said, the one exception pollsters most often found that even abortion opponents tolerated.

Then in June of 1990, an issue that made Democrats squirm in 1989 was back. The Supreme Court, predictably, threw out the congressional statute that outlawed flag desecration. It had been passed in response to the Court's earlier ruling in *Texas* v. *Johnson,* which said that flag burning was "speech" protected by the First Amendment. Though Hoagland had privately indicated he agreed with the court's ruling, he'd voted for the anti-flag-desecration

statute. It seemed a less odious way to respond to the outcry over
the Court's decision than the passage of an amendment to the
Constitution, which would have meant editing the Bill of Rights
for the first time. Now the Court had stripped away the statutory
fig leaf. If Congress wanted to outlaw flag burning, an amendment
to the Constitution was the only way.

Before the floor vote on the amendment, Hoagland held a
meeting with his staff. "Look, guys," Gary recalled him saying,
"I'm thinking about voting against the flag amendment. So let's
just discuss ways to deal with it."

Jim and Paul Landow, Hoagland's top aide in Omaha, had
"heat strokes," Gary recalled. They had visions of attack ads, of
Hoagland's image paired with pictures of flag burners. Voting
against the amendment, for the sake of a principle, could cost him
the election. Was it that important to him?

Apparently it was. Of course, Hoagland didn't vote his conscience on every issue. No politician who wanted to remain one
for long could do that. Like his colleagues, on any given vote, he
weighed the amount of political capital he could afford to spend.

The price of voting against the flag amendment might be
high. But for Hoagland, a vote for the amendment would also
exact a cost in self-respect, one he wasn't willing to pay. "I didn't
want my tombstone inscription to be that I supported an amendment to weaken the Bill of Rights," he said.

Jim didn't give up. He contacted Hoagland's friends, confi-
dants, pollsters, and asked them to talk some sense into the man.
Hoagland was besieged by phone calls. After all his hard work to
get to Congress, why throw it all away on one vote? Hoagland's
aides and friends were overstating the potency of the flag issue. It
had lost a lot of its intensity over the past year. Still, a no vote on
this one took courage.

Of all Hoagland's aides and advisers, only Gary supported his
decision to vote no on the flag amendment. When he did, and the
measure was defeated, the reaction was swift and surprising.
Hoagland was one of five House members featured in a *New York
Times* article about representatives who'd opposed the amendment
"despite the political risk." A couple of days later, the *Times* did
another story, exclusively on Hoagland. Of the twenty-one Democrats who'd won their most recent elections with less than 55 percent of the vote, the story noted, only seven, including Hoagland,

had weighed in against the flag amendment. Soon CBS called Hoagland to set up an interview. He was looking like a hero who put protection of the Bill of Rights ahead of his own political safety.

Still, Jim was not pleased. "We shouldn't be doing national press on this," he warned Gary after the second *Times* story ran. Gary had set up the appointment with the *Times* reporter. "You're keeping the issue alive," Jim told him. "She'll kill us on this thing." The "she" that would kill them was Ally Milder, the feisty Republican who would oppose Hoagland in the upcoming election. Milder had called Hoagland's flag-amendment vote "just the latest example of how out of step he is with the people of eastern Nebraska."

Hoagland did hear it from some angry constituents. But more of them congratulated him for his bravery. Hoagland didn't think the praise was necessarily typical of what Omahans were thinking, since as genial Midwesterners, they were inclined to say something nice or nothing at all. Still, he was feeling good about the vote, especially when letters thanking him for it began pouring in, along with a few unsolicited campaign contributions.

"Although not a constituent, I read of you in the *New York Times* and want to contribute to your campaign by way of acknowledging my gratitude for your vote against the pernicious attempt to change the First Amendment to the Constitution," said one letter, accompanied by a $1,000 check, from a man in Colorado.

"At a time when political considerations dominate public policy more than any time in my experience," said another writer, a Washingtonian, "your vote stands out as an example of real leadership."

Congratulatory letters came in from the unlikeliest of places. Friends of Hoagland's, after reading a reprint of the *Times* piece in the international *Herald Tribune,* wrote from Budapest. A recent college graduate scrawled a thank-you note from "a Spanish ferry" and promised money for the Hoagland campaign. A football coach from Florida said reading of Hoagland's courage "made my day much brighter." He also wrote to his own U.S. senators. ". . . unfortunately, they caved in to the pressure," he said. "Thank you for your vote against the flag amendment and for the Bill of Rights," wrote a professor in the Department of French at New York University. "We cheer you."

Despite all the praise, Hoagland still thought the flag issue could cut against him, especially in the hands of the combative Ally Milder. And he still fretted about the Yanney factor. In May, Hoagland refunded $11,400 in campaign contributions from Yanney-related PACs and individuals, to inoculate himself from anticipated charges of serving special interests on the S&L bill.

Though Hoagland was coasting atop a twenty-to-thirty-point lead most of the time, he got a scare late in the campaign. Congress normally likes to adjourn early during election years. But members were trapped in Washington by a stalemate with the Bush administration over the budget, which had to be resolved to keep the government running. This "budget crisis" got a lot of media attention when Bush shut down the government for a weekend, rather than sign a "continuing resolution" to keep it funded until a deal with Congress could be struck.

Congressional leaders and the president, after reading the latest dire economic statistics, were agreed that it was now crucial to cut deficit spending by hundreds of billions over the next five years. They had even decided how it should be done. But the deal they worked out in closed sessions was rejected by the House, which didn't like its sharp hikes in gasoline and "sin" taxes, and in Medicare premiums.

House members argued that the taxes raised in the package hit the middle class and the poor hard, while leaving the rich unscathed, though they'd profited most from excesses of the eighties. They wanted a budget deal to include higher taxes on the wealthy. Meanwhile, Bush advocated precisely the opposite: a cut in the capital gains tax, to further reduce the burden on the capital-owning classes.

As the stalemate endured, the media did their best to embarrass Washington. As usual, Congress fared worse than the president, though they shared equally in the "blame" for the impasse. Pundits were snarling, "Why can't Congress get anything done?"

But the nasty attacks on Washington weren't entirely fair in this case. At least some of the blame for this sort of paralysis in government had to be assigned to the system itself, not just the people who served it. Because the system, far from being "broken," was functioning exactly as designed.

Nevertheless, Congress took a lot of heat for the current deadlock, though it was just one in a long history of deadlocks in

Washington. Pundits were now certain that with the cost of the S&L crisis hitting home and the public's rising anger over the budget stalemate, the electorate would be out for blood in the 1990 congressional elections. Incumbents, the pundits crowed, were marked for extinction.

Members of Congress thought the media were enciting voters to wheel out the guillotines. Hoagland was getting anxious. While he was trapped in Washington by the stalemate, Ally Milder aired attack ads back home, lashing him for supporting an alternative budget-cutting plan. The plan still called for raising Medicare premiums, along with gasoline and "sin" taxes, though the hikes were less than those called for in the rejected deal. It also raised the top tax rate, to make the wealthy share in the burden of deficit reduction.

Milder's ads seemed to strike a chord. Two weeks before election day, Hoagland's big lead had shrunk to just eleven points. He didn't have to be reminded that he himself had once overtaken an opponent—Cece Zorinsky—despite her huge early advantage. Hoagland seemed desperate, to state the matter as mildly as possible, to get out of Washington and start campaigning.

Finally, just ten days before the polls opened, Congress and the president struck a deal on the budget, freeing incumbents to go home and do what they do best—get reelected. Now Hoagland hit back. Milder, like Bush, favored a cut in the capital gains tax. Hoagland accused her of protecting the rich at the expense of the middle class. The charge seemed to ruffle her. She lashed out, mocking Hoagland's claim. After all, she said, it was Hoagland, the Stanford blue blood, who'd catered to the likes of Mike Yanney.

Hoagland's aides were surprised that Milder didn't play the Yanney card sooner, or with more strategy when she finally did. She didn't even put the charge in an ad, merely used it as a throwaway line in a speech. As things worked out, it wasn't nearly enough. Hoagland won big, with 58 percent of the vote to Milder's 42.

But the victory wasn't as sweet for Hoagland as it might have been. While he was campaigning, people often said things to him like "Boy, I sure can't vote for your opponent." Milder tended to "shoot from the lip," as Hoagland put it. Early in the Kuwaiti crisis, she'd recommended that Bush just "drop a bomb" on Sad-

dam Hussein. It was not the sort of crack moderate Omahans expected from their politicians.

Hoagland, naturally, said he would have preferred to hear
people tell him, "Gee, you're really doing a good job." He'd
already beaten one discredited opponent—Cece Zorinsky—and
might have felt better if he'd won this one on his merits, not
Milder's demerits.

Maybe Hoagland was being overly sensitive and underestimated the affection Omahans felt for him. But even his polls, an
objective, unemotional source, told him that folks still didn't seem
terribly aware of his stands on issues. Perhaps the ringing endorse-
ment he sought would come when they were. On the other hand,
there was always the chance that just the opposite would occur.

Pundits wouldn't be pundits, one must suppose, if they weren't
dead wrong most of the time. Consider their nearly universal pre-
dictions of an "anti-incumbent backlash" in the 1990 elections.
Some backlash. Of 406 incumbents who ran again, 391 were win-
ners.

Despite this evidence of an essentially neutered electorate,
pundits were still predicting a rebellion. It would take the form,
many believed, of a "populist" uprising against entrenched power
and economic inequality that would land with a force on complacent incumbents in, oh, say, 1992.

The term "populist" has many meanings. When used by political journalists, it's often a pejorative, describing the kind of politician who caters to the basest of human prejudices and fears.
Certainly such things were a part of the original Populist movement.

But there was more to Populism than race-baiting and fear-
mongering. A fuller definition of the word would have to include
political leaders who rose out of popular movements, and didn't
just seek to manipulate them with pleasing symbols. "Populist"
politicians would talk to people about real issues—ones that actually mattered to policymakers in Washington—and not try merely
to manipulate their emotions with empty drivel about flags and
patriotism. Turn-of-the-century Populists widely discussed complex issues among their movement's followers. Their opponents,
meanwhile, discussed the flag and "waved the bloody shirt" of
heroism in wartime. In the long run, as we know, their opponents

won, though Populist-inspired ideas have had a way of hanging around.

The only thing approaching a grass-roots or populist uprising on the horizon now is the push to limit the terms of members of Congress, to ten years in the House and twelve years in the Senate, or five terms and two terms respectively. Even that is being orchestrated from Washington, mostly by associates of Republican-affiliated think tanks who want, once and for all, to pry the Democrats out of power in Congress.

After the election, Gary Caruso finally quit Hoagland's staff to look for bigger challenges. Hoagland decided not to replace Gary with another media aide. He planned to hire an issues expert instead. Hoagland said he wanted to have someone on his staff whose advice would have more to do with the substance of issues, and less to do with their politics. He also hoped to spend less time on the phone soliciting campaign dollars—he'd raised around $800,000 since arriving in Congress—and more time on issues.

Hoagland got a new office after the election, on the seventh floor of the Longworth Building. Now his staff wouldn't have to run up and down three flights of stairs between office and annex. And there would be flags outside the office door. Hoagland had splurged and joined the flag club over a year before.

There was some redecorating on Hoagland's political stage too. Between attrition and defections, he'd moved up ten seats on the Banking Committee, which put him a long jump ahead in seniority. But Hoagland's chairman, Henry Gonzalez, still seemed to be holding a grudge against him.

Just before Congress adjourned for the 1990 election, Hoagland's Niobrara bill was approved by the Senate, and the conference report was coming to the House floor. The bill would become law if it passed now. But Virginia Smith was trying to kill it. It would be her last fight on the House floor. She was retiring at the end of the session, in a matter of minutes.

While Hoagland was on the floor lobbying for his bill, he glimpsed the craggy Gonzalez, who turned away and folded his arms on seeing the freshman. "His body language said, 'Don't even think of lobbying me on this issue,' " Hoagland recalled. The Niobrara vote was close, but the bill lost. Gonzalez was one of only four Democrats to vote against it.

In December 1990, after the election, Hoagland signed a letter endorsing Bruce Vento, his Banking Committee colleague, when Vento campaigned to replace Gonzalez as chairman. Hoagland said his decision wasn't personal, at least not entirely. Gonzalez had done an admirable job on the S&L legislation. But committee members complained that he ran a sloppy shop. For instance, he seldom circulated memos on upcoming issues or witnesses. And Gonzalez committed his biggest sin—in the eyes of Democrats—when he taped a TV ad for the reelection campaign of Republican Chalmers Wylie. Gonzalez said Wylie's opponent had lied about his friend's positions. The Democratic Caucus reelected Gonzalez as chairman, 163–89. But Vento's vote total was unusually high for someone who'd only campaigned for a single day, and was seen as a wake-up call for Henry.

Hoagland wasn't sure if Gonzalez had even seen the letter he signed in support of Vento's insurrection. But these things have a way of circulating in the House. So despite his much-improved seniority on Banking, he was looking for another panel—preferably Appropriations—where he could focus his second-term efforts in a friendlier atmosphere. He eventually won a seat on the Interior Committee and a temporary slot on Judiciary.

The Steering and Policy Committee gave Hoagland more votes than any other applicant for an open seat on Interior, making him the first new member of that panel selected. One might think that Hoagland's 100 percent rating with the League of Conservation Voters played a role in all this. But his insistent lobbying for the seat was probably the biggest reason he won it so handily, according to Hoagland staffer Stephanie Cohen. "Everyone knew his name," she said.

Outside of the House Interior Committee, there were still perhaps a few who weren't yet familiar with the name Peter Hoagland. But he'd made an impressive beginning in his congressional career. He'd worked on one of the most challenging pieces of legislation Congress had faced in recent years—the S&L bailout—and made substantial contributions to the finished product. He'd faced down a hometown S&L to vote for tougher capital standards, and pushed through an amendment that had been tarred as a "special interest," because he believed those were the right things to do. If sometimes he seemed overeager for publicity, what freshman guarding a shaky seat wouldn't be? But when faced with a soul searing vote on the flag amendment, Hoagland's conscience won out over political concerns.

Hoagland's decisive reelection—by 16 percent of the vote—indicated that he'd be a force to be reckoned with in Omaha for some time. But he still sounded a little insecure politically. In a December 1990 discussion of congressional term limits—a policy he decidedly did not support—Hoagland observed that the political pressures on members of Congress were already potent enough. The institution had a lot of tough decisions to make in the years ahead, and a lot of powerful interests to offend in making them. To do that, "we need more job security," Hoagland said emphatically, "not less."

It may seem remarkable that a member of an institution with a collective reelection rate of 96 percent in 1990 could still claim to need "more job security." But it's been said that an incumbent's political paranoia grows along with his victory margin—the bigger it swells, the more insecure he or she is liable to become.

But Hoagland was clearly coming into his own. It showed on election night, 1990. Local hero Bob Kerrey shared the victory celebration stage with the resoundingly reelected congressman. But Kerrey didn't share the credit this time. And it didn't seem altogether unlikely that someday soon people might be talking about who's riding into office on Peter Hoagland's coattails.

INDEX

About the Author

ROBERT CWIKLIK was an editor for the Washington Bureau of the Ottaway News Service. He has written articles for the *Washington Post*, the *Christian Science Monitor*, the *Nation*, and other publications. He is the co-author of *The Secret History of Grammar* and the author of several other books for children and young adults.